KU-568-424

Good policy and practice for the after-school hours

Kay Andrews
&
Gwyneth Vernon

with
Mike Walton

LIVERPOOL
UNIVERSITY
LIBRARY

FIAT LVX

PITMAN
PUBLISHING
education
xtra

PITMAN PUBLISHING
128 Long Acre, London WC2E 9AN

A division of Pearson Professional Limited

First published in Great Britain 1996

© Pearson Professional Limited, 1996

British Library Cataloguing in Publication Data
A CIP catalogue record for this book can be obtained from the British Library.

ISBN 0 273 61628 5

All rights reserved; no part of this publication may be reproduced, stored
in a retrieval system, or transmitted in any form or by any means, electronic,
mechanical, photocopying, recording, or otherwise without either the prior
written permission of the Publishers or a licence permitting restricted copying
in the United Kingdom issued by the Copyright Licensing Agency Ltd,
90 Tottenham Court Road, London W1P 9HE. This book may not be lent,
resold, hired out or otherwise disposed of by way of trade in any form
of binding or cover other than that in which it is published, without the
prior consent of the Publishers.

10 9 8 7 6 5 4 3 2 1

Typeset by Phoenix Photosetting, Chatham, Kent
Printed and bound in Great Britain by Redwood Books, Trowbridge, Wiltshire.

The Publishers' policy is to use paper manufactured from sustainable forests.

371
.89
AND

Good policy and practice

012769371

12/1/96

IVERPOOL HOPE UNIVERSITY
HE SHEPPARD - WORLOCK LIBRAR

New Titles from Pitman Publishing

Developing a Whole School IT Policy by Bill Tagg

Effective Governors for Effective Schools edited by Derek Esp and Rene Saran

The Early Years: Development, Learning and Teaching edited by Gillian Boulton-Lewis and Di Catherwood

Primary School Deputies Handbook by Gareth Thomas

Issues in School Attendance and Truancy edited by Dennis O'Keeffe and Patricia Stoll

Leadership and Strategic Management by John West-Burnham, Tony Bush, John O'Neill and Derek Glover

Managing the Curriculum by Mark Lofthouse, Tony Bush, Marianne Coleman, John O'Neill, John West-Burnham and Derek Glover

Bestselling Titles from Pitman Publishing

The Principles of Education Management edited by Tony Bush and John West-Burnham

You Know the Fair Rule by Bill Rogers

Managing Quality in Schools by Christopher Bowring-Carr and John West-Burnham

Managing School Time by Brian Knight

Bullying: A Practical Guide to Coping for Schools edited by Michele Elliott

School Development Planning by Brent Davies and Linda Ellison

How to Cope with Childhood Stress edited by Pippa Alsop and Trisha McCaffrey

Positive School Discipline by Margaret Cowan et al

Contents

Contents

Foreword

Every time there is some mishap involving young people—joyriding, ram raiding, vandalism—earnest investigators are sent in to reach ashen-faced conclusions about the causes of such mayhem. Whatever reasons are eventually put forward, one in particular keeps recurring. In too many places there is simply nothing for young people to do.

This sense of social and intellectual deadness is overwhelming, and it can start early. Young children soon realise whether their town or village is full of life or like a cemetery. They reach their conclusions when they are still at school, especially if their own school offers nothing outside normal hours.

Education Extra has achieved a great deal in a relatively short time. By highlighting good practice where it exists, encouraging schools that are hesitant, and injecting cash and energy into schemes that bring great and lasting benefit to children of all ages and backgrounds, Education Extra has focussed attention on what *can* be done. It is more than a distant pipe dream. It has passed the real test of practical application.

What I like about Education Extra is that it is based on a broad, not a narrow concept. Each of us can become a more rounded person if we develop several sides to our personality. As Schiller put it: *'Der Mensch ist nur da ganz Mensch wo er spielt'* ('People are only full people when they are at play'). Out of school hours, learning often seems like play, whether children are studying topics they might well study during the school day, or developing interests and skills that do not figure on a school timetable. That applies to people of all ages, not just to the very young, or to teenagers.

Local Management of Schools has imposed considerable additional responsibilities on heads, teachers and governors, but it has also brought opportunities to make the best of what the school has already got: the buildings, the facilities, and the people. Amazing ingenuity has been shown by schools, sometimes against the odds, and in the most unlikely surroundings. Parents in some city areas are now petrified to let their children play outside. Education Extra offers the chance for young children as well as young teenagers to be together in safe and happy surroundings. A whole young generation that might be housebound is able to be sociable.

Foreword

This valuable book allows teachers and parents, governors and administrators, to see not just what *might* be done but what is *being* done, in Britain and other countries, for there is widespread interest in after-hours activity. It describes values and principles, working ideas, the distilled experience of those who are making a success of it, and plenty of practical and helpful models for others to imitate or improve.

There has been a long tradition of after-hours activity in British schools. Sadly, many schemes died during the 1980s when teachers felt alienated by the poor treatment they received from some politicians. Education Extra is a great inspiration. May it go from strength to strength.

Professor Ted Wragg
Exeter University

Acknowledgements

Many people have helped Education Extra to bring this book to life.

Our first and greatest debt is to all the headteachers and the many other school staff who wrote and spoke so powerfully of the importance of after-school activities to the pupils they teach and to the school itself. Their conviction, that this extra enrichment is the entitlement of every child and part of the commitment to the best that schools can offer, shines through these pages. Most of our information was gathered in the course of assessing entries to our National Award in 1993 and 1994. Schools change very fast and some of the provision which we describe has changed too. But the details we set out were in practice in these years, and the good practice which they illustrate remains valid.

We are, in addition, grateful to all those people who provided additional information, comment and advice on specialist aspects. We are particularly indebted to Pat Petrie, of the Thomas Coram Research Unit, Professor Michael Barber and Professor Sally Tomlinson for their help and advice. For the chapter on the arts, we have drawn heavily on the work of Rick Rogers. Jack Wilkinson, of the South East Sports Council, read and improved the chapter on sport after school; Brenda Keogh was immensely helpful in preparing the chapter on science, as were Brian Woolnough, Jan Harding and Jackie Zammit of the BAYS. We are grateful to Mike Hacker and Richard Yelland of OECD for their permission to use unpublished material in the concluding chapter, and for Mike Hacker's support and advice since Education Extra began work in October 1992. Per Hansen of the Building Directorate, Ministry of Education, Denmark, and Dr Yale Stenzler and Charles A. Talbert of the Maryland State Department of Education kindly provided additional information on Denmark and the United States.

Eileen Carleton, Allan Randall and Trisha Bennett each provided invaluable help with individual case studies; Ann Longfield of Kids' Clubs Network kindly provided references to the early years of after-school provision—another expression of the partnership we have valued over the past three years.

Creating a National Award for After-School Activities was only possible thanks to the support of the charitable trusts which enabled Education Extra to establish itself in the first instance. We are particularly grateful, in this respect, to the Baring Foundation, the Gulbenkian Foundation and the Sir John Cass's Foundation. Research on which this book is based was also funded in part, through our work on the Out of School Childcare Initiative funded by the Department for Employment (1992–95), and we are grateful for the help given by the staff of the Sex Equality Branch and many of the Out of School Development Officers based in the TECs. The trustees of Education Extra provide excellent advice and consistent support for all we do, and we are grateful, in particular, to our Chair, Ursula Owen, for her sustained support. Michelle Darraugh and Caroline Morgan of Pitman Publishing have been consistently helpful at each stage of the editorial process and have made the production of the book itself a pleasure. Douglas Matthews expertly prepared the index for us, and Anne Watts proved a meticulous proofreader.

Teresa Johnson, Kiffer Weisselberg, Jackie James, Josh Hardie and Aaron Brown all held the fort at Education Extra while we were preoccupied with producing our first book, and without their help and support it would have been a much more difficult and far less enjoyable labour. To our friends in the Institute of Community Studies, we can only say thank you for their consistent generosity of spirit to yet another cuckoo in their nest.

We owe two particular debts: the first, to Michael Young, our patron and founder, now celebrating his eightieth year who inspired us to put into practice an idea which expresses, once again, his conviction that we must make the improvement of children's lives our priority as a nation if we are to realise the best of which we are capable as a community. Our second debt is to the Paul Hamlyn Foundation which has supported Education Extra since the first, has funded the research on which this book is based, and has enabled us to broadcast the good news about after-school activities more widely. We are profoundly grateful to them both.

Kay Andrews
Gwyneth Vernon
and
Mike Walton

Introduction: Education Extra: Life and learning after school

If you ask any adult what they remember most vividly about their schooldays the chances are that it will not be what went on in the classroom. Far more likely are sharp memories of the end-of-term play, of sports days with parents coerced into egg and spoon races, field trips which may have been the first time away from home and family, debating societies which tested nerves to the limit, and the whole range of clubs, outings and activities that revealed teachers as almost more than human.

Education Extra was created in October 1992 with the conviction that the years at school should be as rich and as fulfilling as possible, and that there was an urgent need to rethink and to develop the educational and social potential that the after-school hours represent. It was created partly to celebrate good practice, but also to inspire better policy, in the widest sense. The two are closely linked. There is, as this book demonstrates, a wealth of good ideas and good practice and huge potential to put that extra time and those resources to better use. Yet there is virtually no information about what schools and communities are doing, what role those activities play in the life of the school, or how they are filling some of the gaps in the lives of children and young teenagers.

In fact, as this study shows, schools are opening themselves up in new ways – providing not only essential learning and leisure opportunities, but havens of security after school for young children and teenagers alike. They are also offering volunteering and training opportunities for adults. Many of these 'open schools' are in communities which are marked by multiple deprivation and a lack of confidence in education. These are communities where there is little access to affordable leisure facilities, and where casual crime can become a way of life even for the very young. In this environment schools 'have to work hard to engender a reasonable level of achievement, and much harder again to match the performance of schools in more favoured parts of the country'.[1] In many of those schools that extra effort includes providing after-school activities which also compensate in part for the poverty of the local environment, and help to build closer relationships with adults while raising commitment to school itself.

The issues raised by after-school provision as a whole are, therefore, large and complex. They include, at the broadest, child care as well as education. They pre-figure the relationship between schools, families and communities which are reflected in part in the provision of community education. They touch on the nature and future of learning and employment in a post-industrial society and on fundamental issues of equal opportunities and how they are distributed in Britain today. After-school provision has something to say about the way work is organised and how family life and working patterns are managed. It also has a place in the heart of the debate about a time-squeezed society where overwork and unemployment has turned time into a curse rather than a blessing. As a recent report has expressed it:

> *If the 20th century was about money – and making it and distributing it – the evidence from values, surveys, and systems analysis, economics and psychology suggests that the 21st will be about time and how to achieve well-being.*[2]

These are all large issues, and we cannot address them as fully as they deserve in a study which has an educational narrow focus. But they are illustrated in the issues raised by the good policy and good practice featured at many levels throughout the book and in the conclusions which suggest how the links between them can be strengthened and how after-school provision can become a vital part of a coherent new strategy for young people and schools.

What follows, therefore, is a first-hand account of what has been a hitherto invisible aspect of the landscape of education in England and Wales; one which is both more verdant and more diverse than we anticipated and one which holds great and timely promise for modest public investment.

Why after-school provision matters

What happens in the classroom, and how it is taught, must inevitably remain paramount, but teachers and parents know that:

> *Many children would benefit from a lively after-school programme. So much of education does not occur in the classroom but arises out of teamwork out of ordinary school hours, in the playing fields, in drama, dance, media studies, music, the visual arts and in environmental improvement schemes in which children can take part.*[3]

Indeed, that is precisely why teachers, helped in so many cases by other school staff, parents, older pupils, youth and community workers and volunteers, continue to provide so much for students to do after school.

The relationship between the successful school and extra-curricular activities has already been identified by the National Commission on Education. Its ten point summary declares that one of the key elements of a successful school would be that it provides:

> *Extra-curricular activities which broaden pupils' interests and experiences, expand their opportunities to succeed and help to build good relationships within the school.*[4]

Education Extra was created to assist that relationship by stimulating development in school and spreading good practice. It was *not* created to add more to the already heavy burdens of teachers, or to extend the teaching day itself. Education Extra offers help for schools to draw in the extra support, advice and resources which they will need if there is to be more extensive and more effective provision after school. In particular, we are concerned with the age group eight to fourteen, which falls between the protection offered by the Children Act and the main scope of Youth Services. Yet these are the very years when young people can turn away from learning and when the school can become an enemy rather than a friend.

Education Extra does not see after-school provision as 'extra' at all. We see it as salient to improving and modernising our education service as we approach the next century. We see it as a means of lifting and fulfilling aspirations, and as an essential resource in the rebuilding of community life. We see it as a positive response to Sir Ron Dearing, when he said that the challenge facing education 'is as obvious as it is severe. To survive, let alone prosper, it is necessary, day in and day out, to aim for and achieve standards previously thought unobtainable.[5]

In this book we aim to show, in the experience of people involved in developing after-school provision, how:

- after-school activities can help children to succeed in school, and after they have left school;
- after-school activities can help schools to succeed, and ensure that the resources and facilities of schools are put to more effective use;
- after-school activities can, by providing safety, supervision and stimulation for children, support families in work, and help to create stronger communities.

Most important of all, we see after-school provision as a means of opening more equal opportunities for children threatened with cultural as well as material poverty. Few homes can provide studio or workshop facilities; some homes cannot provide the space or time required for pursuing hobbies, or doing homework; many parents cannot afford the cost of musical instruments or advanced computers, or the cost of specialist sporting activities such as canoeing, gymnastics or horse-riding; some cannot afford a trip to a leisure centre, or even the local swimming pool (if there is one). For children with special needs, the failure to provide these experiences is a particular loss. The result, for all children, can be cultural malnutrition – a poverty of aspiration, experience and imagination as well as the lifelong poverty which comes when skills and achievements are stifled.

That is the challenge facing schools where the motivated child and parent will want to take advantage of all the extras, but where, as in school itself, the child with the greatest needs will be the one who opts out. It is a challenge which faces not just schools but the whole of society. The choice facing this country now lies between becoming a low-skill, low-pay, secondary economy, competing on labour market costs with the most efficient countries of the Pacific, or a high-skill, confident economy, producing the 'added value' goods of the future and abreast of, if not ahead of, the new technologies which will define that future. Part of the prescription for improvement, as Sir Ron Dearing and the National Commission on Education emphasise from different perspectives, is the need 'to broaden the concept of achievement' and to reinforce and liberate the different natural abilities and aspirations of children. At the moment, 43 per cent of all pupils leave school with five or more GCSEs, grades A–C; a further 29 per cent obtain 1–4 GCSEs, grades A–C.[6] Many of these pupils, and the remaining group who fail to achieve a single GCSE, can leave school with the overwhelming sense that they have failed in every area of school life. Many leave with their natural abilities undetected and unrecognised.

For all these reasons, we urgently need to recognise and promote educational 'added value' and to find ways of both lifting and recording the broad range of achievements of which all children are capable. We also need to recognise that, in an age of austerity for education, learning resources have to be as accessible to as many people whenever and wherever they can be used. Not only schools, but also in further and higher education, there is a growing sense that learning must be opened up – whether that means playing fields, kitchens, libraries, laboratories or information technology suites. If schools do close down completely at the end of the teaching day and are not open during the holidays, their facilities can be idle for as much as 50 per cent of each day, and 70 per cent of the entire year. As the National Commission on Education argued:

We would like to see this capacity exploited for a wide variety of purposes, from providing a safe place where children can do homework until their parents return from work, to offering educational and recreational after-school activities for children and the local community.[7]

There is a mood of reception and change in many schools, reflected in the decisions being taken, for example, to restructure their school day to facilitate other demands on time, and in order to expand what can be done and what can be used after school. Headteachers are leading this movement, supported by governors and parents who also want to seek to put an end to the waste of resources. They do this because they recognise the educational benefits which will follow. In fact, what is clear is not *how little* is done, but, despite increasing pressure on the school day and on the teaching profession, *how much* teachers, in some cases with outside help, already do after school, more often than not on a voluntary basis.

There are new pressures on schools but also some new opportunities. Much after-school provision was lost in the 1980s as a result of the teachers' dispute, and the contract based on 1265 hours, which led both to a loss of flexibility and goodwill. At the same time, the introduction of the National Curriculum and assessment at Key Stages have put primary and secondary schools alike under heavy pressure. Open enrolment and the introduction of City Technology Colleges and Grant-Maintained Schools has fostered competition between schools for scarce resources. League Tables, by focusing on academic measures, have diminished the real achievements of those schools which educate disadvantaged children. Local Management of Schools, while it has given welcome autonomy and budgetary control, has also created pressures to lease out buildings for profit rather than for the purposes of the school. The impact of these changes has been compounded by underfunding in many areas, increasing numbers of children in classes, the loss of support for Special Needs teaching, and a wide variation in basic resources – books, libraries, music and art materials, laboratory equipment, and information technology.

There are, at the same time, great opportunities. The revolution in information technology opens up enormous scope for changing the location, means and nature of learning – and work. The jobs of the future will belong to those people who are confident with language, who can access, use and evaluate information and technology; who are capable of updating and transferring their skills, and translating knowledge into practical solutions – either within a co-operative setting or working independently - increasingly, perhaps, in isolation.

After-school activities can provide an instant boost and an extra opportunity to develop key skills for the future. They open up access to resources not only for pupils, but for their parents and other adults in the community. They can fit alongside local training and regeneration strategies.

The benefits do not stop there. Teachers, as well as parents, are only too well aware of the need to provide some alternative to an empty, unsupervised home, or dangerous streets, shopping areas or amusement arcades. Probation officers, the police force and voluntary organisations are becoming increasingly involved in after-school initiatives to divert and occupy young people. Knowing there is a full and stimulating programme of supervised activities after school can free parents from worry, enable them to turn part-time into full-time work, or take up training or shift work. For the one-parent family, this could mean an end to a life on benefit. For the working family, a playcare club for primary-aged children can be the essential route back into training or work, or the means of extending working hours.

About this book

This book celebrates the achievements of hundreds of schools throughout England and Wales which provide enrichment and extra opportunities for children outside the formal school day. Most of the examples were drawn from schools which submitted entries for the Education Extra National Award for After-School Activities in 1993 and 1994. The examples given, therefore, represent what schools were doing during that stage of their development and are offered as good practice from that vantage point. We are delighted to recognise their achievements in this way. The examples are supplemented by information from other schools outside our network, and other schemes, including some of Education Extra's own pilot schemes.

This book demonstrates some of the immense wealth of innovation in schools across the country, from relatively limited but excellent programmes of very high quality to fully-organised programmes of activities, which are available every evening after school and at weekends. There are also holiday schemes for younger and older children. Some of these schemes take place within a community-designated school alongside programmes for children and adults of all ages. The majority, however, are offered within the non-community maintained school.

What is remarkable is the range and diversity of what is offered – from the activities which support the curriculum to those designed to be purely recreational. In effect, however, although the menu may be different, the effect is equally nutritious. Equally remarkable is the pace of change and the extent of commitment – manifest in the different models, and the many different partnerships which are being formed by schools with statutory and voluntary agencies, with experts, enthusiasts and individual volunteers, to enrich and extend what they can do.

This cannot be anything other than a snapshot of how some schools are developing good schemes and good ideas. It is not an exhaustive sample of all schools in England and Wales, or even all of the schools currently in contact with Education Extra. Throughout the country, as we have discovered in the third year of our Award, many schools are working on similar lines, restructuring the school day, creating new partnerships, offering new activities – everything from astronomy to archeology – and facing the same challenges. But many are still working in isolation. The need for communication, advice and the sharing of ideas quickly became so evident that, in 1994, we set up Education Extra Network as an information exchange. Membership is now touching 600. Many of the schools and projects described in the following chapters are now part of the Network.

Given limitations of space, we have been able to quote from only some of the many available examples. In each case, the school illustrates one particular way of providing something extra. Some schools are quoted several times because of the different aspects of their work, and there is some overlap between chapters as examples of good practice reinforce each other. Our aim is that the practice in these schools will both inform the policy-makers and inspire the practitioners – teachers, parents, community workers and others – who can enrich children's lives immeasurably through after-school activities.

Our aim has been for practitioners to speak for themselves. The separate chapters relate after-school activities to the many different ways of learning, the partners involved in supporting learning, and the ways of organising education in different ways and at different times.

Chapter 1 examines why so many schools and individuals are committed to after-school activities, and sets the educational and social benefits they bring against the current background of rapid educational and social change.

Chapters 2–5 show how schools are providing support for learning through enrichment for children in specific areas: arts (Chapter 2), sports (Chapter 3), study support and life skills (Chapter 4), and science, technology and the environment (Chapter 5).

Chapters 6 and 7 deal with some practicalities. Chapter 6 explains how schools have dealt with time management issues and found ways to make time in the day, the week or the year for extra activities. Chapter 7 shows how schools are making the most of resources, and how some are drawing in additional funding and making partnerships to enable them to do more.

The concluding chapter looks at what constitutes a successful scheme, and how other European countries are developing their own policies to draw out the benefits using after school time. From these and from examples of good practice in the UK, we put forward proposals for the future role of after-school provision as part of educational and social policy as a whole.

Kay Andrews

NOTES

1 See the recent report of the Select Committee on Education, Performance in City Schools (HC 247–1, June 1995) para 2.

2 DEMOS, *The Time Squeeze*, 5, (1995), p. 11. *See also* Michael Young, *The metronomic society* (1988).

3 Lord Young of Dartington, addressing the Royal Society of Arts, December 1992.

4 Learning to Succeed, Report of the National Commission on Education (Paul Hamlyn Foundation, London, 1993), pp. 142-3.

5 The National Curriculum and Assessment, Department for Education, December 1993.

6 Department for Education, *Statistics of Education: Public Examinations, GCSE and GCE, 1993*, Table 5A.

7 National Commission on Education, Ibid., p. 169.

1

Approaches to after-school learning: The overall picture

It's good to do things after school. I wish it were open in the holidays!

Pupil in a Manchester primary school

The trouble with the 1990s is that children are not free to play. Play is so essential and we've lost the opportunity for children to play together. Children stay in houses overprotected or are allowed to roam. So we have this great extreme. And we've got to enrich the child as a whole . . . to enjoy leisure activities, to be able to organise themselves, to make them feel satisfied, to raise self-esteem. . . . We can provide that by providing for the whole child, and what you do out of school is as valuable as what you do in school.

Headteacher in a Salford primary school

When there are so many additional demands on school staff, why do schools bother to offer any form of after-school provision which extends after the teaching day? This introductory chapter explores some of the reasons why schools do make this extra effort, and the evidence for the benefits of after-school provision as a whole as it crosses educational and social policy. The link between school, family and community life is eloquently summed up in the words of the headteacher of Trent Primary School, London Borough of Barnet, a school which, in 1993, offered activities which ranged from country dancing to creative writing, touch typing and extra languages, and which brought in people from the local church, the university, sports club and the local community every evening. Sixty per cent of the school's children spoke English as a second language. As the headteacher explained:

We offer after school activities, in order:

- *to extend and increase the children's skills and enjoyment of school life in its broadest sense;*

- *to enhance the image of the school within the community;*

- *to involve the children in after-school hours within the school building;*

- *to encourage parents to offer their talent to enhance the school's programme;*

- *to provide families with safe, sheltered activities in a familiar environment.*

The changing culture of childhood

The context for an interest in what schools are doing must be what *children* are doing after school and what they might want to do. Significantly, while it has never assumed the status of policy, the need for some form of after-school provision can be traced back to the 1880s, barely a decade after the introduction of universal primary schooling. These first steps were inspired by growing concern that there should be more positive choices for children than illegal employment or the life of the streets. By 1906, individual initiatives were overtaken by the concept of a professional play service supported by the state and provided locally.[1] In some areas of the country there was distinctive provision. In London, for example, over 1000 volunteers came together in the Children's Happy Evenings Association to provide play experience and recreation after school for 23 000 children. Significantly, the London School Board gave the CHEA free use of school premises to foster more 'happy evenings'.[2]

In the years before the Second World War, the culture of childhood was essentially the culture of the streets. Gwyn Thomas, inimitably, recalls his own childhood in Wales:

> *It was a calm December evening but the street was full of noise. About a hundred children were at play, playing in their tightly defined territories. Their games were meant to set them screaming and drive older people mad. Doors were flung open and showers of abuse came shooting at them from householders, many of them in their nightclothes, made distraught by the racket.*

> *Football, played with a tin by lads who never seemed to tire, was a game that landed a dozen neurotics in the Mental Clinic. Hop-scotch was played on the chalk-marked pavement and many a hopper poised for a last vigorous hop into home-base was sent spinning by a boy or girl hurtling away in a game of hide and seek . . .[3]*

Today streets are for traffic, not for children. Leisure centres are expensive, often available only for adults and special interest groups for much of the week; swimming pools have been closed; adventure playgrounds and parks vandalised or seen as dangerous. And yet, when they are asked, children are quite clear about what they need: they want safe places to play, space, adventure playgrounds, interesting things to do, a clean and safe environment.[4]

Many are denied such choice. In 1973, Colin Ward wrote of the 'litter-strewn, windswept public places of the future metropolis' providing facilities only for 'more sophisticated forms of vandalism'. Twenty-one years later he observed that:

> What I had failed to anticipate was that in the next decade, instead of watching public policies which elevated the degraded surroundings of urban childhood and adolescence, we were to witness a whole series of decisions by central government that seemed calculated to make matters worse, not least by obliging local authorities to curtail their support for a variety of local and voluntary ventures intended to make towns and cities accessible to their young inhabitants . . .[5]

The growth in family poverty makes this public impoverishment worse. Between 1977 and 1990, inequality in Britain has reached 'a higher level than recorded since the war'. It has grown faster in the UK than any other country with the exception of New Zealand.[6] Chief among the victims of this growth in inequality, fostered by unemployment, low wages and cuts in social security and single-parenthood, are women. As the Rowntree Report on Income and Wealth emphasised:

> The striking feature . . . is the relative concentration of children at the bottom: they are 30 per cent of the poorest tenth but only 13 per cent of the richest.[7]

It is family poverty, linked in many areas to single parent status, which accounts in large part for the pressure on so many women with children to return to work, and for the consequent urgent need for pre-school care for young children and after-school care for older children.

Alongside the increase in poverty has come the loss of urban services and resources, extending the gap between rich and poor. James Watson, describing the facilities available in a Canadian city in 1951, described how a *social Himalaya . . . prevented the city's poor inhabitants from making use of the facilities taken for granted by middle class residents next door'*.

How much higher is that social Himalaya now, given the loss of neighbourhood and the decline of the extended family? As Colin Ward suggests:

> *Children whose universe does not contain an understanding of the topography of the local environment, the manipulation of the facilities it offers and the social assurance to use them, need increasingly as the century ends, the money to pay for them.*[8]

The inequalities are compounded by the loss of personal freedoms and independence. Computers, videos and TV have privatised play. Crime and the fear of crime limit freedom of movement. It is estimated that children of nine-and-a-half have the same freedom of movement as seven-year-olds in 1981. Children do not use public transport, and many rarely go anywhere unaccompanied. Many do not have the opportunity to play or work together outside school. As Ward puts it: *'Children have lost out . . . without society apparently noticing'.*[9]

Parents, though, are only too aware of the loss to their children.

> *Living in the centre of a city I know that my child's freedom is curtailed and the opportunities to play are limited to a pavement on our side of the road and a very small yard. The balancing act between freedom to play and 'death on the road' is always on my mind . . . I would welcome a project that would enrich the lives of our city kids.*[10]

In these circumstances, the resources and facilities of schools have become increasingly important community assets, especially in the life of those communities which are facing massive social dislocation.

After-school provision, motivation and achievement

Any review of the relationship between after-school provision, motivation and achievement trespasses on the vast plains of educational theory and practice. This is not the appropriate place for a comprehensive study. In this section, however, we focus on the role which after-school provision might play in improving motivation and involvement in learning and leisure.

The 1980s and early 1990s have brought massive changes in educational policy affecting management, the curriculum, and methods of financing and organising schools. In particular, the delegation of power over school budgets under LMS has given new powers to school governors to use buildings as they see fit, to lease and rent out facilities and keep the income and to use resources at the end of the school day for care as well as for extra-curricular activities. Limited surveys have demonstrated that there has been a definite loss to pupils, particularly in specific areas, such as sport. A survey of ILEA schools in 1992, for example, showed that financial constraints had affected all types of extra-curricular and out-of-school activities. Two-thirds of headteachers mentioned reductions in the use of theatre groups, puppet shows, etc.; one-third said that playcentre or latchkey provision had been affected, and instrumental music tuition was badly affected in half of the schools surveyed. Schools were relying more on parents and on charities to fill the gaps, and all headteachers expressed considerable concern. One commented that extra-curricular activities were 'an absolutely vital part of the curriculum. The need is very great in inner-city schools, where families do not regularly give children these experiences'.[11]

This may be changing. Education Extra's research for Manchester Training and Enterprise Council showed that, of 131 primary schools in Salford, Trafford and Manchester, 90 per cent were already offering some form of provision, and the majority of schools thought that they were providing more than five and ten years previously. Where there was less provision, teachers offered clear explanations. The problems of space, time and funding were mentioned consistently in response to an enquiry about obstacles:

- An increase in teachers' paperwork has resulted in staff spending more time after school keeping up with it.

- More staff have no non-contact time during the day, so after school is the only time available to mark work, plan, prepare and attend staff meetings and courses.

- The teachers' pay dispute in the 80s has left its mark.

- Staff are already fully committed with the National Curriculum.

When asked what was required to ensure that schools could develop more after-school provision, headteachers replied:

- An organisation which would run it, liaising with the school, the local community and parents.

- Financial support to purchase equipment, extra cleaning and energy bills.

- Our own playing field.

- More than twenty-four hours in the day!

At one level the motivation for providing something extra after school is very simple. As the headteacher of St Alfege with St Peters, London Borough of Greenwich, said:

> Clubs are particularly important at our school to provide our children with opportunities that many children have at home which ours, due to various social factors, do not have.

Most do not have access to playing space, art materials, games other than computer games, or growing plants and animals. Many of them spend their days at school, in their flats or playing out in the streets. We are a small school and the teachers are all very dedicated and caring. The clubs are run willingly by teachers who already have a heavy workload. . . . They are run on enthusiasm.

Adding value after school

Many of the pupils at this school have learning difficulties and they find success difficult to achieve in academic lessons. They can, however, succeed in pottery or art club; they can sing sweetly in the choir or play an instrument in the orchestra, they can score frequently in a variety of sports and leap over a box with great agility. The success and enjoyment gained in these and a host of other pastimes raises morale and increases feelings of self-esteem. It makes the children feel valued and of worth, possibly for the first time in their lives, and this makes them walk tall in school. A positive effect in the classroom often follows this increase in self-esteem. When a club or a team produce something of value the whole school basks in reflected glory and we all, staff, pupils and parents, have a warm glow.

Chris Morgan, headteacher, Goetre Primary School, Merthyr.

The menu of after-school activities available to most schools covers a range of tastes, which extend from study support activities to those traditional and sometimes purely recreational activities which have been common historically. Some provision, particularly homework clubs, can have a direct influence on achievement (*see* Chapter 4). Other specific activities (e.g. science clubs) can also be shown to have a direct influence on motivation (*see* Chapter 5). However, whatever the choice on offer, different after-school activities can prove equally valuable. In summary, after-school activities bring:

1   **Enhancement,** in that they offer opportunities for pupils to learn in greater depth or to develop further a skill which she or he has begun to acquire. One can include under this heading, for example, study skills, learning support, homework and project work, and also any provision which is aimed at stretching those with an already demonstrable ability in a particular area, e.g. computer clubs or clubs for high-flyers, where the express objective is to enhance both their experience and their levels of achievement.

2   **Entry into the curriculum,** when they enable pupils who have encountered some obstacle and who need extra help, a means of overcoming the problem, e.g. through basic skills programmes related to language or literacy (individual or family-based), or basic curriculum support.

3   **Enabling skills,** when they offer clubs or courses which can be connected to personal, technical or necessary career skills, e.g. motor projects, courses on

health and safety issues, personal skills courses such as assertiveness, interviewing techniques, career information. These can be useful for all pupils, particularly those intending not to choose further or higher education.

4   **Extension of the curriculum,** by carrying on where the in-school curriculum has to stop. They can include those activities related to personal interests and hobbies, where the pupil needs time and opportunity to explore interests and enthusiasms at a more individual pace, e.g. to complete or undertake a design or craft project; this would appeal to many pupils, but particularly those with strong personal interests and motivation.

5   **Enlargement of the curriculum,** in effect a recognition that not everything can be achieved within the existing school day. By providing after school clubs, activities or classes, a school can provide opportunities for pupils to discover new interests, to acquire new skills and to enjoy new experiences. Any activity which cannot or does not also take place within the school day, whether it be clog-dancing, juggling, go-karting or gardening is a form of such enlargement. These activities should be available for all pupils of all ages and abilities.

6   **Enrichment of the curriculum,** by adding to what is taught and used in the classroom, by building up personal motivation, and encouraging interest and enthusiasm, and by encouraging greater confidence and skill levels.

This taxonomy can be represented as a pyramid with enhancement at the apex. The danger with such a taxonomy is, of course, that it configures both a hierarchy of skills and a separation of skills. The opposite is true in practice. After-school activities are about *connecting* and promoting skills and talents. They are popular and successful because they show that success and skills come in different forms; that learning is an active process; that it can be fun and collaborative and involve personal choice and responsibility. After-school opportunities can also offer a chance for teachers to bring different skills and enthusiasms to bear: the maths teacher who teaches wood carving after school or the geography teacher running a photography class is sharing not only a personal interest, but also a personal commitment to pupils which they are quick to value.

The opportunities this offers for pupils to present a wider range of achievements and interests, and to experience a different and perhaps more successful form of learning, is not only a step towards a broader and more useful definition of 'success'; it can also help to overcome some of the negative effects of current assessment systems on pupils at risk of failure. A recent report identified those effects as an over-emphasis on normative and summative assessment, a narrow focus on academic curriculum, and a failure to recognise individual personal achievements within a 'global, summative statement of attainment'.[12] These are particularly damaging to the child who is more liable to underachieve or fail altogether.

There are, therefore, two vital points to be made in relation to the benefits of after-school activities. The first is that, in terms of the individual pupil, after-school activities can offer all the benefits represented by each layer of the pyramid and give them all an equal value. The range of skills which can be developed within the different levels can filter through the whole pyramid. The second point is that, by enabling all pupils to show what they can do in different ways, individual successes after school can be identified and recorded within Records of Achievement, and can create a virtuous circle of encouragement and achievement within school.

Participation and achievement

Given the added benefits which can flow from all these forms of after-school provision, what proof is there that participation in after-school activities as a whole can add to the effectiveness of schools and lift achievement? It must be said that, where research exists, it is partial, scattered and often confined to the more transparent links between direct curriculum support manifest in study support. Given the attention now being paid to getting the very best out of the education service, there is now both an opportunity and a need for systematic evaluation of the links between participation and the performance of the individual child and the school itself. The following studies, reinforced by the experiences of teachers and pupils cited in this book, show some of the benefits which participation in after-school activities can bring.

Learning to succeed

The Report of the National Commission on Education[13] listed ten features of effective schools. Included in those ten features was:

> *Extra-curricular activities which broaden pupils' interests and experiences, expand their opportunities to succeed, and help to build good relationships within the school.*

There is, first, the link with motivation. After-school activities, because they provide another arena for success, whether that is football, chess or a games club, provide another opportunity for the child to shine at something different and to be recognised and rewarded for doing so.

As Professor Michael Barber has shown, there is currently a gap between expectations and experience in education. Against the background of consistently improving examination results at GCSE and A levels, and increasing numbers of young people and mature students entering further and higher education, current research offers, paradoxically, a cause for worry about the quality of school life. In 1994, the Centre for Successful Schools at Keele University published an interim report based on the attitudes towards school expressed by almost 8000 young people during 1993-94. Despite many positive findings, the authors of this report found that many schools were 'failing to inspire'. In fact, 'for some young people this is a gross understatement. These are the ones who have opted out of school entirely.' The authors of the report backed up this statement with evidence which showed that:

■ 17 per cent of Year 10 students (14–15 year-olds) and 20 per cent of Year 11 truant 'sometimes' or 'often';

■ 25 per cent of pupils admit that they behave badly 'sometimes' or 'often';

■ 30 per cent state that other pupils in their class disrupt their lessons every day and, for GCSE pupils, this rises to 92 per cent;

■ 15 per cent of pupils say they are bullied.

The authors concluded that:

> as a whole a disruptive minority of 10–15 per cent are seriously undermining the quality of schools for as many as half of all secondary pupils.
>
> This may explain, but may not, the more general lack of motivation among perhaps 40–50 per cent of all pupils in secondary schools. In addition to the disappeared and disruptive, there are the disappointed and disinterested. 70 per cent of pupils agree that they count the minutes to the end of their lessons. 30 per cent believe that work is boring and 30–40 per cent take the view that they would rather not go to school. Over 50 per cent find that, in their school, pupils make fun of those who work hard.
>
> Whichever way you look at it, this is a bleak and disturbing picture.[14]

Among those who are 'disappointed, disinterested and disruptive' are to be found the 30 per cent of children who still leave school with few or no GCSEs, and for whom youth training fails to provide the realistic options of jobs, let alone lifetime skills and careers.

The Keele study emphasised perception. These findings have been reinforced by a recent study on pupil attitudes by the National Foundation for Educational Research which showed that half of all fourteen-year-olds didn't want to go to school, and one in five said that they are unhappy at school.[15] This crucial loss of motivation and the general increase in unhappiness seems to happen in progressive stages which would be recognised by most teachers. Pupils start secondary school feeling very positive, but they become less positive until, significantly, in GCSE year their commitment begins to rise again.[16]

To counter this, the Keele study suggested that the educational opportunities which could unlock commitment and potential would be those which build on the characteristics of adolescents themselves, including the need to establish independence and the need to challenge peer-group attitude. One way of doing this, it was suggested, is to provide additional voluntary classes after school, 'recognising and celebrating *a wide range of achievement*, and ensuring that the school, from the headteacher downwards, is focused on teaching and learning'.

The link between participation in activities after school and achievement itself was examined in 1989 by David Smith and Sally Tomlinson in their study of nineteen schools across four LEAs. The authors found that there was 'a fairly strong relationship between the level of attainment in absolute terms and the level of participation in after-school activities.[17] There were wide variations in the levels of participation, which they concluded opened up 'the possibility that participation in school activities may be bound up in some way with differences between schools in attainment at the end of the second year'.[18] Children with high participation scores tended to attain well in absolute terms and show better progress in attainment. However, there was no evidence that participation helped to explain differences in academic performance *between* schools. The authors concluded that 'This may be because the sample of schools is too small to demonstrate a fairly weak effect'. After-school activities may serve in the first instance, therefore, to raise levels of involvement and motivation across ages and abilities and to support the work of the school during the teaching day. This is something with which schools passionately agree.

These studies strongly suggest that after-school provision should form part of the development plan of each school, and part of the overall strategy of every LEA looking to raise pupils' achievement. This has begun to happen in certain areas.

In the Two Towns Project, in Burslem and Tunstall, three secondary schools, supported by the local universities and post-sixteen institutions, undertook a series of school-based initiatives to lift achievement. Over a period of two years, the project's success was measured in an improvement in GCSE results, staying-on rates and truancy rates significantly lower than the Staffordshire or national averages. Examination performance improved:

by roughly 100 per cent. Among the curriculum strategies adopted (which included an enhanced careers programme, visits to local colleges, residential experience, work experience and the involvement of adults, including parents) was a wide range of extended day or 'Period Nine' options for pupils and extra-curriculum visits which were intended to enlarge the curriculum and offer more intensive learning opportunities after school.

The Report also found, significantly, that 'part of raising levels of achievement is changing the peer-group attitude to achievement . . . Voluntary after-school activities can make a major contribution in this respect'. Moreover, 'the active presence of adults other than teachers, such as an artist in residence, local industrialists, colleagues from the local FE and HE institutions, makes a valuable contribution to the life and culture of a school'.[19]

After-school provision brings success

Schools know from experience that enrichment through the widest range of activities helps them to meet many of the school's direct objectives. In short, it makes for a successful school – and successful pupils.

Among the objectives of every school, priorities tend to be to:

1   provide a broad and balanced curriculum;

2   recognise and develop the potential in each child;

3   provide for equal opportunities at every level.

These, in turn, imply strong leadership, involvement of all school staff in working to ensure the school can meet its objectives, and strong connections both with parents and with the local community.

The examples of successful after-school programmes demonstrate how such activities make a contribution towards meeting those objectives, and, above all, how they can enable *all* pupils to experience a measure of personal achievement and success which can keep them interested in further education. This is the point made consistently by headteachers.

The headteacher of Matthew Humberstone School in Humberside sums it up well:

Most of [our] *students do not come from families with an academic tradition. Because of this the school values the non-academic achievements of the individual. It is aware that sometimes these can best be promoted and recognised through extra-curricular activities. The good staff–student relationship which exists within the school is certainly due in part to this. The staff are aware of the need to widen the experiences of students. It is largely as a result of this awareness that an increasing variety of educational visits and experiences appear in the school calendar. In those areas which are traditionally competitive, particularly sport and the performing arts, all students are encouraged to take part, not just those who will immediately excel.*

Another school stresses the crucial importance for young people in areas of high need:

The enrichment of opportunities for developing individual interests is crucial to young people, particularly in an area of social and economic disadvantage. Preventative approaches to failure – promoting personal and team success and achievement – need to be underpinned by this. A school can contribute to a framework of additional opportunities and relationships across a much wider definition of personal achievement and satisfaction than the traditional definition of achievement through academic success. (Parr High School, Merseyside)

Schools are clear about the relationship between after-school and the in-school curriculum. Studlands Rise School, Hertfordshire, told us that:

Our clubs endeavour to complement as well as enrich the national curriculum. The children do not necessarily attain expertise but certainly they are sociable as well as pleasurable occasions.

And they are equally clear that this brings benefits to staff as well as students. As Patcham High School, East Sussex, told us.

Excellent schools need excellent opportunities and after-school activities provide tremendous opportunities for teachers and students. Just as we are developing student activities, we are exploring the value for staff groups too.

Motivation itself starts with self-esteem and a positive experience in primary school. The Community Education Liaison Teacher at St Anne's School, Rotherham, explains how it works:

Here at St Anne's we consider that one of our biggest roles is to raise the self-esteem of the children we teach. We aim to do this by providing positive role models, by encouraging, by celebrating success, however small, and by offering a broad, extended curriculum which is relevant to the children and their needs. We also endeavour to involve parents and other people from the local community in the after-school activity club, who help with and, indeed, organise some of the activities on offer, including cookery, chess, and soccer.

We feel that each of the activities offered should be, where possible, educationally sound and complement, develop and enhance much of what is learnt in class. However, this is not to suggest that the activity club is merely an extension of the school day, for the activities offered and chosen are the results of requests from children. We aim to present each activity in such a way as to be enjoyable and without pressure, where all children can take part regardless of ability, aptitude or age. In addition to the educational benefits which we feel our children get from this activity club, we also feel that they benefit greatly in both social and emotional ways. We believe that such an activity club gives children a sense of belonging and pride in their school and local community.

From raising motivation, most teachers would agree that it is a relatively small step towards raising achievement itself. Again, schools themselves are very conscious that after-school can bring an additional chance for the child to build up learning and social skills which will support their work in school. For example, the headteacher of Christchurch CE Primary School, London Borough of Lambeth, emphasised that:

Many families cannot afford additional club activities for their children and the range on offer within the community is very limited. We seek to offer . . . the opportunity to experience a variety of skills within a relaxed atmosphere and secure environment. A number of those who attend are lacking in social skills and the ability with this, of working together across the age groups. Although such targets are within all the work we undertake in this school, this additional opportunity helps to enhance self-esteem and develop relationships of co-operation and also an appreciation of the skills of others.

Above all, there is a concern, particularly in the early years of the primary schools, for the development of the whole child, and for the need to stimulate the whole range of abilities. In Winton Primary School, London Borough of Islington, for example, where teachers offer a very wide range of voluntary activities including country dancing, the result is that:

Children are improving in skills of collaboration and concentration, learning new skills and getting additional physical exercise. Seeing them mastering the long sword 'star' or teaching themselves a new tune on the melodeon is convincing evidence of the value of these activities.

Schools which make a powerful commitment are in no doubt about the benefits. Islington Green School, London Borough of Islington takes in students from a wide variety of ethnic backgrounds: 24 per cent are bilingual, and three-quarters are drawn from economically and socially disadvantaged homes. The school places a very high premium on equal opportunities and achievement and sees after-school activities as central to those aims. The headteacher makes it clear how after-school activities can serve these multiple objectives.

Many of our after-school clubs add value to the curriculum. Many departments in the school offer clubs which extend the curriculum, e.g. a science club which gives students the opportunity to take double science in single science time. Less able students are also catered for, especially by the SEN Department, who run both reading and homework clubs for students who need extra help with aspects of the curriculum. Attendance at clubs is monitored as part of the school's commitment to equal opportunities.

The commitment of students to after-school activities is rewarded through the school's system of commendations and recorded through the National Record of Achievement and student and school statements . . . Other rewards include the improved GCSE grades achieved by students in recent years as a consequence of making an after-school commitment to one or more curriculum areas.

The school is oversubscribed and short of space, in terms of rooms, corridors and playgrounds. This further highlights the importance of running an after-school programme which engages a significant proportion of our students in meaningful and relevant activities on an already overcrowded site. The high standards of behaviour of students at the school commented on by HMI is in no small part due to the fact that many students are engaged in such activities around the site.

Raising motivation and reducing opportunities for crime

Whereas after-school provision holds promise for all children taking part, it can offer particular benefits for those who are too old for supervised play, but too young for youth clubs. Strategies to raise self-esteem, and personal responsibility have a role in all community-based crime prevention policies as well as school achievement strategies. Many areas of youth work targeted at young people at risk, whether focusing on truancy or diversionary programmes, have direct links with schools and with what schools are doing after school. At a direct level, many schools have created very successful crime prevention panels in school, to bring an awareness of crime, not least crime against young people, and to foster greater community responsibility. Some of that effort takes place in after-school time.

The simplest argument is the most powerful. Commonsense and experience suggest that, when young people are occupied and engaged in activities which interest them, there is less time or incentive for delinquent or criminal acts. Moreover, persistent absenteeism is often associated with delinquency.[20] On these grounds alone, after-school activities deserve support. Proving the link between boredom and crime is hard, given the failure to fund longitudinal research programmes in the UK, but does not diminish the general case for more provision. Indeed, in 1994, the Prince's Trust study drew attention to 'the large body of subjective evidence which convinces us that there is a linkage' between youth work and crime diversion.[21] Crime Concern (the organisation charged with developing programmes which prevent crime in the community) itself asserts that 'Young people consulted by Crime Concern report that it is boredom and a lack of affordable activities that lead to much delinquency'.[22] Other studies confirm these findings.[23]

Schools themselves exert a direct influence on truancy, disruptiveness and thereby on the success or failure of their pupils.[24] A Home Office review of the literature in 1992[25] summarised the evidence:

> *Overall, research does not provide conclusive evidence to support or refute the notion of a causal relationship between schools and delinquency. However, research does provide clear indications of how schools may inhibit or promote delinquency. Through their capacity to motivate, to integrate and to offer pupils a sense of achievement regardless of ability, schools would appear to have a significant influence on whether or not pupils become offenders.*

> *Pupils who fail, or who behave disruptively at school, or who persistently truant from school, are more likely to offend than those who do not.*

It is not simply that young people need more to do after school. Evidence suggests that, whatever the age, the most effective form of provision is that which offers them both personal responsibility for their own learning, and clear educational expectations. The successful Perry Pre-School programme demonstrated, for example, that, by the age of twenty-seven, people who had gone through the pre-school programme twenty-five years previously, were far less likely to be criminal offenders. 'Only 7 per cent of the former pre-school pupils had been arrested five or more times compared with 35 per cent of the control group'.[26] Significantly, one of the essential components of the pre-school programme was 'a curriculum which allows children to *choose* their own educational activity within a structured learning environment'.

After-school provision can also reinforce effective learning by strengthening home–school strategies. Parental involvement is increasingly seen as one of the key supports to learning – and therefore to effective schooling as a whole. Parents can be invited to participate as caretakers, supervisors, trainers, coaches, explainers and tutors in the informal context of after-school time; as Chapter 7 shows, many do so with enthusiasm.

There is another connection, however. Research shows that one of the strongest predictors of delinquency is the level and consistency of supervision exercised by families over their children, along with low parental involvement in the child's activities, and low educational attainment.[27] Supervision refers to the degree of monitoring by parents of the child's activities and the degree of watchfulness or vigilance of parents.

Many studies have shown that parents who do not know where their children are when they are out, and parents who let their children roam the streets unsupervised from an early age, tend to have delinquent children.[28]

Professor Farrington's own research based on a longitudinal study begun in 1971 on a sample of 411 London males, found that over half of the boys who were poorly supervised at age eight were convicted by the age of thirty-two.[29] The fact that a child may have two working parents does not necessarily mean a lack of supervision or a greater tendency towards crime. The Cambridge Study found that a full-time working mother when a boy was eight was associated with a somewhat lower risk of delinquency (15 per cent versus 21 per cent for boys with part-time or non-working mother.) This, it was speculated, might have been because 'full-time working mothers were associated with a greater family income and a smaller family size'.[30]

These findings stand alongside those of Richard Kinsey, whose surveys of 1200 teenage children in Edinburgh, later extended to a further 2000 young people, showed that a key factor in self-reported offending was *whether or not there was a parent or adult at home after school*. His research showed that, where there was no adult at home after school, the incidence of self-reported offending increased from 46 per cent to 59 per cent. His research led him to raise the crucial question: 'Could it be that the demand for low-paid, full-time and part-time women workers has not been met with adequate after-school provision for young people?'[31]

Against this background of recent research and comment,[32] it can be strongly argued that after-school provision can play a major positive role in reducing opportunities for crime, and encouraging responsible behaviour, in the following ways:

- By offering opportunities for leisure and occupation where none exist.

- As part of effective schooling as a whole, in particular in relation to building closer home–school relationships through extended after-school activities.

- As a means of raising motivation by offering young people a chance to choose and engage in interests which go beyond classroom teaching.

- By offering opportunities for new ways for young people and adults to work together – in groups, or in more interactive and negotiated ways, sometimes out of school.

- By providing new and informal opportunities for parents to become involved in a wide range of after-school activities, both with learning programmes and activity programmes.

- By providing supervision for those who would otherwise return home to an empty house, or who would have no option other than to hang around the local streets or shops.

Some practical responses

The merit of providing young people with more interesting and challenging options after school has been made in several different contexts.

In the UK the Home Office Select Committee investigation into juvenile crime in 1993[33] prompted demands from a variety of youth agencies for more investment in all forms of youth activities, including after-school clubs, summer holiday activity schemes, youth clubs, children's centres and adventure playgrounds. The Committee supported these arguments with a recommendation for more funds for crime prevention methods directed at young people.

Schools have, in fact, been quietly getting on with the task of providing activity programmes and, by so doing, helping to enrich as well as divert the lives of many adolescents who might otherwise be getting into trouble. Many schools who do offer after-school activities testify to the social and community benefits this brings. The effects are seen in a drop in the casual vandalism and petty theft which an empty school, particularly during long summer holidays, attracts.[34]

> A number of authorities, such as Coventry, for example, have recognised that both the intensive use of school buildings and community identification with schools can reduce vandalism.[35]

Schools who do offer after-school activities do not, however, see themselves as in the front line of fighting crime. As the headteacher at Abbeydale Grange School, Sheffield, explained:

> Among other things . . . that we do . . . there is everything from basketball coaching to computers. The idea was not to keep people off the streets, it was to maximise learning. But obviously, keeping them busy is a by-product of it.

Likewise, the headteacher of Charters School in Berkshire, an Education Extra Award-winning school in 1994, and one which runs a very impressive range of after-school activities, emphasises that

> The facilities that Charters offers are more than 'just keeping kids occupied', or 'keeping kids off the street'. The bridges we aim to build involve a pupil's social bonding with peers

17

and also with teachers; both as an ongoing process. This is why over seventeen members of staff, representatives of all levels in the school, have been involved in contributing information [for the Education Extra Award]'.

Some schools have responded specifically to the challenge of the lack of youth clubs for young teenagers.

Oldershaw School, in Wirral, for example, offers a programme specifically for ten to thirteen year-olds in its 425 Club. Established eight years ago, the Club:

caters for youngsters who are too young for traditional youth clubs but old enough to want some independence and freedom from their parents. The numbers attending are testimony to their success. The time is right for expansion. Some youngsters are ending up disappointed because activities are oversubscribed . . . Parents value such a facility. It is not seen or used as a child-minding service.

In some areas of the country it is particularly important. As Foxford School in Coventry put it:

We believe that what we are trying to do would be important and valid in any school. We believe it is particularly important in our area . . . where many of our students suffer from the disadvantages of economic decline and the associated impoverished opportunities and low expectations. An active youth programme is a real need in our area and one we will fight to maintain despite the challenges to delivery of even the basic curriculum.

Many schools have become involved in crime prevention in a specific way.

GRANGEFIELD SCHOOL, STOCKTON ON TEES, CLEVELAND: PREVENTING CRIME IN THE COMMUNITY

Grangefield School, in Stockton on Tees, is one of the largest comprehensive schools (1200) in the North East of England. It runs a splendid after-school programme with about thirty different activities from chess to recycling. The school established a crime prevention panel (CPP) in 1989 'which has now established itself as a leader in the country and . . . involves a lot of work at weekends and during the holidays'. The headteacher described the crime prevention panel as 'one of the most amazing educational developments I have ever experienced in twenty-five years of teaching'.[34] Most of the work goes on after school, during the weekends, and in the holidays.

There was, 'a clear need to channel the energies of young teenagers into constructive crime prevention rather than adding to the crime figures; to help the local community, rather than destroy it; to work with the police force and not against it'. The CPP would provide opportunities for team work, enterprise, and active citizenship – and tackle some of the problems in the school, e.g. graffiti, litter and damage. Over four years 300 pupils and six teachers have been actively involved. One of the most imaginative schemes was raising funds and setting up an enterprise company (with help from the local National Westminster Bank) to buy and donate security devices to elderly people and to local hospital nurses. An exhibition attracting 2000 people was mounted, and a mountain bike was obtained and presented to the police as an alternative to the police car. Within a week, four burglars had been chased and caught by a local police officer; our pupils were over the moon.'

With local partners in support and publicity, the project has gone from strength to strength and the school has benefited in a practical way – raising funds to install time-lapse video cameras has drastically reduced the number of broken windows. Links are encouraged (e.g. using crime figures within a statistical analysis) and 'Ideals, values and attitudes form part of a school ethos – so what better way to realise them than in a junior crime prevention panel?'

There are, of course, alternatives which take place out of school and which are more directly targeted on reducing opportunities for crime and building specific skills.

The SPLASH (Schools and Police Liaison Activities for Summer Holidays) schemes were devised as a way of keeping young people out of trouble during the summer. The overall aims are to reduce the level of youth related crime – and crimes committed on young people themselves. SPLASH aims therefore to provide activities which relieve boredom, to provide opportunities for activity and responsibility, and positive adult role models. Resources are provided from all areas: the police, local authorities, young people's organisations, and members of the local community. Crime Concern helped set up ten schemes in the summer of 1991. Typical activities across the week include sailing, canoeing, rock music workshop, mountain biking, tennis, five-a-side football, multi-activities, driving instruction and swimming. Typical partners include local schools, education welfare departments, youth clubs, youth organisations, social agencies, professional sports clubs, young offender programmes, the Probation and Police Services.

In Bracknell, for example, the Thames Valley Police have run a SPLASH programme for three years for children aged ten to sixteen. In 1993, 1650 children took part over a four-week period in activities as diverse as wind-surfing, potholing, gliding, and snooker. In 1994, over 2000 children enjoyed an even larger range of activities and 1995 'looks to be even bigger'. There is a weekly registration fee (although this is waived in cases of difficulty and for some children nominated by caring agencies). Supervision is mostly undertaken by volunteers from the community.

A preliminary evaluation in October 1994 found that, within the SPLASH area, there was 'an 11 per cent decrease in recorded crime for the relevant Police area during the six weeks evaluation period which was not reflected in the statistics for the rest of the Thames Valley'. There was a 24 per cent reduction in the number of victims aged ten to sixteen; Bracknell Town Council reported a noticeable improvement in the level of nuisance. In summary, the Evaluation 'found that there are strong grounds for believing that the SPLASH scheme is now delivering success on achieving its primary aims as a crime reduction initiative'.[37]

Younger children: play, care and learning

It's dead boring at home and you don't have a lot of things to do. I've got a little sister and she's a pest.

I would be bored at home. Completely bored. Watching TV – and I've had to put up with my brother moaning.

I think they should have after-school clubs in every school because some Mums do work and some children have no place to go . . .

Children in a Salford Primary School

Younger children have different needs from older children, and primary schools offer many different models of how after-school provision both meets their particular needs and, increasingly, the needs of their parents. For the youngest primary-age children (five to seven) the key needs after school, apart from quality care itself, may be for rest, play and recreation and a chance to recover from the school day. For the older age range, play, with its inherent links into child development through social, physical, linguistic, and creative opportunities, continues to be a vital need.

As children grow older, play blends into more structured activities as developed in the majority of primary schools. That traditional model, 'run on enthusiasm' and altruism, as well as a professional understanding of the benefits that it brings, remains, essentially, a voluntary model, with teachers offering clubs and activities after school designed to encourage a wide range of interests and skills.

Women, work and after-school care in schools

Over the years, many different routes have opened up for providing play, care and recreation for pre-school and young school-age children. To an extent, the 'drop in' after-school play and recreation offered by many primary schools sits alongside the traditional play services offered on a voluntary and statutory basis. At the other end of the spectrum from drop-in activities for children, there is a new generation of after-school childcare clubs, registered under the Children Act, and providing play and care for primary-aged children paid for by parents who are in work or seeking work. The number of these after-school 'Kids' Clubs' has grown from about 300 in 1990 to approximately 2000 in 1995. Over 700 of these are in schools. They represent a key departure in policy and practice – and a major and new opportunity for primary schools, if they so wish, to offer more structured play, care and enrichment activities after school, supported directly by parents and other agencies.

Britain has less publicly funded pre-school childcare than any other country in Europe and the need for more is now widely accepted. The case for after-school childcare is not so well advanced. Neither is it so well documented. Nevertheless, for the working parent, after-school childcare can be the vital route back into work. Even if childcare is available for the pre-school-age children it can cease, with devastating effects, once the child goes to school. Once in work, the disastrous mismatch between school hours and the average working day (750 hours across the whole year) causes misery for parents, children and employers alike. Juggling with hours, making complex and time-consuming arrangements with friends and family, reduces incentive to work and confidence and concentration at work. The situation is bad for the family, the child and the economy. As the Employment Department has put it: 'Even part-time workers experience problems – working mornings or afternoons, for example, does not fit well with escorting children to and from school'.[38]

Action is needed to meet the increasing pressures on mothers in work or seeking work. Between 1984 and 1994 the percentage of women of working age in work increased from 66 per cent to 71 per cent. The rise was particularly noticeable among mothers. In 1984, 55 per cent of mothers with children under sixteen were in the labour market. In 1994, 64 per cent were. Women with younger dependent children are less likely to work; and female lone parents, who make up 90 per cent of lone parents overall, are less likely to work.[39] Lone mothers who do work (and the numbers have dropped from 49 per cent in 1979 to 42 per cent in 1992) are more likely than married women to work 40 hours or more a week. It is estimated that, in some areas, such as Newcastle, about one half of children using Kids' Clubs come from lone parent families.[40] The decline in the traditional extended family has reduced the number of alternative (and free) carers available to working mothers. The demand for care for the elderly as well as for the young will intensify pressure on this declining pool of carers.

Working mothers in the UK are more likely to be in low-pay, low-skill, part-time work, and, therefore, particularly if they are lone parents, more likely to be in poverty.[41] As a result, 20 per cent of primary school-age children of working mothers are estimated to be, in the pejorative and judgemental language too often used, 'latchkey' children – 'home alone' after school.[42]

It is, however, not only the very young who need care after school. Young teenagers continue to have a need for care and supervision; returning to an empty home can be a lonely and depressing experience. These young people are too old for childminding, too young for many of the youth services. Many mothers who have returned to the workplace once their children are over eight are faced with an even more difficult search for solutions to the problem of knowing that their thirteen-year-old child is alone and unsupervised every day of the week for two to three hours after school.

The problem of 'latch-key' children and female unemployment has prompted some limited government action. In 1992, the problem was partially addressed by a commitment of £45m over three years to prompt the development of 50 000 new, registered, after-school playcare places for school-age children (focusing largely on the ages five to eleven) across the UK. The initiative was employment-led, and the Training and Enterprise Councils were invited to bid for and deliver the new schemes. The Kids' Clubs Network was charged with the main burden of assisting TECs to do this. In 1992, Education Extra was invited to advise TECs and schools as to how such schemes could cover the additional needs of children over the age of eleven, and how such schemes could draw out the maximum educational benefit for the children involved.

The conditions attached to funding from TECs are strict and complex. Funding is available for clubs for only one year and places created are strictly to enable parents to find or keep work. Parents pay fees, and clubs have to prove that they can sustain themselves, according to their own business plan and targets, within that year.[43]

The target is 3000 clubs by April 1996 . Meeting this target and any future expansion will involve many more clubs being set up in primary and some secondary schools. Logically, schools are, in many ways, the most appropriate place for clubs. Moreover, as participating schools testify, clubs based in schools have additional strengths – not least the fact that parents find them accessible and familiar, and the school, its staff and governors, can offer a host of additional resources which can enrich the clubs in all ways. Similarly, schools which host care-based clubs do so primarily because they know that there are specific advantages in so doing; not least (and important in areas where rolls are falling), they will attract a new generation of parents and children.

For many these conditions have proved too inhibiting. Nevertheless, schools taking up the challenge by providing regular activity clubs across the week recognise that they are offering care and supervision on a regular basis, particularly when a condition of attendance is registration and where fees are charged for certain activities or for club 'membership' as a whole. In these different ways, primary schools, in particular, are playing an increasingly prominent role as direct and indirect providers of care and, therefore, in supporting families.

Provision differs widely between areas and local authorities and the form of provision in some cases reflects different priorities within each authority. Schools can choose to act as hosts to an independent, profit-making or non-profit-making after-school club, with minimal contact between the school and the club, or they can be active partners in the provision. The 'added educational value' in each case depends on the formal links, but also on the way in which the school itself seeks to use and develop the provision. Within the terms of the Out-of-School Childcare Initiative there are, for example, two main types of registered care provision offered in schools:

1   Registered care schemes sited within school grounds, run as an independent business, managed separately from the school, and which have no formal connection with the school, other than the use of the school yard or playing field.

2   Registered care schemes sited within the school, parallel or integrated with the school's own activities, with head or teachers as active partners, involved in setting up the scheme, or represented on the management committee.

In addition, it is estimated that 3 per cent of schemes are run by schools themselves, within their own premises and not registered under the Children Act.

There is no single preferred model. The schemes can be run as parents' co-operatives, as charities, small businesses, or under simple management structures. They can be profit-making or not; they can involve partnerships as diverse as the social services, Training and Enterprise Councils, children's charities, local employers, arts and sports councils, Police and Probation offices. They can be staffed by qualified nursery nurses, play workers, childcare workers, YTS trainees, parents, teachers, and volunteers – or a mixture of qualified staff. Training for playworkers is a key issue and a central element in any definition of quality. Training can be funded through the TECs and provided in different ways.

There is some flexibility with regard to access and activities. Clubs can have a strict policy of admissions limited to working parents, or none at all.

Activities can be planned and provide for everything from homework to rugby practice, or they can be free play with virtually no structured activities. Children can be fully involved; they can decide their own rules, make their own snacks and choose their own activities; or they can be excluded from key decisions. Some schools cater for their own children; others, for example, Franche First School in Kidderminster, Worcestershire, can 'bus' in children from as many as fourteen different primary schools.

Good practice in playcare

Some schools have gone ahead and developed after-school playcare for working parents outside the Childcare Initiative.

Chandlers's Ridge School, in Nunthorpe, Cleveland, explained that they offered an after-school care club simply because: 'We are keen to extend opportunities for serving our community beyond the normal school day.' Cranmer Middle School, London Borough of Merton, put it in a similar way:

> *The purpose of the Cranmer After-School Care Club is to provide a service for the community. As a school, we were concerned at the stress being caused to parents by the need to make arrangements to have their children looked after between the time the school finished and parents finished work. We also had concerns about the suitability of the people looking after these children and the prices they were charging. Parents were in a situation where they were paying out almost all they earned to have their children minded. Many of our parents are also single parents or the only money earner.*

The purpose of this club is, first, to ensure that the children are adequately supervised by an appropriate person and, second, to ensure that the children are engaged 'in purposeful and enjoyable activities which help to develop their social and co-operative skills'. In this case, school governors have agreed to fund the supervisor's salary.

The benefits to parents are noted immediately by schools. An inner city school, with about 30 per cent ethnic minority, and high levels of unemployment and single parent families, Gosford Park Primary School (Coventry) started a Before and After Club for children of working parents. They comment that:

> *The commitment of those involved has been inspiring. The benefits we have noticed so far include:*

> ■ *opportunities for women to take up courses without worrying about children getting to school or away from school on time;*

- *reducing pressure on families by providing an alternative at a harassing time;*

- *providing an emergency service where other childcare facilities break down;*

- *enabling early arrivers at school to be taken care of.*

Other headteachers took an early initiative and have since been awarded funding. In Salford, the headteacher of Monton Green Primary School inspired the establishment of an independent registered care scheme managed by the staff employed by the school itself. The club is situated each evening in the school hall, with its own equipment. The essence of the scheme is flexibility. Parents can register for a day or a week at a time, and, on average, with thirty-six on the register, between sixteen and twenty-six attend each evening. Activities are offered on a six-week timetable, balanced throughout the week and include baking, salt-dough modelling, mask-making, collages, puppetry, sport, printing, free games and craft. The children use the school sports equipment. Activities are not curriculum-led, nor are teachers involved, but they are seen as a reinforcement of learning. The school runs no other after-school activities.

Parents using the scheme on a regular or random basis are enthusiastic:

> *It enables me to work and not have to pay high childminder fees.*

> *The . . . club is always there whereas another parent or family may not be because of sickness or holidays.*

> *[we have] the security of knowing exactly where the children are and who they are with.*

Children, too, were adamant that this was a better alternative than going home after school. As one put it:

> *It's good to do things after school . . . If you're at home and bored stiff and in the holidays you just waste time and get bored and everyone's gone out shopping . . . I wish it were still open on the holidays.*

Other schools have responded to the specific need for after-school care and have accommodated an independent club alongside their own school-based activities. Springfield Primary School in Trafford is an example of a school which differentiates between the needs of children of different ages, offering a fee-paying playcare-based scheme for younger children, organised independently of the school, alongside an extensive programme of specialist after-school activities offered by teaching staff.

The care club is run as a business, and extends from 3.30 p.m. on most nights to 5.45 p.m. The activity clubs operate from 3.30–4.30 p.m. every night. The club is limited to children from the school itself, and provides toys and games suitable for imaginative and creative play. The children have access to computers and activities are structured on a monthly theme and include art and craft work, music and drama, board games, books, indoor and outdoor sports and free play.

The school's own junior clubs are open to all children from the school. They include an arts-crafts club, guitar, recorder, badminton, gymnastics, dance, bookworm club, computers, technology, French, German, Spanish and netball. Most children belong to a combination of three to four different clubs and pupils can belong to both activity and specialist clubs. The music room and library are open after school.

There is no formal constitution for the after-school care club, but there is a statement of aims and objectives which has been agreed between the school and the club. The organiser attends all relevant school meetings. Parents pay for their children to attend the club, which is staffed by qualified play workers. The after-school activities are offered by teaching staff who provide one hour per week as part of their contract to run an activity which is educationally based.

One outstanding example of an after-school club, funded in partnership by the local authority and the TEC, and working within an active and committed primary school is in a Tyneside school:

TREEHOUSE AFTER-SCHOOL CLUB, HOTSPUR PRIMARY SCHOOL, NEWCASTLE: REGISTERED AFTER-SCHOOL CARE

> There are three types of children. There are the ones who come in twiddling their hair who need to have a sit down . . . there's another who comes in walking backwards talking to his collector . . . and there's some who come in, jackets off, and want to run. All seem to fall into three basic characters.

Pat Woodhead, Organiser of the Treehouse After-School Care Club.

The success of this club is that it recognises that children's different temperaments and needs are a key element in whether they are happy to stay in school after school.

Treehouse is a large and very successful scheme in Newcastle. It was started in Hotspur Primary School in September 1990. It is based within the school and has daily use of the school dining hall and playgroup room, with equipment stored in the nursery, medical room, hall, gym, and corridors. When weather permits, the children use an outside field and the garden and gym may also be used. The scheme is registered for fifty places and has fifty children between the ages of three and eleven each night. Overall, 135 children are registered and the organiser estimates that between one-third and one-half of these have single parents. Funding has been obtained from Newcastle City Challenge and from Tyneside TEC.

Apart from the organiser, eight staff are employed, with BTEC and playcare qualifications. It is run as a non-profit making Community Business with a management committee of seven users and five co-opted members. The scheme is open from 7.30–8.50 a.m. and 3.15–6 p.m. every day and all day during the holidays. Parents simply pay for what they use and there is maximum flexibility to fit in with the real needs of parents. In addition, the success and stability of the club means that, to date, poorer parents can be offered a range of subsidies depending on their family and work situation. This has enabled many to return to part-time work, training and education.

There is a very close relationship with the school and with the nursery scheme. The club offers a wide range of activities – sport, craft, role play, chess, gardening, environmental education, a book club, guitar, recorders, games, board games, books, woodwork and outings, and children are free to attend the school's own clubs – Scottish dancing, etc. The children themselves know that the choice is key to whether they enjoy being there – or not. One told Education Extra: 'You have to make it interesting . . . so that it's got something for everyone . . . so if you like having lessons there's some of that and if you like making things you can make things . . . and if you like running about you can do that too.'

The key to the outstanding success of the club lies in large part with the commitment of the school, and the personality of the organiser, who creates an immediate sense of trust and support for parents and children alike. The club is an example of how, in a school hall, an after-school club can be made to feel different and personal for each child. 'They don't want to come home some nights' (parent) – a view reinforced by children who said that they liked being able to 'play out' with their friends. This has been done with some care – with a home corner being created with a rug, sofa, easy chairs; tables covered in check cloths and bright crockery, and children able to make their own meals, and negotiate their own activities and the rules for running the club.

The support for parents is obvious.

'One of our parents – I'm so proud of her. We subsidised her. She did a course and she's got a really good job. Another girl had a baby when she was sixteen. Now she's finished her degree and gone on to do a doctorate in physics. When she passed her exams I felt like her Mum.'

Between the voluntary drop-in provision for younger children, and the registered playcare club, funded by parents and other partners, there is growing scope for innovation and enrichment linked to care.

The following school offers a specialised activity scheme which registers the attendance of children itself, and makes a charge to parents, for a wide range of clubs and activities offered four nights a week.

EARDLEY PRIMARY SCHOOL, STREATHAM, LONDON BOROUGH OF WANDSWORTH
A NEW MODEL FOR PARTNERSHIP

Eardley Primary School is a large primary school (500 children) which serves a multi-ethnic community, including many refugees. In September 1994, a part-time Community Development Officer – assumed to be the first such appointment to a primary school – was appointed with responsibility for setting up a new after-school club for children, geared to a wide range of activities.

An activities programme has been structured across four evenings a week, from 3.30–5.45 p.m. The club does not offer care, but registers are kept, and parents know that, once committed, the child will be expected to be there, under supervision, for the period in question.

What is unusual about Eardley is the scope, the degree of organisation involved, and the system of payment. Thirteen activities are offered across the week and the scheme provides childcare support which enables children from all family circumstances to participate. One hundred and seventy-three children are booked in for the current sessions – and demand is increasing constantly. Four or five different activities are offered each night – including lifesaving, cycling, creative writing, rounders, board games, swimming, chess, drama, junior reporters, karate, gymnastics, roller skating, storytelling, French, football skills, arts and crafts, gardening, and computing.

Children sign up for a block of twelve club sessions, one term, and pay an annual registration fee of £5.00, for which they receive an identification card which indicates whether or not they are to be collected. Each session costs £2.50 per week – £30 per term – and parents are invoiced. Allocation is on a first come – first served basis, and the club is able to offer a proportion of free places or subsidised places. In many cases, parents 'have been very willing to offer their time in exchange for their child's club session'.

The clubs are offered by school staff and outside clubs and individual experts. 'We now have a list of short-notice volunteers to complement our regular army of twelve and have sought assistance from local sixth form pupils'. The caretaker, for example, organises the rounders and swimming clubs; the St John Ambulance offers the lifesaver club. Parents take the children roller-skating; a local tutor offers French; the school's English teacher offers the creative writing, drama and storytelling clubs; the headteacher supervises the junior reporters club which uses school computers to produce a magazine; the local karate club provides the tutors for karate, and the local football club (Wimbledon) provides professional coaches for football skills. Three local sixth form pupils are regularly involved as supervisors and support.

Parents' fees go towards the cost of paying tutors a flat rate of £10 per session. The school has provided some start up funds from its budget and the Parent-School Association made an initial grant of £500. The ambition is that the club should become self-supporting as soon as possible. Sponsors have been brought in from Barclays Bank (Sports), and Adrian Moorhouse supports the swimming club. There is, in addition, supervised quiet time to 'keep up with homework' – a different night for each of the years.

The club is at present only available for the school's own pupils. It is hoped, in time, to bring in children from other schools; and to train staff in key skills (e.g. first aid and playwork). There is, in addition, a Saturday school for specialist subjects and it is hoped to start a breakfast club.

Six months after the start of the scheme, everyone involved is delighted with the scheme. Take up is higher than anticipated. There is evidence that the scheme is already attracting new parents and children to the school.

Conclusion

This chapter sets the scene for those which follow. It has shown how after-school activities can promote successful learning and successful schools and how, in their many forms, they can enrich and add value to the experience of learning throughout the school years. It has also shown, within the wider term 'after-school provision' that there is a link between learning, play and care for children of different ages. As such, whatever schools are able to do after school can also help to support family and community life. The following chapters take up the educational argument and illustrate in detail how schools offer and organise after-school activities to suit the needs of their pupils and their schools.

NOTES

1 For an overview of public policy and voluntary action to develop play and recreation services for children *see* Petrie, P. (1994). *Play and Care*, Chapter 1. HMSO.

2 Cranwell, K. (1994) A century of out of school provision. *Schools Out.* Summer, p. 8.

3 Thomas, G. (1993). *A few selected exits*, p. 16. Bridgend.

4 *See*, for example, Central Statistical Office (1994, August). *Social focus on children.*

5 Ward, C. (1994) Opportunities for childhoods in late 20th century Britain. In B. Mayall (Ed.), *Children's childhoods, observed and experienced*, p. 145. Falmer Press.

6 *Inquiry into income and wealth* (Vol. 1), p. 6. Joseph Rowntree Foundation.

7 Ibid. (Vol. 2), p. 11.

8 Ward, op.cit.

9 Hillman, M., Adams, J., & Whitelegg, J. (1991). *One false move. . . . A study of children's independent mobility*. PSI. (Quoted in Ward, ibid., p.151.)

10 Clark, R., & Wisher, S. (1991) *Out of school childcare in Sheffield*. Sheffield City University.

11 *After ILEA* (1992), pp. 2–5. Centre for Educational Research, London School of Economics.

12 Weston, P.B. (Ed.) (1990). *Assessment, progression and purposeful learning in Europe: A study for the Commission of the European Communities*. National Foundation for Educational Research.

13 National Commission on Education (1993). *Report*. London: Heinemann.

14 Barber, M. (Unpublished report, 1994). *Young people and their attitudes to school*, p. 2.

15 Keys, W. and Fernandes, C. (1993), *What do students think about school*. (Quoted in ibid.)

16 Barber, op. cit., p. 4.

17 Smith, D.J., & Tomlinson, S. (1989). *The school effect: A study of multiracial comprehensives*, p. 163. PSI.

18 The figures imply that a child with the maximum participation score of 4 would achieve a second year reading score 5 points higher than a child with the minimum participation score of 0.

19 *Raising expectation and achievement in city schools, The 'Two Towns' school improvement project*. (A dissemination report for the Paul Hamlyn Foundation.) Centre for Successful Schools, Keele University.

20 *See* OFSTED (1993). *Youth work responses to young people at risk*.

21 Prince's Trust (1994). Avebury.

22 Crime Concern (1992–3). *Evidence to the Home Office Select Committee on Juvenile Crime* (HC 441), p. 14.

23 These findings were confirmed, for example, by the study of juvenile crime in Edinburgh [Anderson et al., (1991) *Cautionary tales: A study of young people and crime in Edinburgh*], which found a quarter of young people interviewed to be 'very bored' and revealed a tendency for vandalism of property and cars to increase with boredom.

24 For a review of the literature, see Graham, J. (1988). *Schools, disruptive behaviour and delinquency: A review of research* (Home Office Research Study No. 96).

25 Home Office (1992). *Crime and its correlates*.

26 Families and schools (1993, June). In Family Policy Study Centre/NACRO/Crime Concern, *Crime and the family* (Occasional Paper No. 16), p. 44. Family Policy Study Centre.

27 For a review of current research and the relationship of these to other factors, e.g. parental disharmony, offending siblings and parents, etc., *see* Farrington, D.P. The influence of the family on delinquent development *and* Junger-Tas, J. The changing family and its relationship with delinquent behaviour. In *Conference proceedings on crime and the family* (Occasional Paper No. 20. Family Policy Studies Centre (1995, January).

28 Farrington, op. cit., p. 10. For a review of research into the role of parental supervision, both in the UK and USA, *see* the whole article, and *see also* Wilson, H. (1980). Parental supervision: A neglected case of delinquency. *British Journal of Criminology*, **20**, July, pp. 203–35.

29 Farrington, D.F. Implications of criminal career research for the prevention of offending. *Journal of Adolescence*, **18**, 93–118.

30 Farrington, op. cit., p. 13.

31 Kinsey, R. (1993, 5 March). Innocent underclass. *New Statesman*. pp. 16–17.

32 For an American perspective on the role of after school strategies, *see*, for example, Carnegie Council on Adolescence (1994). *A matter of time: Risk and opportunity in the non-school hours.*

33 Crime Concern (1992–3). *Evidence to the Home Office Select Committee on Juvenile Crime* (HC 441).

34 There is a need to collect, as a first step, some of the anecdotal evidence available from headteachers of the direct benefits of summer holiday programmes. Hartcliffe School in Bristol recorded that during its three-week summer programme only three windows, compared with the usual tally of 30, were broken.

35 Utting, D., Bright, J., & Henricson, C. (1993). *Crime and the family.* Family Policy Studies Centre.

36 *Managing schools today* (1994). Special Report, p. 56.

37 Thames Valley Police (1995, March). *An evaluation of the 1994 Bracknell and Wokingham SPLASH scheme.* (With kind permission of the SPLASH Co-ordinator, Jill Heywood.)

38 Department of Employment (1992). *Taking the initiative on out of school childcare.*

39 *Employment Gazette* (1994, November). Mothers in the labour market, pp. 403–11.

40 Information provided by Pat Woodhouse, Organiser, The Treehouse Club, Newcastle upon Tyne.

41 The Employment Select Committee (HC 227.1, para. 16, February 1995) emphasised that 'Women suffer discrimination in employment in terms of financial remuneration, promotion opportunities and job security. They are segregated by occupation and concentrated into the lower grades within occupations. Most employed women with dependent children have part time jobs and usually work few hours. . . . Part time work by women is often poorly paid and with limited job security.

42 Smith, F. (1994). To be or not to be a working mother. Paper presented to the British Geographers annual conference, November. (Quoted in *The next step for out of school childcare*, Kids Club Network, 1995.) *See also* the survey commissioned by the Confederation of British Industry (1989, August), which showed that for 79 per cent of mothers with school-age children currently not in full time employment, the lack of high quality, affordable childcare was the biggest single barrier to returning to the workforce. (Quoted in *Rural childcare*, Rural Development Commission, 1990.) For information about the extent of out of school childcare *see* the publications of the Kids Clubs Network, *and* Clark and Wisher, op. cit.

43 *See*, for example *The out of school childcare grant initiative* (1995, January), the interim evaluation conducted for the Employment Department by the Policy Research Unit of Leeds Metropolitan University. A full evaluation is anticipated later in 1995.

2

Creative and expressive learning: After-school arts activities

The fundamental reason why the arts must be taught ... is that they can change the way in which we see ourselves, and the world."

David Pascall, Chairman of the National Curriculum Council, November 1992.

Within the broad meaning implied in the broad term 'the arts', schools carry a particularly heavy responsibility for opening up the parallel world of creation and expression along with that of knowledge and information. Many children, outside school, will never visit a theatre or a museum, will never be taken to a concert or an opera, will never play or even handle a musical instrument, a paint brush or a camera; will never take part in a play, read a poem aloud, play in a band, or sing in a choir. And, since identity is bound up with culture, schools are charged, not only with transmitting enthusiasm and commitment to traditional and new *forms* of culture, but with celebrating, through the arts, the many different cultures represented in our multi-ethnic communities.

These responsibilities are expected to be discharged at a time when technology is pushing out the boundaries of the arts and changing the way that culture itself is consumed. In a 'quick-hit culture when video is king . . .'[1], where will the theatre audiences, let alone the artists and actors of the future, come from? Complaints about cultural illiteracy are balanced by fears of cultural uniformity, not only across Europe, but world-wide.

Those fears are fuelled by the persistent concern that 'in spite of the entitlement established for all children, the arts in the National Curriculum are underrated compared with other areas of the curriculum and under pressure from priorities which allegedly stem from a dominant but narrow ideological commitment to work-oriented instrumentalism'.[2] Successive reports have identified the marginalisation of the arts in primary and secondary schools, and the effect of budget cuts on book-stocks, equipment and specialist material in an area which has never been lavishly provided for.[3] Most recently, the National Foundation for Educational Research, in its study on the participation of young people in the arts, confirmed the popular impression that social class, gender and educational attainment 'remain closely linked to arts involvement and . . . to those demographically favoured young people, arts opportunities appear to increase'.[4] Moreover, some of the findings from that study suggest that the arts curriculum within school, and the lack of personal choice and involvement, can be successfully challenged by out-of-school (youth club) opportunities where young people finally discover their own personal talent.[5] These findings explain others which show that two-thirds of young people would welcome more arts opportunities, workshops, tuition and direct participation, and that the arts create a sense of excitement and achievement missing from other areas of the curriculum.

This challenges policy makers, teachers, parents and all who care about cultural vitality and diversity – as well as human rights. When there is so little scope within the curriculum, after-school activities in the arts provide the only other chance to channel talent and enthusiasm, to present teachers as well as students in a different light, and to extend participation and collective enthusiasm. Even in schools where there is little or no activity after school, there is usually an end-of-term play or concert. More contemporary and populist productions have it should be said, taken over from the classics as the most common offerings, but the nativity play is still going strong and the school year has become richer for the opportunity for children of all ethnic groups to celebrate festivals such as Diwali. The extent and diversity of what is being offered, however, imposes a great problem of choice. In this chapter are given a few examples of how, in specific circumstances, schools are offering after-school activities in the arts to stretch and challenge the natural talents of their pupils.

What price arts education?

Despite the overwhelming evidence of enthusiasm and talent that has been revealed by research, arts funding in and out of schools has never been under greater pressure. In January 1995, for example, in a Landmark Lecture to the Royal Society of Arts (revealingly entitled *Making Do the British Way*), Lord Gowrie, Chairman of the Arts Council asked, 'Can you put a price-tag on human aspirations?' For teachers trying to find the funds to cover the cost of peripatetic music teaching and the time to organise individual music tuition, the question has a heavy irony. The arts in education are at the centre of the debate on the value and the cost of arts in general. That debate has taken a new turn with the creation of the National Lottery as a key funding mechanism for future support for the arts. In the first months there had been 10 000 applications for arts funding for sums ranging from £5000 to £50m – and for everything from rock to opera.

A recent report commissioned by the Royal Society of Arts[6] has documented the drop in resources and provision in schools.

- Almost half the advisory posts in the arts have disappeared from local authorities.

- Only a quarter of authorities have a full complement of full-time advisors or inspectors in art, music, dance and drama.

- Less than a third of local authorities fund schemes to put artists into schools; only a third support theatre-in-education work.

- A quarter of art lessons in secondary schools are not taught by a specialist art and design teacher.

- Infant pupils spend less than half the time on art, craft and construction activities than they did ten years ago.

- One-third of schools rely on commercial sponsorship for arts projects.

- Three-quarters of authorities have devolved, or are in the process of devolving funding for music services.

Between 1991 and 1993 the staffing budget for instrumental music tuition fell in more authorities than it rose (in cash terms). As Coopers and Lybrand revealed in a report in May 1994, the average hourly charge made to schools for the provision of instrumental music tuition between 1992/3 and 1993/4 rose from £5.60 per hour to £11.10. Pupils are increasingly expected to pay for tuition, at a rate which tends to be in excess of £3.50 an hour. In over half of primary schools, parents contribute to funding instrument purchase and maintenance. Schools are increasingly turning to private teachers of music.[7]

The result, according to Rick Rogers, is that

> *There is a growing disparity in the ability of schools to meet the minimum requirements of the National Curriculum. In addition, many schools are unable to go beyond that minimum and offer pupils a more wide-ranging and fulfilling experience of the arts.*[8]

Schools have not merely suffered because of the absolute loss of time and support for arts teaching, they have also suffered from the loss of vitality in general. The regional basis for the arts, music, dance, theatre and opera ought to be a vital source of support for schools. But in recent years the recession has taken a large toll on the regional arts. Despite a small increase in funding for the arts in 1995/6 the outlook for regional and local arts is still poor. Some regional theatres are committed to working with, and enthusing, young audiences. In other areas, however, it may be too late. It is the small venues and companies (such as the now-closed Kent Opera) which could relate most effectively to schools, and prove such a source of innovation and inspiration.

Resources are shrinking outside school and pressures are intensifying inside. There is the expense of materials; the cost of musical instruments and modern sheet music; the higher standards demanded by audiences and performers alike – stage lighting, recording equipment, synthesizers, dance and drama costumes. Moreover, the continual changes and constraints imposed on the in-school arts curriculum have not only reduced the opportunities for dance and drama, but have added to the pressures on arts teachers to find ways of offering more opportunities after school.

Above all, there is the mismatch between the length of time which a school is able to allocate to a given subject (typically in periods of 40 minutes) and the length of time required for the creative process in a particular art-form, or for experimentation to take place within a particular medium. More than other activity areas, the arts in school require *sustained* time if those involved are to get as much out of them as possible. This is where after-school activities have a particular role to play. Here is the time required to bring a performance up to standard; to complete a school banner; a tapestry; a major piece of mural painting; to design, fire and complete ceramics; to experiment and fail with batik or silk painting.

There is, however, reason for some confidence. There is a continuing and outstanding commitment to outreach work in national companies such as the English National Opera, the Royal Ballet, the National Theatre, and the Royal Shakespeare Company, which each year take opera and drama workshops and performances to hundreds of children. In 1994, a performance of *Cinderella* with the Welsh National Opera involved 100 pupils from Hartcliffe School in Bristol, Avon, which has made a special feature in its arts activities of joint ventures with professional companies. Another production, to involve approaching 400 children, is planned for 1995. The school has also managed to arrange visits from the Royal Ballet, D'Oyly Carte Opera, the Ballet Rambert and Sadlers Wells Dance Group.

The National Theatre has established strong links with schools such as Chestnut Grove Comprehensive in Wandsworth , which was chosen to participate in the NT's Stage Door Project, for which they were required to find matching funding of £450. An Education Extra Award for this amount was aimed at facilitating participation. When this is put in the context of the school's general commitment to the arts, evident in its work in the field of dance; its production of whole-school drama/music/dance performances; its steel band; and its recently revived orchestra, then it is clear that the link between the school and the National Theatre is being developed on very fertile ground. The school is aiming to become a centre of excellence in the arts.

Rationing by price and availability is also being challenged by individual philanthropy. Thousands of school children each year attend ballet and opera performances at the Royal Opera House, thanks to the personal generosity of Paul Hamlyn. The Royal Opera House recently brought hundreds of Salford schoolchildren into the Lowry Centre for their first taste of opera-making. There is also the strong tradition of voluntary local arts activities which fosters links between schools and organisations at a local level. The Voluntary Arts Network seeks to serve the 53 per cent of the adult population who regularly participate in some form of arts and crafts activity. It endeavours to give these people a voice in the development of future national arts policies. Its overriding aim is to promote participation in the arts. Significantly, at its Third Triennial Conference in May 1994, a whole workshop was devoted to the theme of 'Linking the Arts and Education Locally'. In the background paper, it was observed that:

> secondary schools form a nationwide network of facilities, services and skills of vital importance to every community in the UK. Their specialist equipment, facilities and teachers provide a unique community resource which is often vital to local arts groups, particularly in out-of-school hours. Moreover, the catchment area of a secondary school is used, in part, as the definition of locality in . . ., and there is a growing collaboration between secondary schools and their 'feeder' primary schools on music days and other arts activities.

The workshop devoted its time to the consideration of two themes within this framework:

1   the opportunities offered by the introduction of LMS;

2   the possibility of enriching the opportunities offered to pupils 'by the development of a closer, and perhaps a more formal, relationship between schools and local artists, arts societies and clubs.'

There is, finally, the support for the arts in education from established sources, mainly the Regional Arts Boards, which maintain an active interest in supporting the efforts of schools in the various fields of arts education.

In the early months of 1995, the London Arts Board collaborated with Education Extra to run an Awards Scheme for after-school arts activities in schools across all London boroughs. The very high quality responses from schools in the capital (several of which are mentioned in this chapter) was a clear indication of the existing levels of activity and the potential for development. The LAB provided the funding which enabled twenty-seven schools to bring in professional artists to work with their pupils on after-school projects. The formula was a simple one, but extremely effective, and will no doubt enhance the educational experience of all the youngsters involved.

The LAB is not alone in its active involvement. South-East Arts, for example, operates an Artists & Craftspeople in Schools Scheme. West Midlands Arts channels its funding for schools through the Arts Education Development Fund (although this primarily supports curriculum development in school time) and provides revenue funding to an organisation which trains playworkers to use the arts in informal settings (such as after-school care). The East Midlands Board operates an Artists At Your Service scheme, whereby the Board provides funding to groups and organisations to cover up to 50 per cent of artists' fees for participatory workshops in the fields of drama (including puppetry, circus, technical and script-writing), dance and mime, literature, music and visual arts (incorporating art, craft and photography); or for multi-media or cross-disciplinary projects. The objective is to encourage long-term arts development strategies rather than supporting one-off events and performances. It aims to stimulate the development of artistic skills and awareness in schools and elsewhere. Yorkshire and Humberside Arts Board contributed to the Education Extra pilot project at East Leeds High School; and the Customs House Trust, to which the Northern Arts Board delegates its funding for that particular area, provided matching funding for the Education Extra Award to King George School in Tyneside.

Other support agencies with similar aims include the National Foundation for Arts Education, which offers both professional support and in-service training, in the form of courses, workshops and publications, to those in the field. Working with arts education practitioners of every kind, the NFAE co-ordinates and supports practical initiatives to improve the range and quality of arts education. Among the matters for which workshops and advice are offered are a number of the features of good practice highlighted within this chapter (eg Arts and the Community; Artists' Residencies; Organisation of Arts Weeks).

It is against this complex background that we have selected a few examples of schools in action for the arts after school, focussing on specific issues such as the arts and inner-cities; the arts and new technologies; arts and special needs; and arts and partnerships. Even within these restricted headings we have had to choose a few examples out of hundreds which would serve equally well to illustrate the personal passion which teachers and others bring to the offer of arts after school.

Commitment and excellence in after-school arts

The arts are vital for both primary and secondary age schoolchildren in the inner cities. As the following examples illustrate, some of the most exciting work seems to be taking place in very unpromising settings.

With the declared intention of providing 'a curriculum which complements the school curriculum', a comprehensive range of activities is offered after school at Acland Burghley Comprehensive School, London Borough of Camden, which covers sports, social and other activities at the on-site youth centre, and discussion groups, one of which is a Black awareness group, and another an after-school girls' group. The arts provision is widely respected, not least for the after-school work in the fields of drama, art and music. The school's art department has always had an open-door after-school policy, which offers the opportunity for pupils to develop their interests and skills at their own pace. Much of the out-of-school provision is offered through the work of the Youth Service, which has extremely close ties with the school itself. As headteacher Philip O'Hear says:

> We provide pupils with opportunities to find what they're good at: at this school you can try anything you want if it's worthwhile.

On the other side of London, the Henry Fawcett Infant and Junior Schools, London Borough of Lambeth, share premises in a very deprived inner city area (65 per cent of the children claim free school meals). There is a tea-time club – an essential resource for parents who are attempting to obtain or keep employment. One hundred and thirty children attend regularly; some for specific activities. There is some funding help from the LEA (parents of present and former pupils are paid a small wage as tea-time club workers), but teachers and parents also give their time voluntarily to undertake extra activities with the children. Sixty children attend the after-school gym club, run three times per week (for different age groups) by one teacher. A parent runs an after-school sewing group every Wednesday. The after-school football club is a recent innovation which proves very popular (forty-eight children attend, and there is a long waiting list). The school's creative and innovative approach is ensuring that the tea-time club is also a great opportunity for the children to learn, enjoy and extend themselves.

In particular, a new art club is being developed as an extension of the existing provision. The two schools have very many artistically gifted children, and there are plans to extend significantly the formal school time spent on art by upgrading and improving the art room and employing a specialist art worker to work with the children after-school on pottery, craft, painting and drawing.

One of the headteachers explains the importance placed on developing arts activities after school:

> We feel that a well run art club will greatly benefit our school and widen our children's horizons. Painting and drawing allow children to use their imagination, and they also teach dedication and self-discipline. Craft and pottery are both technological in the sense that children are finding out what they have to do to make things. It is intended that the art worker should work closely with the class teachers so that the art club can complement and expand on the work in the class-room. However, we all feel that the art worker should, at times, be free to let the children develop artistically in ways separate from the pressures of the class-room.

The schools won an Education Extra Award in 1994, in recognition of their achievements and as an encouragement to their developing work in the arts. As well as a cash prize, the schools received a substantial donation of clay from Messrs Potterycrafts, to use in the art club. (The schools, unusually for primary schools, perhaps, already have a kiln. Tea-time club workers and parents are to be trained in firing the kiln so that the children can take their pottery projects through to glazing and firing.)

Kentish Town CE JMI School in London Borough of Camden has made a particular feature of drama. The headteacher, Kate Frood, started its drama club three years ago.

> Numbers have reached seventy-five and never fall below thirty-five. Our clientele is extremely mixed and includes three statemented children (two with cerebral palsy and one with emotional and behavioural difficulties) . . . Our emphasis is on confidence building, co-operative games, voice projection and essentially having fun!

The drama club has clearly helped achieve the aim of:

> opening the children's eyes and minds to the world beyond Kentish Town . . . Although we have no aim of creating Shirley Temples, we have featured on a recent Radio 4 play, have

tried out ideas for BBC Schools TV, sent groups for Saturday morning TV activities, been on Blue Peter in a Rembrandt feature and done voice-overs for Talking Magritte on BBC2.

The school places a high priority, in all its extra activities, on 'visits, visiting musicians, theatre workshops, art workshops and storytelling'. Piano Circus and Recorder Unlimited have recently visited the school. Twelve children worked for a week with an artist at the British Museum on 'Responses to Japanese Art'. The storyteller Ben Haggarty has been working with Year 6 pupils on the theme of 'The Seven Ages of Man'. Artist Sue Lovell spent a week with Year 6 pupils making wooden icon boxes. And in 1994, Year 4 pupils worked with Children's Music Workshops and the City of London Sinfonia on the Interlude of Storms Opera – culminating in a performance at St Paul's Cathedral. The school received an Award from Education Extra in 1994, which included tickets (donated by Cameron Mackintosh) to see *Cats* – and a visit backstage – together with funding for other resources.

With music frequently the prime victim of recent changes, it is important to record here that, despite the serious difficulty many schools are finding in organising and funding provision, some are trying to meet aspirations by using time out-of-school. Others have simply given music preferred status within the school as a whole.

ST JOHN'S PRIMARY SCHOOL, SALFORD: MUSIC IN THE INNER CITY

This school provides an example of outstanding musical excellence in a small urban school.

The school has existed for 100 years but was moved into a new open-plan building in 1973. It serves a very built-up community where local housing includes many terraced properties without gardens. The primary school-age children can be short of safe places to play once they leave the school grounds. The school is doing its best to compensate for pupils' urban environment by developing its grounds, including a prize-winning nature reserve created by children, staff and parents.

St John's has an outstanding school orchestra, which has built up a good reputation in the area and regularly plays at local churches, charity events, and so on. With a very high level of interest from pupils, the school finds it hard to provide enough instruments for everyone who wants to learn, and especially to afford the good quality instruments the children's talents merit. In 1993, the school won a £500 Education Extra Award to be used principally for the music club. Unemployment in the area is high, and many parents cannot afford instruments or lessons for their children. The school has a special music fund ('built up by busking, bring-and-buy sales, concerts, etc.'). This is used to provide instruments and pay for violin, percussion, brass and cello lessons. Some parents play alongside the children in concerts, participate in Suzuki tuition and help with community visits by the orchestra. The school declares:

Our aim is to encourage children to enjoy both participating in and listening to music, whether it is on the radio, pre-recorded, in the concert hall, club or disco, to gain self-confidence and pride in presenting music to an audience and gain skill and enjoyment from playing instruments alone, with a partner or group, or as a member of a whole orchestra.

In addition to the music offered in class time, the extra opportunities include:

- **the chance to take up instruments such as the recorder, keyboard, flute, clarinet, violin, cello and percussion, through peripatetic lessons and extra-curricular clubs;**
- **the chance to help with or take part in concerts and shows;**
- **the chance to join the school choir and orchestra, both of which take part in festivals and perform at various sites around the community;**
- **the chance to take part in school visits to local concert halls;**
- **the chance to contribute to school concerts, assemblies, religious festivals and major productions;**
- **the opportunity to achieve academic excellence and sound examination standards, in both music theory and its practice.**

The school emphasises that 'Our school is unique in being the only state UK primary school affiliated to the Royal Schools of Music and serving as an accredited examination centre'.

As well as this strong commitment to music, St John's offers children the chance to dance at the weekly dance club; and to take part in sports such as cricket, football and netball. There is also a year-round gardening club which is well supported, with participation from parents, residents of the local old people's home and other members of the community. British Trust for Conservation Volunteers have helped with gardening activities and Lancashire Conservation Trust recently gave the school a £500 prize for its nature reserve.

Extending choice in the arts

Schools are also proving prime sites for all manner of innovation in the arts. They are extending choice in terms of the range of arts offered, the opportunities for performance and participation, and the use of technology as a means of accessing different art forms and extending what can be done within traditional forms. As schools from all over the country testify, the arts are flourishing despite all the obstacles, and there is vigorous growth in the arts after-school.

The Henry Beaufort School, Winchester, Hampshire, for example, is maintaining its commitment to the arts with an extensive programme of activities, with regular attendance figures at after-school dance, drama, and music sessions in the range of 30-60 pupils. The school deliberately describes this provision as 'Curriculum Extension', as the explicit purpose is to extend the curriculum beyond the conventional school day. Indeed, this is one of a number of schools which deliberately compress the school day itself in order to facilitate the after-school programme. Within that programme, there is a heavy voluntary commitment of time by the expressive arts staff, reflecting both their own attitude, and the interest of their pupils.

Winston Churchill School in Surrey has a strong commitment to music. Twenty-five per cent of its 1200 students (from a variety of social backgrounds) have individual music lessons. Ten extra part-time staff are employed and the music department organises a special trust fund which handles the cost of parental contributions to individual music lessons. The school is planning to upgrade its music department into a music school, to run four evenings a week after school. The school emphasises:

> At a time when there is huge pressure to cast subjects like music to the fringes of the curriculum, it is our intention to raise the status of music because of its essential role within the ethos of the school.

The Saturday club at Leighswood Junior School in Walsall, for example, offers pupils the chance to work with clay (the school has a kiln), papier maché and 3–D media. The club has been running for six years, staffed by parent volunteers who are given free use of the school premises and facilities. Chiswick Community School, London Borough of Hounslow, encourages pupils' individual talents through its out-of-school creative writing group. The school is also home to the Chiswick Youth Theatre. Older pupils assist in running many of the lunch-time and after-school sessions at Hillcrest School and Community College in Dudley. The clubs for contemporary dance and jazz are particularly strong and the students taking part in them have won many awards for their performances. After-school activities at Henry Cort Community School, Fareham, Hampshire, include workshops in cartoon-drawing and a 'rock' school. Pupils can also study modern languages in the German and French clubs. Holiday courses at the school include music and drama as well as a wide variety of sports.

During the past four years, the Cardinal Wiseman RC High School, London Borough of Ealing has become a focus for extra classes in life-drawing, photography, print-making and fashion design. The school hopes to add sculpture and three-dimensional studies to the list soon. Its Saturday life-drawing classes, which are open to other schools' pupils as well as its own students, are especially successful. Art lecturers from the Slade are involved in teaching these classes. The lecturers charge £75 per day (1993), so participants pay £5 each to cover the cost.

Some schools are developing performance arts after school as a specific response to pressures on the curriculum. Other schools see this as an opportunity for involvement and fun at the end of term, and a means of bringing in parents and community support. What is impressive about all of these is the high standards achieved by schools and the opportunities seized for performance on a regional or national stage. And, above all, the scale of involvement by staff, pupils, parents and the community alike. Within the good practice is the negotiation implicit in choice and conduct of performances, and the involvement of varied age groups.

In September 1993 the Shaftesbury School in Dorset began to offer the expressive arts GCSE as an after-school option.

> *This is because of pressure from the National Curriculum subjects, and a desire to make experience in the arts available to all – particularly students following double science, who would otherwise be excluded.*

One result has been drama of sufficiently high standard for pupils to participate at the Edinburgh Festival.

Every pupil at King George Comprehensive School in South Tyneside follows a performing arts course and over a fifth of the school's 700 pupils are actively involved in extra-curricular performing arts activities. The drama club meets weekly and the dance club twice a week. The school puts on performances every term. These have recently included *The Little Shop of Horrors*, *Antigone* and *Godspell*, as well as carol concerts and tours of local primary schools with workshops for their pupils. The performing arts work offers great opportunities for pupils to take responsibility and learn to work together. The school says,

> *On the performance side, wherever possible responsibility is put in the hands of the pupils themselves. For the last four years all choreography for shows and all dance training has been in the hands of the pupils. This is not done on an age basis but purely according to talent. Talent, in fact, is very quickly recognised and we have often seen Year 10 and 11 pupils seeking the advice and guidance of someone from Year 8 or even Year 7!*

Park High School in Colne, Lancashire has a clear and thorough commitment to a comprehensive after-school programme. The school's arts activities are especially noteworthy. The school is particularly strong on dancing and has no fewer than four dance groups – the Step Cloggers, Morris Dancers, Colne Lads, and 'Bangles, Beads and Bloomers'. All the groups perform in school and at local and national venues, and pupils have recently performed in Germany. The school's choir also performs in festivals and has won various cups. The drama group puts on three productions every year and students attend English and drama workshops outside school (such as those run at Giggleswick public school). A 1993 workshop was led by Sam Wanamaker. Other young performers play in the school's 'Big Band' or sing and play in its folk groups. The school's deputy head told us

> Park High's after-school activities policy indicates a clear commitment to developing the talents and abilities of every student. It stresses the need to encourage continued participation by as many students as possible.

A large-scale annual musical production is a feature of school life at Sandhurst School in Surrey. Significantly, the production is chosen in consultation with pupils and parents. Work on it starts each April and runs through until the performance the following February. For the 1994 production of *Barnum* over 200 pupils, parents and staff were involved. The deputy head, Carole Chevalley, told us:

> We find that extra-curricular activities are excellent for integrating pupils from different year groups. In this year's production . . . leading parts were taken by pupils from Year 7 to Year 12. No-one is turned away from an activity – open access for all pupils is important and actively promoted.

As well as the large production, pupils can take up outdoor pursuits, juggling, music, science and computer activities after school. There is a dance club which works to 'break down gender barriers, and encourage the appreciation of dance in a great variety of cultures'. Interestingly, this club is not run by a specialist, but by two enthusiasts on the staff, who are actually members of the geography department! Carole Chevalley made the point that

> the school day finishes at 3.00 p.m., and this allows after-school activities to flourish, even in the winter months, when parents are more concerned about their sons and daughters travelling home in the dark.

The high standards achieved by some schools can lead to students participating in major national arts events. In 1994, pupils of the Wey Valley School in Dorset performed an original play, *Still Waters* at the Edinburgh Festival Fringe. A cast of forty-five Year 10 students took part, and many more were involved in backstage and preparatory work. Taking the play to the Fringe cost £6300, which the school managed to raise 'through fund-raising and a cocktail of sponsorship'.

Staff and pupils hope to make the Edinburgh Fringe performance an annual event. The 1995 production of *Harbouring Doubts* (another original play) is already underway and as the school says,

> *All Year 9 are welcome to participate – and are involved not only in performance but in the production of display models and demonstrations to create an event rather than a play.*

Other schools have found novel ways of performing in public and of involving the local community. Pennywell School in Sunderland serves the inhabitants of a large post-war housing estate on the periphery of the old town; an area where crime, and particularly juvenile crime, is high. The school, in conjunction with the local Community Association which inhabits an adjacent building, works hard to offer students worthwhile activities and opportunities. The 'Pennywell Patch Roadshow' was set up to provide pupils with a platform to perform in public. Thirty musicians, fifteen vocalists and over twenty dancers were soon involved. The Roadshow has proved extremely popular; many students are working hard to become part of it. Ex-pupils now in further education come back to support and encourage the younger members. It gives regular performances in the community, and by entering competitions in the north east the group has won national recognition.

Making the most of new technology

Children are responsive to the opportunities technology offers. They are adept at using information technology, and are developing, as a matter of course, the interactive skills which enable them to make their own music, films or videos and other art forms. Music, in particular, is keeping pace with the possibilities new technology offers.

Southfield GM School for Girls in Kettering, Northants provides a fine example of a school with a forward-looking approach to technology in music education. The school's computer suites are used extensively after school, and their plans for a music technology club received the backing of an Education Extra Award in 1994. The school has a three-year plan to underpin developments in technology with the development of expressive arts. Thus the 1994–5 phase is concentrating on computers in music; in 1995–6, the focus will be the development of dance through extra-curricular activities, and in the following year, there will be an integrated arts project (with performance). The overall project is perceived by the school as a vehicle which, by its nature and diversity, includes rather than excludes; its development is dependent on the commitment, dedication and hard work of the *whole* school community. The PTA provided its firm support with a pledge of nearly £1000 for the first year.

Plumstead Manor Girls School, London Borough of Greenwich, is developing and extending the work already undertaken by a music technology specialist within the curriculum. The recording studio (a converted dental suite!) which is being set up at the school will offer opportunities to build on existing successes, in particular in popular music, such as the girls who won a competition and made their entry into a CD, used as part of an anti-drugs campaign. The creative talents shown in the past by the school's pupils cannot be fully realised within school time. The use of modern technology to fulfil their potential is an exciting prospect.

Brampton Manor Comprehensive School, London Borough of Newham, is aiming to become a centre of excellence in the arts, and one part of these plans involves the development of IT in music. The project is a continuation of work undertaken by a professional musician as a 'spin-off' from the Partners in Education programme. It will involve recording all the work on an 8-track machine.

At George Mitchell School, London Borough of Waltham Forest, additional arts funding awarded by the London Arts Board and Education Extra is targeted on the young performers and writers club. Its members will be learning about the composition of electronic music, and producing a music video. The artistic focus for this project is multi-cultural. The members of the club have already produced a multi-lingual poetry video, and have composed music for plays and backing tapes for their raps. The club brings together young people between the ages of 11 and 15 living in Waltham Forest, and especially from the areas of Leyton and Leytonstone.

Celebrating heritage

Keeping up with what is new in the arts is one side of the coin. The other is ensuring that, in a world overwhelmed by change, children have the chance to take pleasure in their own heritage. It is significant, perhaps, that so many schools are offering traditional dance and music and that, in particular, country dancing and folk music seem to be such a popular after-school option in so many schools. Moreover, in a world of diversity, with many schools able to draw on the musical and dance traditions of Asia, Africa and the West Indies, there are great opportunities for schools to foster ethnic dance and music among children.

We have referred elsewhere in this chapter to the excellent dance teams at Park High School, Colne, Lancashire. Pupils at Winton Primary School, London Borough of Islington, can start young by becoming members of Morris dancing and country dancing teams there. Maypole and Morris dancing are also available to pupils at King's Somborne Primary School in Somerset. Lace-making is another traditional skill on offer there.

There have been Morris dancing teams at Hillside First School, Great Yarmouth, Norfolk, for about nine years. There is a girls' northwest clog and a boys' cotswold morris. The clubs are run at lunchtimes and after-school, two days a week. The activity is so popular that not all of those volunteering to participate can be included. Currently there are some thirty girls and twelve boys practising. The pupils have been kitted out by the school and parents. During the school year, a great deal of entertainment is provided by these young pupils for the local community and various organisations, at weekends and during the holidays. Sometimes they travel further afield for specific events. In 1994, for example, they performed at the Bradwell Flower Festival, the Douglas Scott Memorial Concert at Woodlands, the One World Festival in Norwich (when they were featured on both BBC East and Anglia TV) and the Peto Day Festival in Lowestoft. On those occasions when they charge a fee for their services, the money is donated to Save The Children.

It is not only dance which is the focus of such heritage-sustaining activities. In the rural crafts workshop at Danetre School in Daventry, Northants, pupils can learn to turn wood, weave willow baskets, or design decorations for a canal barge, and to use traditional implements, such as pole lathes. When the school presented its major dramatic production of *Lark Rise* in 1992, there were rural craft demonstrations before and during the performances. Pupils have also participated in a number of country fairs, etc.

Crofton Comprehensive School, London Borough of Lewisham, is typical of many schools in the way it reflects its multi-ethnic intake in the range of its arts activities, both within and without the curriculum. Recent projects have involved collaboration with the IRIE Dance Company; Utol Dance members; and with the Horniman Museum, Royal Ballet and an Indian dance company in working on a 'Sacred Lands' project. The London Extra Arts Award received by the school in 1995 is intended to assist with the development of the work, employing the skills available among parents and artists to introduce new dance styles to the pupils.

Equal opportunities for special needs

Equal opportunities to access community heritage is one form of fostering equal opportunities. Another is to ensure that children with special needs also have a chance to experience the pleasure of performance and participation in the arts.

GROVE PARK SCHOOL, EAST SUSSEX:
CREATIVITY AND PERFORMANCE

Dance and drama are central to the arts programme at Grove Park School, East Sussex, where, in 1993 a lunchtime club was running throughout the year and additional after-school meetings for a term of each year culminate in an annual show involving the whole school. Grove Park is a school for children with severe learning difficulties and the staff believe that participating in dance and drama is of great value to the students. 'The majority of pupils work towards and within level 1 of the National Curriculum, so anything which gives them a means of "creating" and expressing themselves in their own ability level is very valuable.'

The school's dance teacher explains how the enormous scope and adaptability of dance as an activity helps to meet the very different needs of the pupils:

'. . . many of the pupils are mobile (some excessively). Some have sight or hearing impairment; some have Downs or other syndromes and some have profound and multiple learning difficulties (PMLD) . . . Others spend much of their time in moulded wheelchairs, unable to use their body without hands-on assistance. Wheelchair dancing certainly has its place in the popularity stakes. My personal aim is, however, to encourage every student to experience bodily movement. It is for this reason that PMLD dance sessions are usually held on floor mats, grouped in an endless variety of patterns. We use props such as silk and chiffon scarves, hoops and balls, ribbons, feathers and music. Students, helped by assistants, work through "aerobic" exercise routines which enable them to experience bending, stretching, shaking, tensing, relaxing . . . exercise progresses to body dancing, where pupils might try rolling, curling, spinning, rocking and so on. Towards the end of the session some of the moves practised might be combined to form a group dance, or perhaps individual pupils will show the rest what they can do.

. . . Whilst sitting or lying down may be the most appropriate way for some to dance, others need to run and jump and make full use of space. There is an enormous scope in dance to combine spatial awareness with large and energetic movements, as well as with precise and lyrical steps, each of these creating new challenges.'

As well as meeting the individual physical challenges of dancing, the students learn through dance to work together, to use and maintain eye contact, and to be aware of social relationships with other dancers, the teacher and an audience. Video has also been used to good effect. Pupils' performances are recorded and, when played back, they can help pupils remember as well as building self-confidence.

The school uses dance to encourage creativity and expression in pupils, and at the same time involves every pupil in the structured effort of putting on whole-school productions. In 1993 Oliver was enthusiastically received by parents and friends. Putting on the productions involves extra commitment from parents as well as pupils and staff, because the school's wide catchment area creates transport difficulties. Parents have had to arrange transport between them to allow pupils to stay on after school hours. Other activities such as the regular workshops in theatre, dance and drama run at lunchtime to avoid this problem. Students' interest in drama and theatre has also led to evening or weekend trips to see London productions.

There are other, collaborative, opportunities for promoting the arts after-school among pupils with special needs. The Youth Service in London Borough of Haringey, for example, has an extensive arts programme, in particular collaborating with the Praxis Theatre Company, the Tellers Theatre Company, the Ujama Art Project, and Haringey Arts Council. They hold regular drama workshops and performances, and have a Greek Cypriot dance group, an Asian dance group, and a Steel orchestra. The Service runs three projects or clubs for pupils with disabilities from across the whole borough. These are: an integrated after-school club for students from Moselle School (for those with moderate learning difficulties); a hearing impaired club for students from Blanche Neville School (LB Haringey's school for those with hearing impairment); and a Greek Cypriot special needs support group for Greek Cypriot young people with physical and learning disabilities.

They plan to bring in a professional artist to run creative movement and art workshops with the Bruce Grove Area Youth Project during 1995. This proposal received an Award under the London Extra Arts Awards Scheme for 1995. As Bill Hickey, the Head of Youth and Community Services in Haringey points out: 'Movement workshops are helpful when working with children with special needs, since they combine both physical and psychological experiences.'

In support, he quotes the words of Veronica Sherborne: 'Movement experiences are fundamental to the development of all children but are particularly important to children with special needs, who often have difficulty in relating to their own bodies and to other people.'

Hugh Vivian, teacher at Gayhurst School, London Borough of Hackney, commented after a workshop with his Year 2 class: 'Those children involved in the performance experienced something very positive which developed their confidence and self-esteem.'

Special times for the arts

Artistic work sometimes requires a concentrated burst of activity, but equally often, it requires dedicated and collaborative effort over a long period of time. The chance for children to spend a whole week, even a whole day, working on a project of their choice is rare and valuable. Seeing through the creation of a mural or a piece of ceramic work, writing a musical composition or a story from beginning to end, taking a dance from choreography to performance in a weekend or a week of full-time work can bring immense satisfaction. This is where specialist arts workshops and arts weeks come into their own. This concept often overlaps, in practice, with that of a festival, involving the whole school in celebrating the arts. The heady atmosphere of a festival or carnival is an exciting way of switching young people on to the arts, and all-inclusive, whole school events draw in the shy, the diffident and the nervous, giving them as well as the naturally extrovert performers the chance to participate and perhaps discover new talents.

Arts workshops and weekends

Arts workshops make a special time and a special place for the arts. They can also provide an excellent opportunity to bring in outside specialists. The input of expertise can be an inspiration to school staff and students alike. They are becoming a regular feature at many schools, offering extra opportunities for students to explore new avenues and teachers to share their special skills and interests.

ALLERTONSHIRE HIGH SCHOOL, NORTH YORKSHIRE: WORKING THROUGH THE WEEKEND

A special feature of the out-of-school provision at Allertonshire School is Weekend Workshops. These feature artistic and creative activities and come at the end of two days with performances for other children and parents.

The workshops were started five years ago, as an experiment to broaden the horizons of school students. They are a very special added extra for students who already participate in a full programme of out-of-school activities during the week. The opportunities for dance, drama, music, English activities at lunchtimes and after school (as well as sports, technology, music, computers and environmental education) are well established parts of school life. But the Weekend Workshops further extend the children's work opportunities for challenge in the formal curriculum and other out-of-school activities, because they operate by buying in a very high level of expertise. Over the years the school has formed close relationships with a number of very effective groups and individuals who come in to lead the activities. They include the Rejects Revenge Theatre Company, which leads Drama workshops, and Skylight Circus in Education, which runs the Circus Skills weekends. National coaches are also brought in to run Gymnastics weekend workshops.

Allertonshire School has gained some funding from Yorkshire and Humberside Arts, the District County Council and the County Youth Service to subsidise the cost of the weekend workshops, so the cost to students is heavily subsidised. The grants cannot cover the cost completely, and up to now each student has been charged £7.50 per weekend to help make up the difference. Every single workshop is oversubscribed. However, this cost, although nominal, has had the effect of excluding some students from the workshops as they cannot afford to pay. The school feels that this is in conflict with equal opportunities and is now looking for ways to meet the extra cost for future workshops, so that there can be completely open access for all the students. The Award they received from Education Extra in 1994 will hopefully contribute towards this process.

In the school's annual survey of parents' opinions, the Weekend Workshops were highlighted as a much-valued, unique extra opportunity. 'Many parents have spoken of the dramatic change of confidence that they have observed as the result of one of our weekend workshops.'

Three-day arts workshops in the holidays have become a feature of the provision at Abbotsweld Primary School in Harlow, Essex.

We wanted to offer something that would include a learning experience as well as having fun. Little opportunity is open to children of this age (8–12) to work in the Arts, and our projects have included music, fabric, video-making and photography. All of these have been a real hands-on experience.

Oakwood High School in Salford organises Saturday morning workshops for circus skills and music, alongside its sports workshops. And at Cradley High School in Dudley an Activities Week in July 1992 featured a three-day workshop for students to make their own pop music. Two bands were formed as a result, and they have continued to be part of school life, inspiring more pupils to get involved in making music.

Interest is now such that demand far exceeds the availability of equipment, and practices have spilled over into some Saturday mornings as well as the more usual after school time on up to three nights a week.

There are also unique opportunities for collaboration in the arts, especially between secondary and primary schools involved on joint initiatives. Many primary schools join up with secondary schools for after-school musical or dramatic performances. What is less common is a continuing link between primary and secondary schools on a long-term creative project.

Pupils from eight primary schools are involved in the weekly creative arts workshop held at King Harold GMS in Waltham Abbey, Essex. Parents and other community members get involved alongside teachers. The workshops offer a choice of 11 different activities, including puppet-making, dance, clay and dough craft. One hundred and twenty children are involved every week.

Carnivals and festivals

Some schools make a feature of celebratory carnivals and festivals which focus on a theme, or on the place of the arts in the school, or relate to a special week in the year.

At Shenfield High School in Essex the annual Arts Festival is an opportunity 'to invite professional men and women to come into school to judge, share, talk, display and lead'. The festival here is held on an inter-house basis. Like the school's regular programme of arts and other activities after school it is seen as 'an integral part of the education process' . The Helena Romanes School in Essex is home to its local authority's Music School as well as having a Community Education Centre on site. The school hosts summer holiday music schools and also Easter music schools. In addition, it hosts the Dunmow Summer School of Performing Arts. Following the restructuring of community education in Essex, the school will be pioneering the idea of a School of Community Arts. Through the out-of-school activities young people are encouraged to 'major in the performing arts'. And Pen Park School in the Southmead area of Bristol, in Avon, as well as providing after-school activities on a regular basis, also makes a feature of an arts-and-crafts-focussed Activities Week with a great range of activities, which include jewelry-making, model-making, 'favourite experiments', shirt transfer design, baking, circus skills and landscape painting.

Friends and partners in the arts

Within the general scope of arts development after school, there is a whole range of outstanding examples of innovations in individual schools which are clearly replicable elsewhere. These adventurous projects often involve a working partnership with others, and all of them accept the principle that schools are not meant to be isolated within the community.

Artists in residence

One means of providing added value is to bring artists themselves into residence. The London Arts Board, in conjunction with Education Extra, has recently sponsored awards for the arts in London schools expressly designed to bring more artists into schools as a means of direct enrichment. As with the weekend workshops, this brings school students into direct contact with arts practitioners from potters to poets, whose inspiration and skills are a source of significant educational enrichment for young people.

At Brannel School in St Austell, Cornwall, the principle of extending the curriculum and of working in partnership with the local cluster of primary schools was well illustrated by the special fortnight in January 1993 with Desmond Carty, Commonwealth Artist in Residence. His classroom work was extended out of hours, and led to a very successful joint public presentation by pupils from the different schools. Artist-in-Residence visits are so much an accepted part of life at Brannel that they are considered 'almost routine' now. The school also uses workshops regularly. In the school year 1992–93 workshops with the Performing Arts groups Attic Dance, Transitions and Les Saxons were held in school. Work done in such workshops has led to groups from the school taking their own performances outside, to as far afield as the Barbican Theatre in Plymouth. In 1993 two of the school's pupils were selected for the Cornwall Youth Dance Company.

The Gwyn Jones Primary School in London Borough of Waltham Forest speak warmly of the effectiveness of their Artist-in-Residence, who ran a week of workshops, working throughout the school. They tell us that the artist in question, Anthony Glenn,

uses very little in the way of props, but concentrates on his skill at telling stories and acting skills. He is liked by the children, and pupils are eager to participate. We have on a few occasions had him perform to the whole school, giving extracts from Romeo & Juliet *and* A Christmas Carol. *He raised the level of interest in Performing Arts from both staff and pupils. He is very clear in his explanations, and has good control. Therefore, large amounts of work can be achieved in a short time.*

These are just two of many accounts from schools in contact with Education Extra extolling the merits and special benefits of using Artists in Residence.

One of the key partnerships for the arts has, always, been founded on the support of parents who have found themselves in many schools active participants in after-school performances, making costumes, scenery, providing music, technical expertise, or even taking part in school performances. One more extended form of partnership, however, is when parents come together as tutors and sometimes learners alongside children in arts programmes.

CWMRHYDYCEIRW PRIMARY SCHOOL, WEST GLAMORGAN: 'CEIRW BACH': PARENTS AS PARTNERS FOR THE ARTS

CEIRW BACH (Little Deers) is an Education Extra project which started in January 1994 at Cwmrhydyceirw Primary School on the outskirts of Swansea. The project is funded by the Gulbenkian Foundation and is now supported in part by the LEA's Community Education Department.

The intention of the project was to set up an After-School Arts Club where parents are teachers, tutors and learners alongside the children themselves. Once the funding from the Gulbenkian Foundation was confirmed a coordinator – teaching at the school – was appointed. Parents readily and enthusiastically agreed to support the idea.

The headteacher, Julie Jones, writes:

> When our first club evening arrived, to our astonishment, eighty-six children attended. On the second evening it was sixty-three. These numbers have remained constant. A number of staff members were keen to be part of Ceirw Bach – and no fewer than forty-six parents agreed to help. The way mothers have organised and supervised activities has been extremely impressive.

The emphasis has been firmly on the arts. Mothers are involved, for example, in drama classes, calligraphy, ceramics and silk-screen printing. The standard of the crafts made is extremely high and it is hoped that it may be possible for some parents to take childcare qualifications as a result of their involvement – and also other qualifications which may become available with the expansion of the scheme into the local Comprehensive School – which has now appointed its own after-school coordinator.

The headteacher is very keen to emphasise that 'Ceirw Bach (Little Deers) is not a child minding organisation. The club aims to encourage children to work imaginatively alongside adults in a relaxed but structured atmosphere so that they can discover the joys of a prolonged experience at a chosen activity. There are opportunities to rotate through the activities so that the child can concentrate, experiment, succeed, and then move up'.

By going forward with the Comprehensive School and being able to use its computer facilities and sports facilities, for example, Ceirw Bach is now extending its choice of activities. It will also be offering a successful model of how resources for children across the age range can be put to better use.

Other schools offer excellent examples of how links with local theatres or arts agencies can be formed.

L'Ouverture, a local professional arts group, has a long association with The Reay Primary School, London Borough of Lambeth. The group has worked with the school over many years, bringing to the children a variety of new skills, relevant to the curriculum and at the same time great fun and always 'hands on'.

L'Ouverture runs workshops in all aspects of performance arts and media technology. Children and adults alike attend these sessions after school and finally a performance is staged for the community. Through working closely with L'Ouverture over the last three years, many of the children from the school have acquired substantial skills in modern lighting and sound technology, and computing skills, all in relation to performance. At all events at the school, children can be seen operating this equipment confidently and safely on their own.

The association between school and theatre group has now been brought even closer as the theatre company has moved into the school building. From this base they operate a series of after-school projects throughout the year in Theatre Studies, including performance arts, lighting, sound and computing technology and design.

The Queen Elizabeth School in Middleton, Rochdale, is a good example of how after-school arts activities can bring together the schools in an area and draw in the local community. Adults work alongside pupils in the Art Group, and local college students have brought their help and expertise in lighting and so on to the school's recent dramatic productions. The school is now working to develop a Brass Band, to involve six local primary schools as well as Queen Elizabeth School pupils.

Holly Hall Community Comprehensive School in Dudley is another school reaching out to its local neighbours, in this case through a scheme to introduce

Shakespeare to primary school pupils. Twelve- and thirteen-year-old pupils at Holly Hall have formed a Youth Theatre which will perform for the younger children, and are establishing themselves as the Youth Theatre in Education Company. Staff believe that the Shakespeare for Primary Schools Project

represents an exciting challenge . . . the opportunity for worthwhile cooperative work, whether administrative, support or on the stage, is immense.

The school hopes that the new theatre company will become well established and so benefit many future generations of students in the area.

Agencies such as Community Music East, which is based in Norwich, provide a good working model for others who may wish to collaborate with schools. This venture began its life as an MSC Community Programme, training unemployed musicians. When MSC funding for this project ended in 1988, CME was not large enough to obtain funding under its successor, and therefore set up its own independent company which operates in harness with Community Music (London). Its activities include peripatetic music workshops, especially focussing on disadvantaged groups; and an integrated schools project, running 12-session series of workshops for clusters of schools, including special schools. They bring together the skills of professional teachers and of volunteers; and the potential of pupils in mainstream schools and of those in special education. Their near-neighbours, the Norwich Community Workshop provide a base for after-school and holiday activities for local pupils, including an upstairs studio where a variety of visual arts may be undertaken under the supervision of a tutor.

The work of the National Early Music Association (and the Regional Early Music Fora) is typical of the way in which voluntary arts organisations, most of which are within the voluntary arts network can develop productive working relationships with schools. One early music enthusiast in the north-west records that he has for several years been running an early music workshop for young people on a voluntary basis. This has been made possible by the valuable support of the local school, where they meet each week in term time. This particular forum even has a fund 'especially for the promotion of early music among young people' . They run a special day each year at which young people can have hands-on experience of playing early music under the expert tuition of professionals. These sessions regularly attract sixty to seventy participants. This is not the only one of the Fora which is so directly in touch with schools; and this is certainly not the only organisation which has established such relationships. It must be true that there is enormous potential here for further expansion, to the great benefit of pupils of all ages.

Conclusion

We have focused in this chapter on only a few among hundreds of different schools and on selected ways in which they are working to unlock the talent of their pupils. The overall picture is one of genuine optimism which both challenges and reinforces the general concern about access to and enjoyment of the arts among young people. The after-school culture offers another way forward. It also emphasises the need to provide and encourage choice for young people – especially those who are disadvantaged in many other ways.

The participative activities described in this chapter not only put young people in touch with their own creativity; they also connect them to the past and future of a collective culture. There is another equally powerful argument. Investment in the arts is not just about leisure and pleasure – although it would be justified in those terms alone. The cultural industries will provide a large segment of the jobs of the future. Making time for the expressive and creative arts after school as well as in school will prove, therefore, as useful as it is pleasurable. As such they deserve to be publicly supported on economic as well as on cultural terms.

NOTES

1 *Daily Telegraph*, 24 December 1994.

2 Harland, J., Kinder, K., & Hartley, K. (1995). *Arts in their view: A study of youth participation in the arts*, p. 4. National Foundation for Educational Research

3 Calouste Gulbenkian Foundation. *The arts in schools: Principles, practice and provision* (2nd edn), p. 61.

4 Harland et al., op. cit., p. 279.

5 *See*, for example, the case studies on young people and youth clubs in Chapter X.

6 Rogers, R. (1995). *Guaranteeing an entitlement to the arts in schools*. Royal Society of Arts.

7 Coopers and Lybrand/Mori (1994, May). *Review of instrumental music services*.

8 Rogers, op. cit., p. 5.

3

Physical learning and healthy living: After-school sport[1]

. . . in London we have lower participation rates than in any other region in the country. Something's not right. The answer has to be to start with sport for our young people, to make sure they all have positive experiences of playing sport from the word 'Go'. It is those early experiences which shape a child's attitude to sport in later life – to opt in – or to opt out.

Fred Smallbone, Chairman, London Council for Sport and Recreation.

In 1993 the Sports Council set out the key changes affecting sport in school, and, by implication, extra-curricular sports-based activities.[1]

Over the past decade there has been something of a revolution in both education and sport. The education world has had to face up to new ideas and legislation placing it firmly in the market place with sport at school perhaps taking second place to economic and academic considerations.

In this chapter we shall be looking at some of the ways schools are offering all manner of sports, and we will look at some of the issues which are contextual to after-school sport. The choice of what to include is problematic, given the sheer volume and diversity of what schools offer. There is, also, a relative wealth of published material about sport in and out of school. This chapter therefore focuses on a few issues where schools are developing after-school sport in particularly innovative ways – for example, in promoting individual activities and sports; in fostering community links, and new forms of partnership and in developing a healthy life-style. Other major opportunity issues, such as gender equality, which run through the whole of after-school provision, are largely illustrated within these issues, rather than as an artificial sub-division. We shall also be looking at some of the ways in which the schools are seeking to build or participate in the new partnerships recommended by the Sports Council.

Issues in after-school sport

Sport is a phenomenon somewhat set apart within the context of after-school activities. The traditional public school ethos which saw sport as vital to building character through team work, determination and often, physical pain, has, in the past, been reflected in the structure of a school day usually geared to an afternoon of sport. That commitment to 'sportsmanship' mirrored in national life, particularly in the imperial role of cricket as a means of spreading a common culture throughout divergent colonies, has also been historically reproduced in state schools. The key difference has been that whereas the public school has set time aside each afternoon for sport, the state school has usually had to make time available *after* the school day and at weekends for sports practices and competitions.

One common adult memory is, therefore, of staying after school for team sports practice. Even this particular form of collective activity was, however, usually confined to those who were particularly keen and talented enough as children to be selected as members of the school teams. This guaranteed a sense of exclusivity which has probably inhibited many adults from taking up sport in later life.

Given the 'added value' which sport can bring to those who participate, wider access becomes critically important. This is, after all, one area of education where talented children are particularly likely to be spotted and selected for extra attention and training over and above what the school day can offer; they are conspicuously successful within the community of the school, and their special talent is seen as something to be nurtured and developed by the school. That could not have happened without the support of specialist teaching staff who have made a collective commitment to after-school sports themselves.

Moreover, changes in access to sport exemplify differences in the lifestyle of today's children.

25 years ago children in London walked to school and played in parks and playing fields after school and at the weekend. Today they are usually driven to school by parents anxious about safety and spend hours glued to TV screens or computer games. Meanwhile , community playing fields are being sold off to property developers at an alarming rate.[2]

'This change in lifestyle has, sadly, meant greater restrictions on children,' says Neil Armstrong, Professor of Health and Exercise Sciences at the University of Exeter. A five-year research project based at the University of Exeter, concluded in 1990, found that, of 700 eleven to sixteen-year-olds, 48 per cent of girls and 41 per cent of boys exceeded the safe cholesterol levels set by the American Heart Foundation for children. Moreover, 13 per cent of boys and 10 per cent of girls were overweight and, over a 4 day period, half the girls and one third of the boys did less exercise than the equivalent of a brisk ten-minute walk. The authors of the report concluded that:

if these symptoms are being uncovered in pre-teenagers, there is a strong possibility they will track these children into adult life.

Evidence suggests these warnings are already too late. Leisure habits among the adult population in Britain show an emerging picture 'not of an active and busy population, but of one that is extraordinarily passive', spending their leisure hours reading, listening to music, and slumped in front of the TV.[3]

Evidence of the poor health of the adult nation is already available. A series of recent reports have demonstrated that poor health is linked to poor diet and lack of exercise. In 1992, for example, 8 per cent of Royal Navy recruits failed their fitness test, and 17 per cent a swimming test, compared with 5 per cent and 15 per cent who had failed in 1984. This report concluded that the main reason for this was 'a lack of fitness and . . . individuals being overweight'.[4] The New College Durham Report on the Decline in Physical Education amongst sixteen to eighteen-year-olds also observes that

Over the past five years there has been a noticeable decline in the physical education and sporting skills within the 16–18 year-old age group entering for sports – specific studies at colleges of further and higher education. Overall, there has been an increase in overweight students who are lacking the basic skills of running, catching, jumping, mobility and hitting. Few appreciate the health/fitness factor.[5]

The Government itself is concerned at the incidence of coronary heart disease (CHD), which is the single largest cause of death in England and accounts for 25 per cent of total NHS expenditure. It is clearly related to the lack of physical activity. The national target is to reduce the number of deaths from CHD in people under sixty-five by at least 40 per cent by the year 2000.[6]

It is relatively easy to suggest that one of the reasons for this interest in physical activity in adults is the decline in the numbers of youngsters taking part in school. sport, or to the proven gender difference in participation in sports.[7] Regional and national sports councils are making strenuous attempts to promote more access to sport, stronger links between schools and clubs, and stronger community partnerships. Research also suggests that young people, far from being uninterested in sport, are positively interested in a wide range of sporting activities and want to try out and take up new sports both during their school careers and once they have left school.[8] In particular, adventure sports figure highly in their expectations, as do health and fitness activities. Few youngsters show a total lack of enthusiasm for sport, and in many cases, this can be balanced by a 'burning passion' for other leisure activities in the arts or music.[9]

Schools and sport

In recent years, the future of school sports and its significance within and outside the timetable has come into increasing question. This has been partly due to the recognition that the pressures on physical education and school sports have led to a serious reduction in time available; at the same time, the sale of school playing fields by hard-pressed schools has become a political as well as an educational issue.

On 15 March 1994, *The Daily Telegraph* reflected on the fact that:

> Between the wars Denis Compton's genius was first earmarked when he played for London Elementary Schools. Few London primaries now play any organised cricket. A survey of Derbyshire state secondary schools revealed that only half the schools that replied to the survey said they still fielded cricket or rugby teams for inter school matches. The most popular alternatives were dance, gymnastics and table tennis. There has been no such decline in the independent sector.

In practice, time and resources are tight; physical education and sport have been affected, successively, by changes in the curriculum, by cuts in budgets which have forced the sales of playing fields, by the introduction of the Local Management of Schools, the lack of physical education specialists in primary schools, and by the impact of the teachers dispute in the early 1980s which cut down extra-curricular activities.

In fact, as the Sports Council observed in its document *Young People and Sport: Policy and Frameworks for Action, (1993)* many schools had broadened their physical education curriculum to include a wider range of activities during the 1970s and 1980s, including minority sports and health-related fitness. But a lack of resources and time inhibited effective programmes in many schools and 'the provision of a wide range of opportunities for all, at the expense of teaching a limited number of traditional activities in depth, became a point of contention both within and outside the PE profession'. Issues such as sport and the community, the place of dance and outdoor education, special needs, equal opportunities, cross-curricular links, and qualifications were all urgently debated.

Physical education is now included in the national curriculum as a Foundation subject. In principle, according to the Sports Council, therefore, the guidelines ought to promote positive changes.

The National Curriculum is one of the best things that has ever happened to PE. We have a curriculum that is progressive from 5–16. There should be an improvement in quality across the whole country.

The debate is not yet over. More recently the proposals drawn up by Sir Ron Dearing, will mean, according to Chairman of the Select Committee on Education, Sir Malcolm Thornton, that sport will take up just 5 per cent of the curriculum. This is 'little more than half the physical education they need to keep fit' say doctors, sports authorities and teachers. The Central Council for Physical Recreation has drawn up a charter for school sport, supported by the Conference of Medical Royal Colleges and the teachers associations which has suggested that pupils should spend at least two hours a week doing PE . Under Sir Ron's plan they have just eighty minutes. Sir Malcolm Thornton says 'Teachers should be given incentives to run sports clubs . . . [because] We are not addressing the problems of physical illiteracy.'[10]

In recent years the perceived decline of traditional school sports and the question of incentives for teachers has become a hotter political issue. Successive Ministers for Sport have called for more team sports in schools. Ian Sproat, Minister for Sport in 1995 declared that 'the most important thing I can do' is 'to get team games and competitive sport widely played in schools again . . . I do not mean lessons on the history of sport, or stepping on and off benches or going for countryside rambles . . .'[11] In April 1995,[12] he suggested that state schools might be required to publish sporting as well as academic information in their annual school reports and has opened internal government discussions on special payments for sports coaching after school – proposals which, by May 1995, had not met with positive response within Government.

The Labour Party has not been idle either. In September 1994, the Opposition Spokesperson, Mo Mowlam, launched a campaign calling for more arts and sports education quoting the case of Highbury Grove School where cricket is no longer played, and where football can be played for only limited times and on municipal pitches. In contrast, it was observed that Eton had just spent millions of pounds on rowing facilities.[13]

The loss of traditional sports is explained in part by the loss of playing fields for development. It has been estimated recently that 5000 school playing fields have been sold off since 1979.[14] 'We are notified of five land sales a week', says the Director of the National Playing Fields Association. 'That means somebody is selling a playing field somewhere in the UK five times a week . . . So much land is being looked at in terms of development. If land is lost for play, sport and recreation, local communities have a poorer quality of life.'[15]

Along with the loss of playing fields has come the loss of swimming lessons. Many schools no longer have access to regular swimming practice and pupils do not learn life-saving skills.

All these changes have had an inevitable effect on extra-curricular activities.

In 1991, the Secondary Heads Association published a survey which showed that over the previous ten years 70 per cent of state schools had suffered a decrease in voluntary extra curricular sporting activities over the weekend, and 62 per cent had lost activities previously offered in lunchtimes and after school. The reasons given for that decline varied: 82 per cent of teachers said that their workload had increased following the introduction of the National Curriculum; 63 per cent cited the effects of teacher contracts; 32 per cent the position of teachers; 23 per cent the state of facilities; 21 per cent the new charging policy and 12 per cent the lack of facilities.

Not all bad news

Local Management of Schools increases the scope available for schools to make existing and improved resources available to the local community and to local sports clubs. Opening the school for more sporting activities can be an attractive option for schools – especially where enhanced facilities can attract local sports clubs. Moreover, schools can now keep income generated from non-school use. Costs must be covered and any surplus can be used to enhance the school budget. This could strengthen both the community base of the school, generate more income and more interest in sport.[16]

Other positive developments reflect the commitment, led nationally and regionally by the Sports Councils, to bring more opportunity for sport, particularly for young people who lose out in the luck of the draw, starting in 1993, with the adoption of Young People as the major, primary target in national and regional shortages. Policies have evolved since then to reinforce, at the highest political level, the commitment to open up sporting opportunities for young people, to encourage excellence, e.g. the 'Tops' programme – Top Play/Top Sport and Top Club. There is also the new opportunity represented by the National Lottery to fund new developments. One result of this increasing political emphasis on sport and other factors leading to change has been, for example, that, more curriculum support is being provided at a regional level (e.g. the South East) and many schools are becoming more receptive and innovative and are looking at ways of stimulating excellence in specific sports.

The emphasis is on creating a framework with all community partners involved in extending sporting opportunities for young people. The Sports Council sees this as a model for what schools themselves will have to do to develop extra-curricular sports.

> *Teachers have traditionally provided many additional opportunities for school pupils, including competitive extra-curricular sport. However, at a time of considerable change, including the introduction of the national curriculum for PE, there is a need for schools to find new ways of working, developing new relationships and partnerships with local sporting communities.* [17]

Above all, the good news is that there is an enormous variety of new and appropriate sports activities which tap into the enthusiasm of many students who have never found their feet in traditional team sports. Adaptations such as kwik cricket, short tennis or tag rugby give many more children the chance to try out the game; trampolining, mountain biking, orienteering, fencing, archery, table tennis and go-karting can become a life-time's interest for children of different abilities. The Prime Minister's explicit commitment to promoting competitive sports, sufficiently important to command a place in his personal manifesto for the July leadership contest of the Conservative Party will, however, hardly be sufficient to match or fulfil the far wider interest and talent children and young people show. It may well not ensure that all children have equal access to developing competence or excellence, let alone a guarantee of health, activity and fitness during their years in school.

Good practice

Traditional team sports still provide the backbone of many schools' sports provision. Schools in the Education Extra Network are, however, trying to provide maximum choice for their pupils. They offer team sports and individual sports, 'new sports' and traditional sports, outdoor activities offering both individual challenges and group activities more inclusive for those with different talents and abilities; indoor sports and fitness activities.

This diversification may to some extent reflect the introduction to a wider range of activities via the National Curriculum. It stipulates that all pupils should experience dance, gymnastics, swimming and outdoor adventurous activities, as well as games and athletics, in their primary years. It certainly reflects the wider interests in different sport and fitness activities in the community at large and schools' desire to introduce pupils to a wide range of them.

The schools in our Network are evidently striving to make sport and physical activity accessible and attractive to more pupils; increasing the variety of sporting activities to all who like them or who want to try them; not only the small numbers likely to 'make the team' in football or netball. Schools are seeking to cater for those pupils who like to be active but who don't take to ball games; or who like to challenge themselves as individuals without being in a team. They are looking ahead, attempting to stimulate young people's interest in activities they would easily be able to continue with after leaving school – indoor sports like aerobics, squash and badminton as well as outdoor activities such as hill walking and cycling. Many of the activities offered reflect the particular interests of staff as well as pupil demands.

As important are the links that sport itself makes into the community itself. The link is often symbiotic. Sport offers more opportunities for community links than most areas of the curriculum – ranging from the simple dual-use facility represented by school sites which include a leisure or sports facility used by the community, to very close links fostered by the school to link up schools with local clubs and coaches. Another obvious link is into parents' interests and activities. Fathers, in particular, who are likely to be reluctant to volunteer for other forms of parental participation, are much more likely to participate in sports activities – from supporting school teams to coaching. Opportunities for pupils can turn into opportunities for training for parents themselves. Training in Sports Leadership can be the first step for the individual to a new interest or even a career in specialist sports, leisure management and related careers.

The schools featured in this chapter have found many different ways to surmount particular difficulties. Extra fuel for the school bus is allocated from the main school budget to transport pupils to a sports centre or outdoor activities venue. Joint ventures between the school and the youth service allow for the pooling of resources and provide a valuable source of qualified staff. Governing bodies waive lettings fees after school where activities are for pupils' benefit. Primary schools are invited to use secondary schools' facilities if their own are insufficient. Local sports teams are involved as coaches in return for the use of the school field for their training. Some schools find time in teachers' contracted time for the after-school activities; teachers are offered training at the school's expense so that they may become qualified to lead a sporting activity. Special fund-raising helps with the purchase of expensive items of equipment and in some cases local businesses help out with support in kind. Ex-pupils and older pupils inspired by their own involvement return as volunteers to help younger children enjoy the sports and physical activities they had themselves taken up after school. Above all, the evidence shows the great extent of the voluntary commitment made by school staff to after-school sports, despite increased workloads and pressures on time after school.

The choice of sport

The importance of sport

School has long been seen as important for its civilising and socialising properties. The Clarendon Commission on Education in 1864 reported that in public schools 'the cricket and football fields . . . are not merely places of amusement. They help to form some of the valuable social qualities and manly virtues, and they hold, like the classrooms and the boarding house, a distinct and important place in public school education.'[18] One hundred and thirty years later, the headteacher of Fircroft Primary School (London Borough of Wandsworth) which offers many different sports after school, has put it in contemporary idiom:

> *If children are to learn how to participate in games and activities then the school can play a very important part. What is often forgotten is that there are ways of playing a game. There are such things as sportsmanship, being a good winner, and even being a loser. These are not things that one is born with, but things that have to be taught. At Fircroft we believe that we should help children to develop in many ways. We want the children to develop good technique, good attitudes and social skills, like reliability and an awareness of others.*

Participation in sport can raise self-esteem even in those children who simply enjoy it for the fun of it. Enthusiasm often has little to do with skill. As the headteacher of Archbishop King Middle School (Isle of Wight) put it: 'We try to promote games for all abilities and many of our most enthusiastic players are B or C team members.'

One way of doing this is to ensure that wherever possible all pupils are encouraged to take part, irrespective of ability and alongside excellence. The senior teacher of Marple Hall School, Cheshire, which offers, among other sports, golf and fencing, explained that in his school:

All pupils are encouraged to attend and enthusiasm and commitment are perceived as being of greater importance than ability. Representation is always from a squad, for sports teams . . . Excellence is also encouraged and the school is represented at county, national and sometimes international level at most sports . . . However, our real aim is to create a life-long enthusiasm in a wide variety of activities for the majority of pupils.

Harrow Gate Primary School (Cleveland) is fairly typical in the emphasis it places on providing sporting activities which children would otherwise not have the chance to experience. The school says that:

Many of our children do not have access to pencil and paper at home, let alone tennis racquets, cricket bats, rugby balls, etc. The activities in our programme are designed to encourage cooperation, to build a team spirit, to adopt a caring and sharing attitude (skills which our children often lack because of parental attitudes at home) . . . We run many extra-curricular activities to provide our children with experiences which they otherwise would not get at home.

In many cases, that access to sport is provided simply because of the determination of staff to provide it. In Low Hall Primary School (Wigan), an area 'often described as disadvantaged', the headteacher has personally created a Games Club geared to each season of the year with different sports on offer and as much parental involvement as possible.

The Winter, Spring and Summer Games Club is my own small attempt to . . . help to develop the habit of exercise through games and other forms of physical activities (and) to promote parental involvement in their own children's learning. The practical difficulties centre around the present lack of additional adult support and help. The area the school is situated in means that portable play equipment is essential otherwise it would be vandalised or stolen.

And, as some schools emphasise, sport has the unique ability to 'alleviate much of the aggression commonly exhibited often due to frustration or a sense of failure or disillusionment communicated by family situations'. Thus Hawbush Primary School (Dudley) provides a wide range of activities 'to give [our children] the chance to achieve real high levels . . . in developing their ability'.

And, of course, as the headteacher of Nunthorpe Primary School, Cleveland, emphasised 'children that are introduced to sporting and leisure activities at primary school continue with their interest beyond their school years [and] everyone benefits'.

That possibility alone is a powerful reason why sports clubs as well as schools should nurture young people as future members.

Different sorts of sports

Team games, while still seen as carrying the team spirit, are now more often than not accompanied by a choice of individual sports tailored to suit the

67

school and the child. There is, however, still a strong commitment to the team element. Many schools are drawing in the support of local sporting clubs to enhance what they can offer – and the skills of parents. Even small schools can, in this way, expand what they can do.

Saint Thomas' CE Primary School, Groombridge, East Sussex, is a small, rural primary school six miles from the nearest town. The village

> *has few activities for the children with only established scouting, guides and Church Sunday School as an alternative to school activities. The school has therefore focussed on providing sports after school and its 120 pupils have a choice of football, netball, tennis, athletics, cross country running, cricket, and gymnastics.*

Parents are keenly involved in supporting team games, 'and our local cricket club are very helpful offering some help with coaching and letting us use their cricket ground'. Professional coaches are brought in for cricket and tennis and in 1994 the headteacher was well pleased with the success of all the school clubs, especially sports:

> *Our cricketers have progressed from the plastic cricket kit and now need a more serious kit . . . We are just starting to make links with local Rugby and Hockey clubs which may develop into further sports activities. I am very keen to encourage parents and members of our community to provide activities using their own gifts as well. My aim is to involve the children in purposeful activity and provide opportunity to find excellence in a recreational skill that for some may become a lifelong interest. The other major objective is to give the children opportunities of socialising and finding team spirit and pleasure in the community of the school.*

Sports can be particularly successful, too, in stimulating a far wider range of after-school activities. The very successful after-school and holiday scheme at Hartcliffe School in Bristol was inspired by a desire of Hartcliffe pupils to play cricket. Vic Ecclestone, Head of Extra-mural Studies at the school, explained how it started:

> *I suppose it was natural to try and meet the request. Phoning around we found we could find no local facilities to teach cricket indoors. There was little kit and coaches proved elusive to say the least. John Budd, President of Bedminster Cricket Club thought the idea so outrageous that he agreed to coach what were by now twenty-two 14–16 year-olds in the local Sports Centre's five-a-side Court – considered the only safe area for coaching. An immediate problem was the need to fund £180 for the court hire and thus started the fund-raising process. The cricket project developed and the programme extended to cover swimming, outdoor pursuits, rugby, football (with Bristol City coaching forty youngsters of both sexes), weightlifting, canoe training, orienteering, fishing and tennis.*

Schools which serve rural areas have particular difficulties in offering after-school sports – and have to make an extra effort to create and sustain enthusiasm. East Bergholt High School, in Colchester (Essex), has a very strong commitment to sports – with clubs promoting badminton, gymnastics, basketball, juggling, netball, hockey, football for both girls and boys, cricket, tennis, athletics, swimming, volleyball. With virtually no alternative public transport, and a rural catchment area stretching from the Ipswich suburbs to the Essex border, the school offers most of its extra-curricular activity during the lunchtime. Swanmore Secondary School, in Hampshire, offers another example of a scattered rural catchment area – which means that 'commitment has to be genuine for pupils to stay behind and become involved'. In answer to a question about take up for sports activity the answer was simple: 'hundreds'.

Many Community Schools take particular advantage of their status – and use their sports facilities to offer opportunities across the age range. Wayland High School, for example, in Norfolk, believes

> *that every student should have the opportunity to extend their education beyond the basic curriculum. We also believe the school is an integral part of the community and that we should offer the same opportunities to the children from our partnership primary schools and to those young adults who have left our school but who may still need such opportunities. [Thus] in our planning, we have targeted those areas of activity which can only be given a limited amount of time during the school day, but which students can continue to enjoy in their adult lives. The rolling on of Community Sport into later evening activities for the adults in the community demonstrates this to the students . . . We believe that such activities should challenge young people; they should be able to test their abilities and strengths in a safe environment. Our Duke of Edinburgh Award scheme and our Community Sports Programme offer both physical and mental challenges.*

Some rural schools have developed their Community links through sport with impressive effect. Okehampton College, Devon, described its facilities, the way it has organised them to greatest effort, and the links between sport and other after-school activities in the following terms:

OKEHAMPTON COLLEGE, DEVON:
COMMUNITY PARTNERSHIP AND SPORT

Okehampton College is a rural comprehensive school with one of the largest catchment areas of any school in the country. Many people live in outlying villages with few social or sporting facilities and the nearest leisure centre is twenty-five miles away in Exeter. The school's 1200 students travel (mostly by bus) from as far afield as the North Devon Coast and North Dartmoor. In the opinion of school staff some of these young people are in danger of suffering 'rural deprivation' because of their lack of occupation and facilities for them outside school hours. The College is working hard with the local community and statutory services to make up for this.

The College has designated Community status and as such it seems to make provision for both the adults and the young people in the catchment area.

. . . it is regarded as the focal point in Mid-Devon for Sport and the Performing Arts as well as providing mainstream education eleven–sixteen, post-sixteen education and a full Adult Education programme covering a range of leisure and vocational courses.

The College has excellent facilities and is seeking to make the fullest possible use of them after school. As well as good sports fields and sports hall the College has recently managed to add a full size all weather astro turf pitch (with support from West Devon Borough Council) and the new Octagon Theatre – a 250 seat theatre with associated music practice rooms. Other facilities include a multi-gym, two music rooms and a Drama Studio.

A wide range of sport and fitness activities are offered after school and the more traditional sports are supplemented by programmes of outdoor and adventurous activities. Dartmoor is on our doorstep. Associated activities are the Duke of Edinburgh Award Scheme Ten Tors expedition training and the use of Reservoirs and fast flowing rivers for Windsurfing and Canoeing. A water sports programme is supported by a fleet of canoes and boards.

The School's Arts programme includes a Youth Drama group run one evening a week by the local Wren Trust (an Okehampton-based Arts group). The flourishing Community Orchestra also meets after school each week. Most of its members are pupils but parents and other adults also take part. The College has been particularly successful in drawing community members and organisations to spend time in after-school activities alongside young people.

College facilities can be used free of lettings or service charges after school for activities which benefit the pupils and many of the school's teachers are involved on a voluntary basis with activities provision. In 1993 the College decided to formalise the commitment to arts and sports provision after school further. A member of the school's Community Education Department was seconded to the newly created post of Leisure Manager with the specific brief of maximising the use of the college recreational facilities on campus. At the same time, the College formally launched the concept of 'Period 6' a further hour and a half between 3.30 and 5 p.m. following on from the formal school day. The idea behind this was to encourage fuller participation in after-school activities and to make participation feasible for more pupils by addressing problems such as transport. Formalising 'Period 6' also allows the programme of provision to be developed in a more co-ordinated way, ensuring that a balanced programme of activities is available each day from Monday to Friday.

New sports and activities

There has always been a place in the sports curriculum for individual athletic sports as well as team games. Cross country running, athletics or gymnastics are not new activities. However, in recent years the range of activities on offer in maintained schools has extended well beyond the traditional. Trampolining, fencing, table-tennis, archery and martial arts are common; as are the activities linked to fitness – aerobics and weight training. The boundaries between sport, fitness and creative art are in many ways beginning to merge.

Some sporting activities reflect the location of the school and the determination to use the local environment as much as possible. At the St Gerard Primary School, Cleveland, the headteacher told us that: 'From the beginning we wished to encourage in each child a respect for the environment. To this end we take the children on outings to the North Yorks Moors with our popular Walking Club.' More recently, whereas cycle proficiency tests are still conducted in many schools and are vital to maintaining safety and awareness on the roads, mountain bike clubs are also becoming equally popular and training and bike-maintenance can be offered alongside opportunities to explore local countryside.

Many schools specifically refer to the great value of individual sport as the key way into other sports for many pupils – and as a way of lifting the boundaries of achievement in general. This was well expressed by Heysham High School in Morecambe which is seeking to develop more individual sports alongside its team sports.

> We particularly want to encourage the development of sports and games suitable for pupils who do not do well in the traditional competitive team ball games – e.g. archery and fencing.

King Edward VII Upper School in Leicester – a Sports Council Centre of Excellence, and a school recently visited by the Minister of Sport as an example of good practice in relation to in-school and out-of-school activities – is in no doubt that sports such as kiting, fencing and archery are 'initially aimed at increasing participation of pupils at school who do not take part in the "normal" sporting activities'. Among the 'normal' sports offered at the school are hockey, soccer, girls' soccer, cricket, rugby and basketball.

At East Leeds OASIS Project one sport more usually associated with the public schools – fencing – has proved particularly popular with young people in a deprived urban area. An OASIS co-ordinator and teacher has become qualified to teach fencing and pupils are now at a level where they can

71

compete. The nearest opponents they have found are at a school in York, twenty miles away. One of the young people involved described the personal benefits as follows:

> *Fencing is a respectful sport that needs a lot of concentration, thought and technical skill. Fencing builds up all of your emotion inside then lets it out. It brings out the person you really are.*

Martial arts have a particular appeal to all ages – and both sexes. At the Eardley Trojans Club in Eardley School, Streatham, over forty primary school children across the full age range are offered a karate class one evening a week, lasting from 3.30 to 5 p.m. The class is taken by two qualified karate teachers who run the local Bushido Academy of Martial Arts and who expect the highest standards of commitment from the children themselves. (The programme at Eardley is described more fully in Chapter 1, pp. 28–9)

Individual sports can also sometimes lead to specific community benefit. For example, Fleetwood High School in Lancashire offers pupils a wide range of sports, gymnastics and games after school, as well as environmental activities such as surveys and bee-keeping. However, the school is particularly proud of 'One of our more unusual activities . . . our Tandem Club which offers a service to the community.' Much to the great pleasure of all those involved, pupils in the Tandem Club team up for tandem rides with blind adults and handicapped children.

Individual sports do not necessarily involve physical activity. One of the most popular individual and creative school activities is, of course, the school Chess Club. It is placed well within the spectrum of sporting excellence, for example, by Christ Church CE Primary School, in Purley (London Borough of Croydon), which told us that:

> *we have continued to encourage children to strive for excellence in particular in sporting fields . . . The development of the chess club has involved children from age 5 with Junior Age children playing in school matches . . . To get an even broader base of children involved we need to utilise outside expertise to train children to play effectively.*

Education Extra was able to help chess clubs in 1994 by providing over twenty chess sets for two London schools, and an outside chess set for Failinge Park High School, Rochdale where the popularity of chess is spreading rapidly.

Partnerships and people

Sport after school has been a traditional way of linking schools through competition and, in recent years, as a means of sharing resources. Those resources now often involve bringing into school the support of local clubs and local coaches. Sport also offers wide opportunities for local and national partnership, through the National and Regional Sports Councils, through funding schemes such as SportsMatch and through targeted schemes such as Champion Coaching. Moreover, through Dual Use arrangements with Community Associations or Leisure Centres, the basis for partnership and contact with the community already exists in its easiest form.

At Saddleworth School at Uppermill in Oldham, for example, a very strong after-school Sportslink Programme brings in youth workers and community workers and involves fifteen other schools. At Holywells High School in Suffolk, the Sportslink scheme has meant that 'local Clubs are encouraged to use our facilities at a discount rate in return for running junior activities which are of benefit to our students'.

Where there is a community sports centre on the campus as part of community links or dual use arrangements sport is encouraged throughout the school. But even schools where there is no such advantage develop excellent after-school sports provision. At Wayland High School in Norfolk, a community sports programme runs from 3.45 until 10 p.m. with student activity merging into adult activity (see also p. 69 in this chapter). The Community Sport Programme was set up with the help of initial funding from the Sports Council and is now self-supporting. Matthew Humberstone School in Cleethorpes, Humberside, has good school sports facilities which are available for use by the community outside school hours through a joint use agreement with the LEA. A shift caretaking system has recently been introduced to encourage and enable more twilight and evening use of the school buildings. Also, the excellent local sporting facilities, including the King George V stadium, an astroturf pitch and Cleethorpes Leisure Centre are used frequently by the school.

Ventnor Middle School on the Isle of Wight operates a special system where all local people can buy a permission ticket for £1.50 a term allowing them to use all the school's outside facilities at any time that the school is not using them. The school is currently in the process of improving these facilities and extending the use of the school field by converting a mobile building into a sports pavilion. Future plans include floodlighting the playground to extend winter-time community use for basketball and other sports.

73

And community sports in school can generate community interest in sport outside school. Mountfield School, Robertsbridge, East Sussex, demonstrates how a rural Victorian school covering a large area can revive its own village sports through extra-curricular activity.

Three years ago the school had no recent experience of after-school activities for its pupils. Since then we have, despite our small pupil and staff numbers, developed a range of opportunities through the year. We are now extending that to outside expertise. We offer a range of activities but the sporting ones have been a driving force. We compete with great success in local matches and tournaments but more importantly we compete against much larger urban schools and still enable every junior child who shows interest and sporting attitude the chance to represent the school. . .

We re-established the playing of cricket in school after a very long period of abeyance. In so doing we have revived the village square and led directly to the reforming of the adult village team which had folded eight years before.

One of the most extensive community sporting ventures is the Youth Activities Programme (YAP) drawn together by Campion School, Bugbrooke, Northants.

The Youth Activities Programme is an amalgam of 'various independent initiatives – Bugbrooke Youth Activities, Wackies Sports, Bugbrooke and St Michaels Football Club, Campion Arts, school sports and Bugbrooke Out-of-School Club.' Campion School is a mixed ability rural comprehensive school drawing its intake from twelve feeder primary schools. Northants subsidises the use of premises out of hours. Wackies Sports (a voluntary sports club) runs a full programme of activities in the school each weekend. An Out-of-School Care Club operates each holiday along with a summer school. The Youth Activities Programme runs karate, gymnastics and soccer, and there are also trampolining, badminton, tennis and dance clubs, complemented by Wackies Sports which runs sessions in volleyball, netball, cricket and archery. The school itself is renowned for its prowess in 'the usual school sports – hockey, basketball, netball, rugby and soccer' and also offers art, pottery, chess and music. YAS groups start at 4.00 p.m. and continue until 7.00 p.m. and are open to the whole community, including pupils from other schools.

In some instances new sporting activities have been possible only because of investment from the Sports Council. At East Leeds OASIS Project, individual as well as team sports have been developed thanks to the Sports Council's investment. Support from the Sports Council has encouraged table tennis among primary and secondary school pupils involved in the project. The Sports Council grant to the project has meant that new tables and equipment could be bought, including competition level lighting equipment for a school hall. An OASIS co-ordinator ran a 'Come and Try It' table tennis fair which was attended by hundreds of youngsters over a three day period and led to new table tennis clubs being set up in East Leeds primary schools. A Regional Coach in table tennis offered his services free to encourage and train young people in the sport. Future plans include training older pupils to instructor level so that they can begin to coach the younger ones.

Another excellent example of how a range of partners, including the Sports Council, can be brought in to boost sports development is given in the following example.

BLACON HIGH SCHOOL, CHESHIRE:
FUNDING PARTNERSHIPS FOR SPORT

Over the past several years Blacon High School has gained a central place in the life of its local community, with facilities and activities for both adults and children after school and during the holidays. Although the school has no official 'joint use' status in the community it has worked hard to develop community links and its efforts and success have been rewarded by some outside assistance e.g. grants from the Sports Council and the Football Trust to improve facilities, and wages for a Community Sports and Leisure Officer from the Blacon Project (funded by Social Services).

The school's programme of self-help and expansion really got under way in 1987 when surplus space was converted into a Health and Fitness Centre. Staff got involved in raising funds and local craftsmen gave their skills to help convert redundant changing rooms. When a proportion of the £5000 needed had been raised in this way the Sports Council added a contribution of £1500 to help the scheme succeed. The centre is open to the public each morning and evening, charging £15 per year membership and £1 per visit. The salary of the supervisor was originally funded by the MSC community programme and now comes from the Social Services Community Action programme. Apart from this the scheme is self-financing and provides an excellent facility for pupils in school time, as well as for the community.

Inspired by this success the school went on to fund and develop a Dance and Drama Studio (equipped to a high standard, with a sprung floor), in a similar way; this, too, is heavily used after school as well as in school time. The latest development project is a floodlit synthetic turf pitch which has recently been installed with the aid of grants from the Sports Council and the Football Trust, and help from the Local Education Authority. The latter was obtained after a long campaign by the school's head to persuade the LEA to integrate Youth and Adult funding in on-site management. The LEA eventually agreed to do this on a two year pilot basis and the school is now working ever more closely with the local community to provide activities for all – its own pupils and people of all ages locally – all the year round. Pupils introduced to the facilities through school are encouraged to go on and use them on their own initiative as community facilities. Year 10 and Year 11 pupils are given membership cards to promote this; the cards can be used both in PE lessons and after school.

Activities in the Fitness Centre range from Step aerobics to weight training; the Sports Hall is used by a tennis club and at least ten different football teams throughout the week and other areas of the school provide space and facilities for classes in painting, yoga, first aid, music and languages. The classes are all offered on a pay-as-you-learn basis (1993 rates were £1.20 per hour or 50p for senior citizens and people receiving benefits). The Sports Hall is rented out for £15 an hour and the Gymnasium and Dance Studio for £10 each per hour.

After-school activities for pupils are particularly strong in sports; badminton, tennis, basketball and karting are the options, as well as football, hockey, netball and so on. In addition, different music activities such as a band, choir, and keyboard club take place every lunchtime and the school has the district's only handbell ringing team.

Activities do not end with the school term. A summer activities programme is run for a week or fortnight each year in association with Chester Community Police and Chester City Football Club's Community Project. Children can sign up for activities from football and netball to treasure hunting, orienteering and dance. Film shows and a TV room are also available and the programme includes a talent competition, a disco and a 'Super Team of the Week Award'.

Other schools have developed full scale Community Sports Programmes.

WITHLINGTON SCHOOL, BATH, AVON: THE SPORTING COMMUNITY

Withlington School, Bath, every week offers a wide range of sports every week and involves the local sporting community as widely as possible. Activities cover school teams, courses, clubs and community courses in sports. In holiday courses 300–400 pupils a week are involved at peak time, taking into account all courses. Moreover, the school not only offers traditional sports. The school also has a juggling club; while the school's unicycle hockey team has made local headlines. 200 pupils per week participate in all school sport.

There are a range of activities for school pupils immediately after school. Around this time there are also courses for primary and junior age pupils, e.g. short tennis. Evening activities bring in adults and family members for such activities as fitness, aerobics, and trampolining. The activities cater for all ages and both sexes.

The school has also worked during 1992–1994 on developing links with the community on the sporting front. Funding was given by the County of Avon and the

SW Sports Council towards initiating a project by the school in developing links between the school and the local community. The project commenced in 1992 with the appointment of a sports coach to develop these links including a Holiday Sports programme every school holiday. The school says that 'we are trying to establish a tennis club at the school for families and local clubs are using the facilities now, e.g. the archery club and they lay on courses for the community. There have been FA leaders and coaching courses and the local hockey club now uses the facilities to train.' As the school has made clear the scheme has been 'a tremendous success'.

Sports and parents

Sports can play the key role in bringing parents into school on an informal and effective basis. Our Network Schools demonstrate time and again how parents are involved in setting up and running team games and matches, acting as referees, coaches, drivers, supervisors and much more. A few examples show how parents are involved in some schemes – and being trained to do more.

As the Headteacher in St John's Primary School, Coventry, told us:

At the moment we have one parent who has taken a coaching course for our running club and another who is at present taking a coaching course for gymnastics. If we had help with funding the training of willing adults we could perhaps get even more support from parents. Despite the fact that Willenham is one of the most deprived areas of the City of Coventry we are fortunate in having an excellent relationship with most of our parents and they do support the school as much as they possibly can.

Another primary school – Prospect Vale Primary School, Cheadle, Cheshire, gave the following illustration:

One of our parents . . . set up a football club for the community which now involves children from all the local schools. This club uses our school facilities and football fields. It was set up in consultation with the school about three years ago through liaison between parents and teachers.

Sports also offer the opportunity for whole family involvement. At Withywood School in Bristol, Avon, for example, there is an established period before school for family aerobics; while in Cornwall, at Brannel School, St Austell, they have organised family membership of the tennis club.

But sporting activities offer even more to the parent who becomes fully involved, and that is the possibility of additional qualifications which can actually lead to a new job or a change of career. Hartcliffe School, for example, relies heavily for its summer programme on parents and local young adults who are trained during the year to supervise and run the Summer School. 'They receive a small payment but . . . all fees and costs are found. We now have a core of sixty trained locals who are anything from lifeguards to cricket coaches.'[19]

Health and equality

As research is beginning to show, one of the most alarming of contemporary trends is evidence that children are becoming increasingly less active and less fit. In this context, many schools are developing projects specifically linked to health and fitness. These have the added advantage that they often appeal as much to adults as to children.

Fit Kids is an organisation which trains instructors to run fitness classes for children and to promote a more active lifestyle. Nunthorpe Primary School, Cleveland, for example, experimented with a Parent-Child Skip Fit Club in 1991.

We were practising for a Skip-a-Thon activity for the British Heart Foundation at the time. Parents and children were invited to turn up between 8.25 and 8.45 to skip to taped music. The response was tremendous and our hall was full on the mornings when Skip-Fit was organised. Parents and children were charged 20p for the session. We received a bagful of ropes from the British Heart Foundation.

HARTLEY BROOK PRIMARY SCHOOL, SHEFFIELD: HEALTH AND ACTIVITY

Hartley Brook Primary School in Sheffield is the largest combined nursery, infant and junior school in a socially deprived areas of Sheffield. There are 630 children on the roll. It is situated on an outer city council estate with two units attached to the school to enable integration of children with special educational needs. The surrounding estate is a socially deprived area. One quarter of the school's pupils take part in sport after school – including football, cross country, games, hockey and Outdoor Pursuits. Local sports teams are involved in coaching children. The school is also a pilot scheme for 'Fit Kids'.

Hartley Brook School wishes to get as many children involved in after-school activities as possible. They believe that these social and leisure events foster a sense of community and well being. As well as organising school-based activities for children the school can see the benefits of reaching out. As a result, over 300 children have seen local sports teams, in action, thirty children have been involved in orienteering competitions in Sheffield, and both boys and girls have taken part in numerous football and hockey competitions throughout Sheffield. Hartley Brook School, in conjunction with the C'mon Everybody Project and MacDonalds, has organised girls and boys football tournaments for local schools. The C'mon Everybody Project is a Home Office-backed project concerned with reducing crime in the area. The school has just put into place an Outdoor Education Policy. Sixty children have participated in weekend and week residentials. As a result Hartley Brook School is looking at ways of enabling more children to experience these activities through residentials and developing a school-based approach. Their residentials have had an active involvement from the C'mon Everybody Project and the South Yorkshire Police. During school hours local sports teams and Sheffield Recreation Dept have organised coaching sessions for all children.

In particular, twenty children have been involved with the National Fit Kids scheme. This occurs after school and has been a huge success. 'Fit Kids' provides instructors and instruction in activities which are designed to develop heart and lung capacity – and which are also creative and fun. They involve games with parachutes, skipping ropes, volleyballs, space hoppers and much more.

As well as providing an enjoyable and safe atmosphere for children, all activities complement and enrich the National Curriculum. Hartley Brook explains how all its activities can be linked into the curriculum to draw out maximum value. It has developed a 'topic approach', based on a grid which has been drawn up to make sure that all Statutory Requirements are covered, including PE and outdoor education. Our activities fit in with the cross-curricular elements of Citizenship and Health Education. Children who may not particularly excel in academic areas have their own skills and self-esteem built up. All children who compete at events are rewarded as their efforts are appreciated by friends, parents and the school. Any achievement or involvement can be noted in the child's primary records of achievement.

In inner city areas such as Salford, gymnastics and indoor activities which can improve fitness are particularly popular. St Clements Primary School, Salford, offers, among a wide range of activities for different age groups, a gymnastics club with an external coach, and a jazz-dance club both of which are equally popular with boys and girls. The competitive element in gymnastics is particularly appealing to children. In a neighbouring Primary school in Trafford (Our Lady of Lourdes) regular cross-country running before school, organised by a parent, was extremely popular, not least because as one child emphasised, without it 'your legs would get floppy'.

One particularly successful after-school project dedicated to health and sport was the 'Ready-Teddy Go' project in Manchester.[20]

READY, TEDDY, GO:
SPORT, DIET AND HEALTH FOR PARENTS AND CHILDREN

Ready, Teddy, Go was an experimental project based in Sandilands Junior School, a Manchester primary school, and was designed to integrate physical activities, a healthy diet and active leisure. It was implemented and monitored by a partnership consisting of the LEA sports coordinator, the health promotion officer for schools, the coronary prevention officer, community dietitian and local park wardens.

The aim of the project was to raise the awareness of teachers, parents and children of the need for a more active and healthy lifestyle, and to help them take appropriate action. The project included:

- *an after-school activity session*

- *a diary to record activity and healthy eating*

- *a healthy food tuck shop*

- *a parent aerobic session*

- *an outdoor activity session in the local park at the weekend.*

After a four-week pilot in a local junior and infant school the activity project was sustained from January to May 1994. Heads and staff designed diaries appropriate for the ages of the children involved, and invented the title, Ready,Teddy Go! Teaching staff encouraged children to attend the activity sessions, keep the daily diary and think about their diet. Twenty to thirty children participated at each session of the exercise class held one night a week. Activities chosen reflected the need, for example, to:

- *raise the heartbeat, lose breath and sweat*

- *warm up and cool down*

- *experience progression over a period*

- *stress co-operation and individual effort*

- *develop spatial awareness*

- *raise the awareness of health eating in relation to a healthy body*

- *develop a wider use of existing, local outdoor leisure facilities.*

- *offer an opportunity for parents to enjoy being active themselves, and to promote better understanding of the need for physical activity.*

Parents' exercise sessions were timed to run simultaneously with the after-school activities for children and were led by a coronary prevention officer who worked with individual parents on personal exercise programmes. Small numbers were involved but parents taking part were very positive about the experience. A Saturday activity session, organised by the Wythenshawe Park wardens involved the use of an athletics track, environmental games, and many enjoyable activities.

Children were asked to keep a record of daily activity and diet by colouring paws on a Teddy bear to show they had 'become puffed out' (energetic) or when they had eaten fruit or vegetables. A diary format as also produced for parents to use if they wanted to record their own diet and activity.

The community dietitian worked with a group of parents over a period of weeks before the Tuck Shop was launched. With her help and the support of the Headteachers the parents bought fruit, carrots, celery, cheese, bread sticks, low fat crisps, and sugar-free cordial. The food was sold cheaply in small portions.

Feedback on the project suggested that the healthy eating and the activity sessions had been successful and well supported. Younger children in particular responded well to the activity sessions; some older children wanted something 'more strenuous'. The evaluation study observed that:

> Self-esteem and confidence are apparent in the enthusiasm and sheer pleasure shown by the children in participating. The development of positive attitudes, increased self-esteem, co-ordination and stamina have enabled the children to take part in sport either at the school coaching session, or to join voluntary sports clubs.

Children themselves reported, for example:

- *'I do karate on a Saturday now.'*
- *'I do lots of exercise at home.'*
- *'I've joined Sale Harriers.'*
- *'I can kick a ball.'*
- *'I can skip now.'*
- *'I can keep going at football better.'*

The experience gained from the project has been recorded and distributed to all Manchester Primary schools in the hope that it will enable them to develop their own schemes based on the ideas trailed in Ready, Teddy, Go.

Equal opportunities

A healthy lifestyle is only one of the full range of opportunities which cross sport and which raise issues of equal rights and equal access to benefits. There is, for example, the right to excel versus the right to participate. And there is the issue of equal opportunity for children with special needs whose access to sport is often unnecessarily limited. In special schools, sports and physical activities can be of particular importance. Hence, in Worcester, in the Alexander Patterson School, they make a special feature of gymnastics after school. The school takes from a wide area but its commitment to gymnastics extends beyond current pupils to past pupils. It says:

> This is the only extra-curricular activity on the school premises due to the catchment area of the school, but it is offered to ex-pupils as well as present pupils. Therefore, the facility could be extended to involve more children, maybe running a second night.

The cost of gymnastics is, however, significant. As the school emphasises, if it expanded its activity more adults would be needed and they would have to take British Amateur Gymnastics Association (BAGA) courses. 'These would need to be funded.' This would add to other costs:

> We do not make any charge for our club so we have to fund raise or rely on donations when we need to buy equipment. Also, parents have to pay entry fees, travelling expenses and sometimes overnight accommodation to attend competitions and displays.

In South Tyneside pupils at Greenfields School have both physical disabilities and learning difficulties.

> Senior pupils regularly attend the school's Youth Club each week after school which is based largely on athletics. The young people go to Monkton Stadium for a weekly coaching session run by the staff there. This lasts until about 5.00 p.m. then they return to the school for tea and other social activities until 6.00 p.m. Going off site is a very positive feature of the scheme for the young people. They spend a great deal of time in the sheltered environment of their school. The change of scene and the opportunity to work with athletics coaches is good social as well as sporting experience.

After-school sports can also address equal opportunities issues for those children who would otherwise be prevented from participating by social disadvantage or the limitations of their environment. St Anne's Junior School in Rotherham has an After-School Activity Club which offers soccer, athletics and cricket, and indoor sports such as table tennis. The Club is regularly attended by 70 per cent of the children at the school, which is run by volunteer teachers and relies on the funds raised through a Club snack bar.

Mrs Williamson, the teacher in charge of community liaison, told us: 'We feel that here the children are able to socialise and play in a safe and secure environment, something which in an inner city area such as ours, is not always possible.'

The gender issue is particularly acute, starkly symbolised until recently, by the lack of opportunities for girls to play football. Indeed, the issue is sufficiently important to have prompted a policy statement on Women in Sport from the Sports Council itself. It is significant, in fact, that in the schools in the Education Extra Network, girls' football teams or even rugby teams are so unexceptional that they rarely rate a special mention – other than for a particular reason. The girls' football team, at Stewards School in Harlow, for example, is very popular with pupils from all year groups. 'Fixtures have resulted in resounding victories and local press coverage. The team has been led and trained by members of the local community.' Waldegrave School in Richmond-upon-Thames, a girls' comprehensive, drawing pupils from a wide range of cultural, religious and ethnic groups, has successfully started up a girls' Rugby Club which is very popular.

Sport and the great outdoors

The ultimate after-school activity is the chance of getting away from school (and home) – usually for Outdoor Pursuits. In recent years opportunities for taking pupils away for a week or even a few days have, according to the experience of many schools and LEAs, decreased significantly and have often vanished for some schools. Yet every teacher involved knows that those opportunities are unparalleled in the transforming effect they can have on personal relationships between staff and pupils, personal interests and enthusiasms, and attitudes towards schooling. Those schools which still have access to an outdoor centre of their own are seriously concerned about upkeep and anxious to use them for as many different learning opportunities as possible. Stewards School, in Harlow, Essex, for example, emphasises the importance of Outdoor Activities for building good relationships. The school has a cottage in Northamptonshire. The Headteacher told us that

> Past trips to the cottage have been extremely successful as not only is it a time for pupils to mix but they also benefit from seeing their tutors and teachers in a different setting. We have also used the cottage to take groups of special needs pupils away . . . and the results have been a joy to see.

Mark Hall School, in Harlow, Essex, offers an outstanding example of how Outdoor Pursuits Activities can become a central part of school life – and how an effective support service can strengthen the school's own capacity. Built up over the past two years by three enthusiastic members of staff the school has built up a close working relationships with Harlow Outdoor Pursuits Education Centre. In 1993/4 staff had arranged seven weekend/holiday time residential trips, and had used the services of HOPEC for both weekly club activities and the school's Activities Week programme, and for canoeing and sailing in Year 11 lesson time. The school has a written Outdoor Education Policy. In 1994, Education Extra was able to support the school by providing support for outdoor equipment.

At the Dorothy Stringer School in Brighton, East Sussex, which is very strong on sports, bringing in ex-pupils and pupils from six other schools, they have just formed an Outdoor Centre Trust and are using funds from the school tuck shop to develop their outdoor sports opportunities. The school encourages junior pupils to join in their clubs, 'in the belief that good habits regarding education and leading an active life style should begin long before children reach secondary school age'.

In another and more difficult context, Barton Moss Education Unit (*see also* Chapter 4, p. 110) also has a secure and an open residential unit for young men, mostly aged fourteen–sixteen. Staff encourage participation in outdoor pursuits and have made arrangements with the local branch of Fairbridge (an organisation specialising in outdoor education for young people in difficulties) so that boys can go away on intensive courses using outdoor pursuits to challenge them and encourage personal reflection and development. Some of the unit's residents have completed the Yorkshire Three Peaks Walk. Residents interested in football also have the opportunity to attend training with the Salford Boys Football Club and other local sports facilities are available free of charge to residents in the open unit (or allowed out of the secure unit) so they are encouraged to go swimming and use sports centres. The unit's teachers hope to raise confidence and create long-term sports and leisure interests for the young men in their charge.

Conclusion

What is encouraging about the good practice demonstrated by schools is not only the enduring commitment to sport but the range of innovation which is extending opportunity through new individual and collective sport, and indoor as well as outdoor pursuits which can be overlooked or lost completely in a fevered political climate. More important than the search for ways of boosting team sports artificially is, we believe, the need to provide an entitlement to a sport which will prove of lasting personal benefit in terms of fitness and interest throughout their lives. That entitlement should include at least one residential outdoor experience during their years in school.

The selective examples of good practice given here show schools, often in partnerships of a strong and imaginative character, offering a menu of sporting choices which provide something for everyone, and which encourage physical, social and personal development in the widest sense. It also shows schools making the most of their halls, fields and other facilities to bring in young people and adults from a wider community. In short, it shows what schools can be doing to put their resources to the widest use and for the greatest benefit.

NOTES

1 Sports Council (1993). *Young people and sport: Policy and frameworks for action.*

2 *The Independent* 31 August 1994. *See*, in particular, National playing pitch strategy (Sports Council), National Playing Fields Association and the Central Council for Physical Recreation).

3 Tyrell, B. (1995). Time in our lives: Facts and analysis on the '90s. In DEMOS, *The time squeeze*, p. 24).

4 Royal Navy (1993). *Healthy lifestyles.*

5 Quoted in Labour Party Press Notice, September 1994.

6 Department of Health (1992, July). *Health of the nation. See also* Allied Dunbar (1994). *The national fitness survey: More people, more active, more often.* This revealed that national activity levels were 'well below those necessary to improve health and well-being' and it pointed to the clear correlation between exercise and participation in sports when young and better health in adult life.

7 *See* Sports Council (1993). *Women and sport: Policy and frameworks for action.* This policy document addresses the need to reduce inequities at all levels of sport.

8 *See*, for example, McDonald & Tungatt (1994). Young people and sport: Myths and realities. Quoted in *Young people and sport: A strategy for London*, p. 12.

9 Awdrey, L.E., et al. (1989) Young people's leisure and lifestyle, Report of Phase 1, 1985–1989. Scottish Sports Council. Also in Sports Council Research Unit, NorthWest (1985). *Active lifestyles.* Quoted in Sports Council, op. cit., p. 32.

10 Quoted in *The Independent*, 25 March 1994.

11 *Daily Telegraph*, 9 February 1994.

12 *The Times*, 10 April 1995.

13 *The Independent*, 14 September 1994.

14 Ibid.

15 *The Independent*, 31 August 1994.

16 *See* Department for Education statement (1993). *A sporting double: School to community.*

17 Sports Council, op. cit., p. 19.

18 Quoted in Petrie, op. cit., p. 19.

19 *Extra Time*, Education Extra Newsletter, Issue 4, Spring 1995.

20 Information kindly provided by Eileen Carleton.

4

Learning to learn and learning for life: After-school study help

Among the 35 per cent in Great Britain who leave school at the earliest opportunity, the great majority would not do so with the right kind of support and direction . . . If this doesn't come from the parents it needs to come from the school, and if it doesn't come effectively enough from the school, failure is the consequence.

The Prince's Trust, *A Place for Success*, by Professor John MacBeath (1993).

In this chapter we look at the different ways in which after-school activities relate directly to the school's daytime curriculum and, therefore, more broadly to learning and life skills. Of the six key ways in which after-school can link with in-school, this chapter is, therefore, concerned with Entry, Enhancement and Enlargement.

To recapitulate on the meaning of these terms in practice:

Entry is the accessing of the curriculum, or parts of it, for those who need extra help to overcome their difficulties in coping with it (through study skills programmes, curriculum support work, homework clubs, or family literacy projects).

Enhancement is providing opportunities for a pupil to learn in greater depth, and to develop further a skill which he or she has begun to acquire – and refers therefore to any activity which stretches those pupils already showing ability in a particular area.

Enlargement is the opportunity for after-school activities to provide learning experiences which normally fall outside the scope of the daytime curriculum for some reason: by providing such opportunities (clog-dancing, go-karting, gardening, or whatever!), the school is giving the pupil a chance to discover new interests, acquire new skills, and enjoy new experiences.

The case for study support

At home it's difficult to do homework. Brothers and sisters keep asking us for pens and things and big ones boss you around.

Student at Sarah Bonnell School Study Club

In the past few years, as concern about overall educational performance has increased, there has been growing interest in the relationship between study support, homework, project work, etc. and overall performance in school. The recent OFSTED report on Homework, found, for example, that many pupils and parents saw work done at home as a valuable and essential part of school work. Schools saw the benefits as bringing an improvement in learning, increased independence, and more additional time for study and, therefore, for higher standards. There was, however, wide variation in the time spent, on monitoring and on guidance. In conclusion, however, the report was clear that:

Where staff, pupils and parents treat it seriously it has the potential to raise standards, extend coverage of the curriculum, allow more effective use to be made of lesson times, and improve pupils' study skills and attitudes towards learning.[1]

With this and much other evidence, it is therefore, all the more vital that children should have equal opportunities, simply to complete homework and to get the most out of it, and to access and develop study skills themselves. But this is one area of schooling where the playing field is not only not level – it is steeply graded against those children who lack the support, the space, and the resources to make the most of their own commitment to doing well in school.

In 1990 The Prince's Trust commissioned research to follow the progress of two study support initiatives in Belfast, two in London and two in the Strathclyde region. Some of the initiatives were school-based, others community-based. Some were Study Support clubs run during or after school; others offered focused help on residential courses away from the school. The Report (*A Place for Success*, 1993), demonstrated the remarkable success of these different initiatives, funded through the Prince's Trust and British Telecom, and the benefits in self-esteem, motivation, and relationships between teachers and pupils. The results demonstrated that attending a centre where homework can be done in a supported environment can lead to better performance in examinations. In one sample school GCSE pass grades increased from 38 per cent to 62 per cent in maths and from 35 per cent to 75 per cent in science.

Parents have a key role to play in ensuring that homework can be, and is, done. The importance of time, space and encouragement is even more vital, given the emphasis within most GCSE subjects of an element of project work across the curriculum. The problems of children who do not have the right conditions to do their homework well are compounded, and inequalities can be intensified, by the fact that they are now required to present project work of a high order, on time – and the need for additional support for children on the threshold of success or failure at 16 has become an increasing preoccupation among teachers.

One teacher in an inner city school in Newcastle, where the homework club run in the school library is full to overflowing every night, put it graphically: '50 per cent of our children would not have use of a table to work on in their own homes.' Teachers know that some of their most promising pupils would not even have the basic necessities – the pens, paper or materials – or the parental support and interest to complete their project work.

Some children have great problems doing homework at home. A lot of our pupils come from large families. The home can be crowded with no peace and quiet. When they are at home they often have to be looking after younger children or doing chores. Even with children who work well in school, getting homework from them is by no means automatic – it's hard work.

Headteacher, St. Wilfrid's RC Comprehensive School, South Tyneside.

For many children the problem is not that there is no space or support at home, but that there are rival demands and domestic responsibilities – social and religious observations, evening and weekend jobs, and childminding chores – to be done once the child returns home. As the headteacher of Churchfields High School (West Bromwich) put it:

a large proportion of students have part-time jobs; have to collect younger siblings; have commitments at temples, mosques, churches; are themselves carers of older relatives; or have leisure interests outside school. Our policy is to affirm and support the conscientious fulfilment of these obligations.

This school offers a wide range of homework clubs and opens its own premises to many other community partners:

The school's policy is to give outreach support to existing organisations and activities in the community . . . We also encourage students to join clubs and activities out of school by promoting youth organisations.

As the experience of schools demonstrates, there are many different ways to enhance both learning and life skills. In terms of study support, school strategies can range from the most general – ensuring that the key resources areas of the school are open to pupils whenever possible for individual and supported learning beyond the school day – to specific revision and study courses, linked to GCSEs or special projects, and offered on a regular basis, or on occasional weekends. Moreover, study support can mean much more than supporting the individual pupil; it can mean helping whole families to acquire more confidence with literacy and learning; it can bring in volunteers, mentors and learning tutors to assist in many different ways; and it can make exceptionally good use of modern technologies as an aid to teaching, and as a means of overcoming some of the inhibitions adult illiteracy imposes.

Apart from learning skills, however, practical life skills are equally important. Pressure on the curriculum has meant that many important life skills, such as cooking, sewing or First Aid are pushed out of an overcrowded school day. These are skills, moreover, which many parents themselves acknowledge that have lost or are in danger of losing. Enlarging the curriculum through after-school activities is perhaps the only – and very important – option. Putting a high value on these activities is particularly important for young people who have these gifts but who are unlikely to do particularly well at academic life.

For many LEAs and schools, study support is coming to the top of an agenda which is focused on making the most of academic potential as a way of opening up all existing and new routes into qualification for the future. As unskilled jobs and lifetime careers disappear, employers will look intensively for people who are literate, numerate, articulate, adaptable and capable of developing their inherent skills. While jobs may not be transferable, skills certainly will be. It is against this background that many LEAs are putting in place deliberate strategies which are designed to raise self-esteem, reduce truancy, lift motivation and lift achievement. After-school study support, provided inside and outside schools, could be at the heart of those strategies. Schools are giving it increasing priority when planning new after-school provision. But they need support to do so – and to be able to bring in key staff such as librarians, technicians, classroom assistants or specialist tutors who are often needed to make the opportunity most effective. Because study support can offer the key to achievement, investment in study support also has a key place in TEC-led strategies for meeting the National Targets for Education and Training.

Provision and strategy are at the moment, however, very fragmentary and idiosyncratic. Where they can be provided they bring great benefits. Those opportunities must be available to all – particularly those who are struggling against an indifferent home background and who need the extra support and extra motivation. The next few years will, we hope, bring more emphasis on the strategic support of learning for young people in primary and secondary school.

Entry and access: opening up the curriculum

In some LEAs, after-school study support is encouraged as an explicit part of local strategies to raise achievement all round. This may be a part of a wider strategy, involving in-school as well as after-school input.

DUDLEY LOCAL EDUCATION AUTHORITY:
RAISING STANDARDS ALL ROUND

The Raising Standards Project in Dudley LEA, working in four linked schools, and using GEST funding, covered a wide variety of strategies designed to meet specific needs. These included lunchtime and after-school study sessions, reading groups, classroom support, extra reading tuition, enhancing access to the library (Castle High School); a Five O'Clock Club, offering reading, computer work, topic work, spelling and handwriting help, as well as drama, playing games, and listening to stories (Priory Primary School); an after-school book club, a mini-enterprise stationery shop run by Years 3 and 4, 'Early Risers' sessions for Year 6 pupils, who also produced a newsletter, and a home study group giving extra help where needed (Kate's Hill Primary). These three schools, together with the other school involved, Wrens Nest Primary, also formed a group consisting of thirty more able pupils from Years 6 and 7. This 'Quest' group met on a regular basis, and undertook extra activities, including a residential weekend, designed to enhance and enrich the in-school provision in such areas as music, art, drama, poetry, and science.

Given this growing interest in study support it is not surprising that so many schools in our survey were offering opportunities for study support and independent learning which varied from opening up the library more extensively to providing access to school computers after hours, running Easter revision clubs or setting up fully fledged homework clubs where every child could get additional support and stimulation for project work.

Study support is a proven way of helping focus and develop skills which are essential to good examination technique. It also provides support and guidance for project work, for self-supported study and for independent learning which is a part of social and personal development. In some cases, the study support offered is targeted on the examination classes, on particular interests or problem areas of the curriculum; in other cases, it is open to all students of all ages and abilities, as a means of lifting their chances of later success.

Entry and access

For most schools the first step towards making entry into the curriculum easier for many children is simply to open up existing facilities as extensively as possible. There are many different ways of opening up school resources to provide that extra additional support for study which can make all the difference.

Many schools offer access to books and software, contained in normal library resources. Many offer access to computers and DTP facilities after school. Some have refurbished classrooms or halls, and set aside space for GCSE and A-level classes; others have divided off space in their school hall, for study clubs, opened their technology suites, and allow entry into the school from as early as 7.30 in the morning until late at night. Teachers, technicians, and parents are found alongside pupils working at different projects and tasks. Libraries in schools can be both centres of learning and enjoyable focal points for all kinds of interests.

MORNINGTON HIGH SCHOOL, WIGAN, LANCS: OPENING THE LIBRARY DOORS

This school has over 1000 pupils. The focus for the after-school programme is the school library, which is the size of four large classrooms. The headteacher invited a local educationalist who was retiring after many years with the LEA Careers Service to take on the position of resources librarian. With the help of the manager of the adjacent print room, a plan was devised to divide the library into four areas:

(a) a Quiet Area, for homework, study, research;

(b) an Exhibition Area;

(c) a Careers Library; and

(d) a Teacher Section.

The task of converting the existing facility into the envisaged resource-base was to be carried out immediately: during the summer holidays, in time for the pupils' return.

An acute shortage of funds was balanced by a great deal of inspiration and enthusiastic help. The exhibition area proved a problem, because of the high cost of display cabinets, but a little ingenuity, involving the local DIY store, and an obliging school caretaker, meant that several home-made cabinets materialised, at a fraction of the catalogue price! Charity Shops were the source for a large stock of low-cost boxed games and jigsaw puzzles. Education Extra's Network and Advice Sheets showed the school that other people were facing the same problems.

Once the next term began, the library was opened at lunchtimes and after school till 4.30 p.m. The pupils flocked in. After school the average attendance has been thirty; one lunchtime there were 200 pupils present. In the first eighteen months there have been six exhibitions, ranging from the Egyptians to Space, with exhibits provided by the Schools' Library and Museum Service. There is now a thriving chess club, and a space club. The next venture has been to introduce old-fashioned games, such as bagatelle, skittles, and shove-ha'penny, all made from school scrap. The careers section is kept well-stocked and up-to-date by the careers officer: it now boasts three computers containing MicroDoors and TAPS. The teachers section is fully used; it is now full of directories and research material. The school has a large throughput of trainee teachers, and there is therefore a library of books relating to teaching. Parents use the facility, too: some pupils go home, and then return with younger siblings. Doing homework at school has increased, and there are always two adults on hand to help.

Literacy and life and the role of the family

Literacy is a second key area in accessing the curriculum. There can be no doubt either that there is a national problem in relation to adult literacy levels. A recent ALBSU survey reported:

13 per cent of those interviewed said that they had difficulty with writing/spelling; 4 per cent with reading; and 4 per cent with numeracy. The figure was 17 per cent overall.

The age group claiming they had least difficulty were 72–74 year-olds (the oldest group interviewed).

More men than women claimed they had difficulties with literacy; the reverse was true for numeracy.

80 per cent of the people who said they had these problems said they had always done so; but very few said they had had special help at school, or that they had attended special classes since leaving school.

Significant numbers of those who said they had literacy/numeracy problems also claimed to have difficulties with everyday life (especially in relation to employment).

When tested on basic skills, the difficulties actually experienced were greater among those over 52 than among those under 44; the poorest results of all on the assessment tasks were those of the 72–74 age group, contrary to their own self-assessment.

In fact, a major finding of the research is that there is an evident relationship between performance in the literacy and numeracy tests and self-reported problems, with those stating that they have difficulties performing worse than average; equally, many poor performers do not perceive themselves to have basic skills difficulties.

People from households classified higher on the socio-economic scale did, as expected, have better literacy and numeracy than those lower down the scale; and those in full-time employment, and white collar workers, also have higher ratings. Nevertheless, significant proportions of all types of individuals fail to reach the high score level for basic literacy and numeracy.

We believe that we have had a major basic skills problem for some years and that it is not of recent origin. We also believe that standards are not good enough for an industrialised country towards the end of the Twentieth Century, and that concerted action will be needed to raise levels of performance. There is no 'quick fix', no 'magic bullet' to deal with a problem of long standing.'[2]

It is not at all surprising that, even without the prospect of discovering and applying an overnight cure, there should currently be a major thrust in the direction of Literacy improvement schemes, and that most of these should have a *family* focus. The problems of several different generations may be seen as parts of one larger problem, rather than as separate issues. And it may be that the solution lies in attempting to tackle the problems together. Furthermore, it is certainly arguable that there is a process of inter-generational transfer of literacy and/or numeracy difficulties: that a pupil with problems is likely to have at least one parent with similar problems, not least because there will have been a lack of influential input in the earliest years during all those hours spent in close proximity at home.

Given this context, and this reading of the problems and their scale, it is not surprising, either, to find that there is increasing activity and commitment in schools, not merely for pupils, but also for families as a whole. Schools have thus become a major focal point for a national initiative.

ALBSU – now re-named as the Basic Skills Agency – have been charged by the Government with the task of stimulating work in this area, and their Small Grants programme has certainly resulted in a significant blossoming of Family Literacy schemes. Many of their grants have gone to schools. Many of these projects take place after school, either in the teatime period, or later in the evening. It was through this initiative that Education Extra obtained some of its funding for the pilot scheme at Brampton Manor School, London Borough of Newham

BRAMPTON MANOR COMPREHENSIVE SCHOOL:
FAMILIES TOGETHER

Brampton Manor, a comprehensive school in Newham, is the site of an Education Extra project in after-school Family Literacy. The project aims to improve the literacy skills of a group of Year 7 pupils by involving their parents and carers in their learning and is jointly funded by the London Docklands Development Corporation, East London Training and Enterprise Council, ALBSU, the LEA and the school itself.

In consultation with the Head of Year 7 and the form tutors it was decided to base the targeting of students on their Suffolk Reading Test scores. An initial list of twenty-five students was drawn up with care being taken to give a representative race and gender balance. The target group were not those with the most extreme needs, since the in-school support systems were considered to be catering for them. Those other students with low scores who were considered by their tutors to be best able to benefit from the project, with sustained support from their parents and the project tutor, were invited to participate.

A project co-ordinator (Prodeepta Das) was appointed. His account of the first stages of the project demonstrates both its purposes and its progress:

In the first session each student chose a book to read with their parents. The time taken to read and the number of mistakes/hesitations were recorded and the parents were shown how to facilitate reading without excessive intervention. It was agreed that each family would give at least two hours every week to reading. The students showed interest in working on personal projects on subjects which interested them. For example, one student decided to undertake a project on West Ham Football Club. With help from his parents he made up a questionnaire, copies of which were sent to his three favourite players. To his delight a few weeks later one of the players wrote back enclosing a signed, complimentary photograph of himself. This has, of course, done wonders for his motivation.

The abilities and needs of the participants vary widely and individualised learning programmes have been developed. Adults with good literacy skills have readily helped by listening and encouraging other adults and students to read. Both students and parents/carers feel that their interest in learning has been reawakened. Because he has so enjoyed his work on this project, one parent has decided to seek qualifications in the teaching of basic literacy.

The Brampton Manor Project now serves as the model for six other projects Education Extra, with funding help from the Roald Dahl Foundation, has initiated in Merthyr, Rochdale, Salford, Ipswich and Dudley. All are due to begin during 1995. Each of these schemes has a distinctive characteristic (e.g. one of the schools is secondary; one is concentrating on its ethnic minority parents; another is using interactive IT as the focus; yet another sees two schools in harness within the same LEA), with the objective of providing useful information and feedback for other schools who may wish to follow suit in their own circumstances. All of these schemes will endeavour to learn from those which have already been in operation, including some which are not run under the aegis of a school: the need for appropriate intervention is too serious for anyone to be able to afford the time to reinvent the family literacy wheel.

One of the delights of the family approach is the way in which it harnesses the potential of other family members (such as the father referred to above) and in many instances benefits from family relationships, while fulfilling individual family members. The image of an older sibling, sitting close to a younger one, giving intense and unselfish concentration and practical help, and so completely engrossed in the work that the arrival of an outsider remains totally unnoticed, is a powerful and lasting one.

An unique feature of after-school activity at Townley High School, in Burnley, Lancashire, was its recent Fun in Learning event. This included both parents and children and was designed to emphasise methods of learning in the home with parental participation to improve literacy and numeracy.

Schools in areas where there is a high proportion of ethnic minorities have developed intensive strategies to assist literacy. McEntee School in the London Borough of Waltham Forest has a high intake of refugee students and a multi-ethnic school population. It is in an area of urban deprivation. The library is kept open for a homework club five evenings a week after school. In the summer term of 1993 the school also ran a pilot course in English through drama, involving an adult education tutor who was paid for the work. Other teachers from the school also got involved on a voluntary basis.

> We believe we are the first school in Waltham Forest to operate a joint venture with the Adult Education service to support ESOL and refugee students . . . We recognise that the acquisition of competence and confidence in English is the single most important challenge the target group face. We also feel that they fail to benefit from traditional after-school activities particularly in their first terms at school . . . In the normal classroom environment beginning learners often find expressing themselves in a new language threatening and the language intimidating. In the drama group they have the confidence to express themselves freely.

The key role played by families is also enhanced on occasion by the support given by outsiders from local businesses, or simply from the local community, who enter into mentoring arrangements with pupils at the school – or perhaps just help by listening to pupils reading on a regular basis. This work may take place within the school curriculum, of course, but will often find a more convenient place at the end of the school day – and towards the end of the commercial day, when the firm may spare some employee time for this purpose.

Basic literacy and language skills can also be accessed through other activity:

SWANLEA SCHOOL, TOWER HAMLETS:
SKILLS THROUGH ACTIVITIES

Swanlea School is in one of the most impoverished areas of Tower Hamlets, East London. Yet it has many advantages. It took up occupation of impressive new premises in 1993 – widely featured in architectural and educational journals when it opened its doors to Years 7 and 8. A new school and two-years intake offered the opportunity for experimentation – and for developing a model for other schools starting after school provision from scratch.

The school took up the opportunity with enthusiasm. There were already some partnerships in existence – local business employees hear pupils read during the lunch hour, for instance – and many after-school and lunch hour clubs. Every member of staff has thirty minutes of after-school activities built into his or her budget of directed time (1265 hours). Where activities go on beyond this time, staff are paid for them.

In addition, however, the school saw that after-school time offered potential for some curriculum support in the area of homework/literacy, languages and the arts. A scheme was devised to be directed specifically to the improvement of literacy levels among its younger pupils. The target group for the scheme were those pupils in Years 7 and 8 who have reading difficulties and those at risk of underachieving. Other pupils are not excluded. Unusually, the focus was to be on activities which would develop the confidence and communication skills of pupils involved. The club meets two nights a week for one extra hour. Over the year 200 pupils and 10 members of staff have been involved in activities which range from a sports leadership course, the creation of a newsletter to a Botswana school, a drama group, a debating society, a video-making club and aerobics training, with pupils training teachers. The technology faculty are running a multi-media club and a clock-making mini-enterprise. Each mini-project has clear aims and outcomes and language and literacy is fostered in as many forms as possible.

This project has been realised by the fact that the teacher/co-ordinator has been funded to carry out the preparatory work and to ensure that the classes run as planned with sufficient resources and activities to meet their objectives. The co-ordinator receives an enhancement of salary by one point on the salary spine. Funding has been obtained from the local East London Training and Enterprise Council, which sees the project as an effective way of improving skills; and by the local Aldgate and AllHallows Trust.

The LEA have been enthusiastic in support. With the funds obtained, staff have been paid on an hourly basis, and resources have been provided (materials, stationery, software). Provision has been made for needy pupils to be subsidised and for adults to be trained to lead sporting activities.

It is hoped to run the project for a second year with funding from other local community and business partners.

It is also possible to use after-school activities to improve the accessibility of the daytime curriculum for some – perhaps specifically targeted – pupils.

Enhancement: greater depth and effective learning

The next stage of a school's strategy involves building into after-school provision opportunities which enable students to explore their interests in greater depth, and ensure that they are as well prepared as possible for project and examination work. Again, many schools respond to the needs of pupils by opening their libraries after school as the first step towards a fully fledged homework or study club, and for developing revision facilities.

At Werneth School in Stockport, for example, 'the social and study facilities of the school are open to pupils at the end of each day. The Library is open and staffed by a chartered librarian. The large common rooms are available for help with general study skills or specific homework queries.' A range of school and community activities from sports and art to technology and computers takes place after school at the Chesterton Community College in Cambridge. The College is currently extending its provision to include a homework club in the library and extra curricular GCSEs funded by the Further Education Funding Council.

Charles Edward Brooke School, London Borough of Lambeth, is a girls' comprehensive, voluntary controlled CE school in the poorest ward in Brixton, with a 'truly comprehensive intake' of pupils from about sixty primary schools.

> *There is little tradition of pupils in our community going on to Higher Education; in fact Lambeth and Southwark have traditionally had one of the lowest 'staying on rates' after the age of sixteen. The school feels that it must actively support its pupils in this endeavour by ensuring they get the best possible facilities to achieve in their GCSEs.*

The school supports its pupils through after school groups in art, science, history, maths and English, and also through holiday time provision:

In the Easter holiday before our pupils take their GCSE exams, the school holds a revision centre for our students. Subject teachers come in and take classes on specific themes which are central to the exam courses. These are particularly important for our students as many of them come from backgrounds which make it difficult for them to organise and carry through revision. In order to make this revision as effective as possible we invited an experienced teacher now working as an educational consultant who spent the first day on study skills, outlining ways of revising and building the confidence of our students in their ability to learn and do well in exams.

The school is now aiming to start an after-school homework club so that its support for independent study can extend through the school terms.

Some schools have already taken that step.

Homework is just another opportunity

At the Holt School (Berkshire), a large comprehensive for girls in Wokingham, pupils can stay after school to do homework, get access to computers, play games, watch TV and have refreshments. There is a charge to parents of £2 an hour which covers rent, salaries, insurance and refreshments, and the facility is run as a limited company. Where pupils are in need and their families cannot pay, the school covers their costs. The headteacher says

The service has added a very valuable dimension to the caring side of the school. Girls who are not regular users of the facility recognise it as a haven in times of difficulty or emergency. The girls who go regularly have formed firm alliances . . . Girls across the age range and social spectrum mix, play and communicate together. The girls mostly do their homework in a very co-operative way. They use each other and the supervisor to work out worries and problems.

When they are offered, homework facilities attract large numbers of students. At All Saints Catholic School in London Borough of Barking and Dagenham, 300 pupils regularly make use of homework facilities in school. The school has 'a marvellous Learning Resources Centre' including a CD-ROM centre, and is working towards extending the school day in such a way that the children see using the homework and learning resources facilities as 'a natural part of the school day'. The after-school activities programme at Thomas Telford School in Shropshire, described in Chapter 7, p 184, 'attracts between 80 and 150 students each evening. Its central feature for pupils is the Homework Centre which is open on four nights a week from 5.30 to 8.30 p.m.'

The following two examples show how two secondary schools in very different areas of the country are using study support to raise achievement.

SARAH BONNELL SCHOOL, LB NEWHAM:
LEARNING SUPPORT ACROSS THE SCHOOL

Sarah Bonnell School, in Newham, East London, is an all-girls school with 1100 students. In early 1993, the school was successful in its bid for local authority money to develop its already strong technology work. During the course of 1993 the ground floor of the school was converted to become a Technology Village.

The school has developed a Resource and Study Centre, open before and after school and in the lunch-hours, which has been completely refurbished so that students can drop in of their own accord to read, study or use the computers. The library opens at 8.15 a.m., and stays open an hour after the last class in the evening. It is also open at lunchtime. The morning and lunchtime sessions stretch the library more or less to capacity, whereas the evening session attracts between half a dozen and a dozen young people on a regular basis.

As well as this resource provision there is a study club which means that the whole of the top half of the school is given over to quiet study areas. The 'hall' is a large space with eight classrooms opening on to it around its periphery. The centre part has been carpeted to make it more inviting and a few easy chairs have been installed. Free-standing screens separate it from the tables and chairs moved up from the old library. Students use the study area to do homework, to complete GCSE assignments, and to study for exams. There are always two teachers present to offer help and advice.

Over 500 students have now passed through the study club and fifty attend on a regular basis, to read, do project work, share ideas and help each other. Students are quoted as saying:

> The supervisors are nice, trying to give us a nice atmosphere.

> I am fasting, and I come to the study club every day – not only because I'm fasting.

Thirty students completed questionnaires as part of the Prince's Trust Study Support Initiative. They describe the benefits as:

- *peace and quiet away from distractions*
- *getting more work done*
- *getting it over with*
- *getting help when you don't understand.*

The strengths of the Sarah Bonnell Study Club are defined by the Prince's Trust as:

- *a whole-school atmosphere*

- *the provision of opportunities for study as an integral aspect of the school day*

- *a planned and purpose built library and study centre*

- *effective use of existing space*

- *voluntary help from teachers and involvement of head and adviser*

- *parental involvement.*[3]

Another secondary school in an area of high deprivation puts its study support programme explicitly within the general framework of raising expectations.

LANGBAURGH SCHOOL, CLEVELAND: STUDY SUPPORT MAKES THE DIFFERENCE

Langbaurgh School is in an area of high unemployment. 'Education is not highly valued in the area and most of our pupils enter the school with low reading ages, poor self-esteem and little ambition.' The school sees supporting the students in their studies outside class time as a priority.

Some of the parents would like to help their children to succeed academically but do not know the best ways to do it. We would like to be able to go some way to fulfilling the role that is played by more middle class homes and families. We see this role as providing a comfortable quiet place to study, the possible solutions to work associated problems, talks and sources of information about current affairs, encouragement, a support network of teachers and pupils to help withstand peer-group pressure which decries study and an improved self-image of the pupils as students.

To work towards fulfilling these aims the school has set up supported self-study groups, first for Year 11 students and now also for those in Year 10. Currently (March, 1994) it is looking at making similar provision for pupils in Year 9.

The school has been able to obtain funding from the TEC and City Challenge – the latter providing technological equipment. As a COMPACT school Langbaurgh receives some extra financial and human resources. Local business has responded generously to requests for help in equipping the school library. The scheme also, however, relies heavily on the valuable help of adult and young adult volunteers.

For the Year 11 pupils we have a mentors scheme; people from industry come into school regularly. Each is assigned about six pupils whom they will see individually, and talk through careers advice, options for broadening horizons and so on. We have managed to get young, lively people from industry who will be acceptable role models for our pupils. We have also arranged for young professionals such as solicitors to come in and talk to our study group members.

Parents of the pupils have also been invited to discuss their children's study needs.

We seek to show the parents that we have high expectations of their children and that the demands we make on them for homework are real. Parents have reacted very positively to this. They are more convinced that when their children say they have homework to do this is a genuine and worthwhile use of their time and not for instance an excuse for getting out of other jobs at home.

Pupils starting out in a study group are initially given study skills questionnaires. 'These help them to identify what particular areas they need to work on – it might be essay writing, or another particular area of study skills.'

While the initial emphasis of the groups is on methods and skills for studying and has a cross-curricular emphasis, inevitably the concerns of pupils about particular subjects are also identified through their involvement in the study groups. School staff have responded to this by putting on extra – voluntary – lessons in their subjects after school. This is proving particularly helpful to Year 11 pupils worried about their course work. Extra lessons in science and maths and also languages are particularly in demand.

A new venture the school is now attempting is to involve its ex-students now at sixth form college as peer tutors for current pupils. 'We hope the ex-students will get involved in helping pupils with their particular subject interests as well as general study issues.'

It is not only in secondary schools that there is a need for study support. Learning habits are being developed in many primary schools, too.

WOLLESCOTE PRIMARY SCHOOL, DUDLEY:
WHOLE-SCHOOL POLICIES FOR LEARNING SUPPORT IN THE PRIMARY SCHOOL

Children at Wollescote Primary School can complement their classroom learning with extra learning at home, thanks to the bank of resources available to them from the 'Extra Club'.

The Extra Club is a special library of resources in maths and language, which are closely linked to classroom work. Children take them home and use them under the guidance of a parent. The scheme has quickly proved to be very popular. A survey of parents when the scheme was first devised, asking about interest in using the Extra Club facility, showed 120 families keen to participate.

The maths resource was set up first, and now the language resources are being built up – with the help of a 1994 Education Extra Award. The Extra Club is not entitled to any LMS funding and has to rely on school fundraising efforts and the goodwill of teachers to exist.

The school sees the language resources as 'vital enrichment and extension of the main curriculum for our pupils in an area in which underachievement is closely linked to poor language performance, both for indigenous and ethnic minority populations'. Wollescote School serves mainly an area of social deprivation, where there are high levels of unemployment. Over half the children come from families in ethnic minority groups, and in the last two years one-third of children entering the school at nursery level have known no English.

The school works hard at being a fully involved part of the community. It hosts an early morning crêche for working parents in the nursery. A programme of adult education runs throughout the day and evening, with classes including office skills, English for Asian mothers and aquarobics. Teachers run extra curricular activities for the children – sports, music, youth club and so on, at lunchtimes and after school. This tradition of community involvement has helped the Extra Club. Not only have many parents been keen to get involved but the PTA has contributed funding to help build up the learning resources.

In a school which every year recently has seen pupils entering with fewer language and social skills, and more emotional and behavioural difficulties, the Extra Club is making a vital contribution; extending pupils' educational opportunities and empowering local families to help their children learn.

Study support also opens up opportunities for extensive extra-curriculum support in specialised subjects, extra support for students with learning difficulties, and specialised enrichment programmes. A growing number of schools are offering a range of such opportunities.

Elizabeth Garrett Anderson School in the London Borough of Islington is a growing comprehensive for girls, drawing pupils from over seventy primary schools. As well as providing homework support for a small number of pupils and after-school groups in computers, science, textiles, maths, English and humanities, the school ran an Easter holiday revision programme for Year 11 students in 1994.

Pupils at South Dartmoor Community College, Devon, can take after-school extension lessons, which involve studying either new subjects or subjects already on the timetable in greater depth. In 1994 ten hours of additional teaching was available after school for pupils in Key Stage 3; subjects included Latin (aiming at GCSE Latin), beginners Latin, Spanish, electronics, cookery, the Basic Food Hygiene Certificate course, support for learning, computer programming and art. The principal writes, 'We are committed to offering the widest possible curriculum for all children who are prepared to take up the challenge.'

Peers School in Oxford serves a broad intake including young people from the large council estates of Blackbird Leys, Rose Hill and Littlemore. The school tries to be a focus for the local community, and at present 'some 5000 people use the campus in the course of a week'. Joint Use arrangements with Oxford City Council enable the school to be the site of squash courts, a fitness centre and swimming pool.

Peers runs an 'Education Plus' programme of extra classes every Tuesday and Thursday for an hour and a quarter after the end of the school day. It started in 1991 when 'we identified the need to provide a broad range of after school activities for students in the intake year' (Year 9, thirteen to fourteen-year olds).

The deputy head told us, 'The programmes that we offer, in addition to the National Curriculum, are based on increasing the range of experiences and the number of people who use the campus.'

The Education Plus programme involves about 120 students and Saturday Focus brings in some 100 young people.

The school now aims to go further in supporting independent study.

> *Our next major project is to work in collaboration with Unipart and The Prince's Trust to develop a self and supported study centre in the library block of the school. We will appoint within our current staffing provision a co-ordinator of supported study whose role will be to co-ordinate provision after school from 3.00 to 5.00 p.m. each day, during the lunch break and on Saturday mornings. We plan to staff these sessions and additionally provide sets of complementary resources for all areas of the curriculum that students will experience during the school day.*

Study support and programmes which enhance skills can be equally helpful to children with special needs, and those who have outstanding abilities. Charters School in Berkshire has a large catchment area and is a Group 11 school, with an intake containing a full range of ability. Twenty-five per cent of pupils receive some direct assistance from the special needs department. In addition the school is fully resourced to cater for physically handicapped children. The school runs a comprehensive programme of after-school activities for students of all talents and inclinations and supports this by providing a late coach, leaving school at 4.30 p.m., so students can get home after activities have finished. A special feature of the school's learning support provision is the Smudge and Chewpen Club. This uses books, tapes and personal stereos in a programme to help students who have reading difficulties. The aim is to help improve their reading skills in a caring environment.

Some special schools are leading the field in the provision of specialist after-school clubs.

FOXDENTON SPECIAL SCHOOL, OLDHAM: GIFTED MATHEMATICIANS GET TOGETHER

The needs of those with special abilities as well as those with special disabilities may be catered for within after-school projects. It is highly appropriate, therefore, that it is at a Special School in Oldham that a club has been formed for those in all the neighbouring schools who demonstrate outstanding abilities in the field of Mathematics.

Foxdenton Special School caters for pupils who have special needs arising from a physical disability, which would prevent them coping or being adequately catered for in mainstream education. Nevertheless, more than 20 per cent of these pupils make sufficient progress to transfer eventually to mainstream schools. On the other hand, some are transferred to schools catering for those with severe learning or emotional difficulties. 60 per cent of the pupils have wheelchairs. 80 per cent need speech therapy; some have hearing or sight problems. The school has a varied programme of after-school activities, including an Under-5's Club, meeting fortnightly, for those with special needs across the whole town; a series of field study weeks, and a weekend away; and a summer playscheme. The Oldham young mathematicians club is run on Saturday mornings at Foxdenton, from 9.30 to 11.30 a.m. It provides for children in Years 4–6 who show exceptional talent in mathematics, and aims to give them access to a similar peer group and the opportunity to explore advanced mathematical ideas and concepts in an enjoyable way. The club receives financial support from the Rotary Club and from Trusts; and earned an award from Education Extra in 1993. Pupils pay a termly fee, which contributes to covering the costs of supervision and refreshments. As the headteacher, Mel Farrar, comments: 'It is fitting that the club meets in a special school, because we think that youngsters who are way beyond their peers also have special needs which sometimes go unrecognised. This club enables them to spark off a similar peer group, and pursue ideas in a relaxed and friendly atmosphere.' The school received its Charter Mark Award for excellence in 1994 – the first special school to do so.

There is a similar link between special educational needs and the most able in a scheme running at Chaucer School, Sheffield, where the learning support teacher is in charge of a club making special provision for some of the most able pupils. 'Club 9' targets about twenty of the most able young people in

Year 9 – students who have the ability to achieve at A-Level and university, but who are unlikely to aspire to do so without help and encouragement.

The school draws most of its 960 pupils from an area of severe disadvantage. The area has the highest level of juvenile crime in South Yorkshire, high unemployment, and many children in statutory care or registered as at risk. When they come to the school, 40 per cent of the pupils are reading at a level two or more years below their chronological age.

Many of the school's energies and resources are therefore, rightly, targeted at the least able and most disadvantaged pupils. But the school has also recognised 'that the most able pupils are in the minority at Chaucer and are just as deserving of support'. In mixed ability classes of thirty children the two or three most able often 'keep their heads down' and do not wish to draw attention to themselves by overt displays of ability.

> Many of our able youngsters have to be pioneers, beating a new path through the educational system and battling against ever increasing odds.

This is where Club 9 comes in. It meets once a week after school and allows the able pupils from different classes to meet and 'share experiences, hopes, fears and challenges in a way that is supportive but not elitist'.

The pupils can take part in curriculum extension work; areas of interest such as astronomy can be explored in the Club, which could not be covered in classroom work. More importantly the Club works to increase the confidence and self esteem of students – and their parents – to enable them to make more of their abilities. The Club aims to bring members into contact with undergraduates and visiting speakers, to facilitate visits to nearby universities and colleges – to make them aware of possibilities for the future. The headteacher writes:

> This is just one way of fighting the low self-esteem and low expectations which blight the area the school serves. It's a small effort but worth it if it opens up the horizon for even one pupil.

Enlargement: doing things that don't fit in

Extras in the after-school curriculum

A good deal of after-school provision sets out to provide learning opportunities or experiences which would not normally feature within the daytime curriculum, and thus extend the Curriculum to add value to the whole educational experience.

Bretton Woods Community School, Cambridge offers an in-school curriculum enrichment programme which merges with both the activities available for pupils after school and the community provision, both on site and in the adjoining community centre. The school is open fifty weeks in the year, including weekends, and this whole range of work is perceived as a means of adding value to the daytime curriculum.

Duffryn Comprehensive School, Newport, Gwent offers an extensive after-school programme, developed in recent years, both at lunchtime and after school. In 1993, for example, a typical lunchtime 'menu' offered basketball club (Years 7 and 8), swim club (Years 7 and 8), soccer, hockey,and athletics clubs; textiles, painting (Year 8) and art clubs; two choirs; public speaking practice; a drum club, school magazine club, and the school's crime prevention panel. In addition, there is a linked programme of extra-curricular support which can involve literacy and basic English tutoring, history and economics, maths, modern languages, biology, geography, science, and geography – for those pupils who have general queries, classroom problems, and project difficulties. And Furzedown Primary School (London Borough of Wandsworth) in south London has two well-established French classes after school, for beginners and intermediate pupils. The classes (for which the French teacher is paid) are popular, and both have waiting lists.

Some schools offer enrichment programmes on a partnership basis, bringing in primary schools wherever possible.

HEATHFIELD COMMUNITY SCHOOL, SOMERSET: FUN FRENCH FOR FEEDER PRIMARIES

Heathfield Community School offers after-school activities throughout the year in response to curricular as well as extra-curricular needs. The basic belief is in learning as a lifelong process, and the aim is therefore to encourage all students to attain their personal best. Some 'open learning' activities are included within the offer. Most important, one of Heathfield's initiatives – Fun French – has brought the secondary school into a joint project with nine feeder rural primary schools.

> The origin of the 'Fun French' was in the community. A local primary school requested extra-curricular French classes. We then conducted extensive research both at that primary school and in other areas. The result was a clear community need for primary age level modern languages programmes.

The School's Director of Community Education explained that many primary schools, especially small village schools, have no resources to pursue a modern languages programme individually. At the same time the communities are scattered and it would have been difficult to bring all the children who wanted to take part together to a central location. The solution was to keep the Fun French programme based in each primary school, as close to the children's homes as possible. 'All but one of the nine schools involved are in villages.'

Heathfield Community Education organises the training and staff development for the programme. Language tutors are recruited in consultation with the local communities and primary schools. Participants have to pay for the classes but fee concessions are offered for those from families on low incomes.

'It is quite clear', says the headteacher, 'that children, parents, primary schools and the secondary school staff can all see the benefits of such an innovative, activity-based programme. It enhances the curriculum work of both primary and secondary students; it involves the community either through parents, as paid staff, or volunteer assistant tutors. Training and staff development is organised by Heathfield Community Education . . . Recognition of student achievements so far has been done through presentation events and the awarding of certificates.'

In 1994 the school was hoping to add German to its programme.

Many Enrichment programmes involve parents and volunteers as guides and helpers. Parents and high school students are involved as tutors in the after-school activities at Sandown CE Primary School on the Isle of Wight. Pupils have the opportunity to learn lace-making and needlework as well as clay modelling and gardening. Gosforth Park First School in Newcastle

> *has a policy of providing extra-curricular activities to enable the older children to sample activities or develop talents which will hopefully provide them with purposeful leisure activities to carry on at home or to start the children out on a hobby they could carry through to adult life.*

Activities include lace-making and a stamp club, table tennis and other sports, drama and dance. The lacemakers club in 1994 was run by a member of staff and one parent who was learning alongside the children in preparation for extending the club to more children.

Personal skills, life skills and lifetime interests

After-school clubs have the potential for offering activities which can fairly be said to cover the gamut of life skills. Indeed, the list of personal skills which will be important tools for pupils to use in order to master a world of change seems endless. Under this heading we would include, for example, both some domestic skills and practical skills (such as car or bike maintenance); and some life and personal skills (such as health and safety, money management, or assertiveness). But, in addition, to these specific skills there are some relatively unusual club activities which offer in themselves a range of invaluable life skills as well as those specific skills associated with a particular activity.

LAPAL PRIMARY SCHOOL, DUDLEY:
LAPAL STATE CIRCUS – LIFE SKILLS WITH A DIFFERENCE!

The circus club at Lapal Primary School in Dudley is a case in point. The school has just over 300 pupils, aged five to eleven, with some 15 per cent being from outside the immediate area. It is situated approximately seven miles from both Birmingham and Dudley town centres.

The school already had a wide-ranging programme of extra-curricular activities, based essentially on teachers' and parents' personal interests. These activities occur on three evenings a week. They include football, netball, rounders, athletics, gym, art, music and drama. There is also a specific after-school care club.

The origins of the circus club were within the class project undertaken by Chris Ogden with his class. The children were keen to carry on with their newly found interest, and so raised funding for the activity by washing cars, and engaging in other sponsored activities. The new club was called the Lapal State Circus. The admission charge was used to repay a loan taken out to fund a workshop run by a professional juggler, to buy equipment for the club, and to part-finance a trip to London. The State Circus has now performed at several schools, at fêtes and other social occasions. As a result of the further publicity given by the Education Extra Award in 1993, they have made TV appearances and been featured in the national press.

In a circus club, there are the more obvious, and extremely difficult, skills to tackle, such as juggling, balancing plates on sticks, walking tightropes, putting on clown make-up – the circus skills themselves, in short.

Then there are the indirect and associated skills which clearly feature in the programme. These would include the theatrical skills, of relating to and working on an audience, timing one's lines, or miming one's thoughts, planning a routine, and making an entrance.

To these may be added a list of vital life skills – qualities which are certainly evident in the work being done at Lapal. Among these one might list: an awareness of other people's presence, intentions, wishes; timing one's actions to fit in with other members of a team (look at the concentration required for a successful slapstick routine!);

responding to the pressures of an audience; the value of practice; perseverance; co-operation; formulating and expressing constructive criticism; acceptance of such criticism from others; responsibility; willingness to help others less skilled; learning to acknowledge that one's own sense of the ridiculous might not be universally accepted; confidence in front of an audience of one's peers or an unknown audience. The list is actually much longer than this.

And in the case of Lapal, a great deal of effort is also put into a third and perhaps most significant set of skills and abilities, which are enhanced through the organisation of the State Circus. The club is run by a pupils' committee, so that decision-making is real. They design and market their own T-shirts; they raise their own funding by voluntary efforts; they decide what equipment to buy. And they learn, incidentally, all kinds of specific skills which may not be as obvious as these: minute-taking, for example, and telephone competence.

All of this makes it quite clear that it isn't just a matter of clowning around (indeed, even that aspect requires the highest levels of co-operation, planning and timing if it is to be truly effective!).

For pupils with particular needs, personal skills programmes bring particular benefit. Chapel Grange Special School in Bradford, for instance, makes efforts to provide opportunities (through exciting days out) for improving the social skills of pupils with serious learning difficulties. Details of its young adventurers club are given in Chapter 7 on pp. 182–3. Young people in trouble have an equal need of help. Barton Moss Secure Unit, in Salford, offers an extra-curricular programme of outdoor pursuits, sports training and handicrafts to give serious offenders the chance to develop practical skills and a sense of social responsibility. Despite the special circumstances, these young men are thereby able to register achievements and raise their self-esteem. To reinforce this, Education Extra's Award provides funding for a small-scale internal achievement scheme, to enable awards to be presented.

There are many different types of life skills being promoted after school – from the most basic, such as survival cooking, to personal skills, health and safety, and the like. Some schools are using after-school activities to offer students the chance to develop some domestic skills, such as sewing or cooking. Such classes may provide the means for important social contact as well as learning life skills. Marlborough Road Infants School in Salford has been acting, for three years, as a focal point for local teenage girls through its Saturday morning sewing class. The school itself is in an area of high deprivation; 725 of children are on free school meals, and 17 per cent come from the local ethnic minority (largely Sikh) community.

The headteacher explains, 'In this area there are several families with children from ethnic minorities whose teenagers (especially girls) are not given any community provision. This class provides a social contact, a meeting point, and an opportunity to learn new skills.' Local Sikh families expect their daughters to leave school for an early marriage – at seventeen or eighteen – and discourage social contact in the year before marriage. Unlike their white equivalents they cannot go to youth clubs or community centres after school.

The sewing class is taken by an Asian instructor who is paid out of the community education budget. The class brings into the school not only the young teenagers, but younger siblings and, sometimes, mothers who help with open days when the clothes made are displayed and modelled by the girls and Asian food is available for the community. The girls learn how to cut patterns, traditional embroidery, crochet, knitting and how to use sewing machines. About twenty-five girls are now involved on a regular basis and two classes have had to be offered some Saturdays.

Many after-school clubs also use this time after school to focus on issues of personal health and safety. Some, such as the Sandhurst School, Surrey, incorporate this within another club – in this instance a mountain bike club for boys and girls to promote responsibility for off-road cycle-riding and to develop off-road cycling skills. And as described below, Connaught School for Girls, London Borough of Waltham Forest, uses a car maintenance club after school as a means of breaking down gender barriers and providing essential extra skills.

Some personal skills can prove to be either life-enhancing or even potentially life-saving for many young people. George Orwell School in the London Borough of Islington, which has a high percentage of refugee pupils, has addressed the need to improve the assertiveness skills of its pupils and is therefore developing a course in self-defence and assertiveness with a trained worker. (This forms part of a systematic wide-ranging after-school programme, including photography and other non-curricular projects, aimed at combating the potential boredom of pupils during the lunch-hour and immediately after school.) Similarly, Stewards School, Essex, has launched an assertiveness training programme for Year 10 pupils, preparing for their future responsibility as prefects in Year 11. This has been introduced within the context of a school-wide focus on bullying. The project involves working with other agencies, including a theatre-in-education group.

CONNAUGHT HIGH SCHOOL, LB WALTHAM FOREST:
ASSERTIVENESS TRAINING FOR A RACIALLY MIXED COMMUNITY

Connaught High School is a Girls' Comprehensive School, which serves the local multiracial area of Leytonstone. One of its (split-site) buildings nestles very awkwardly in the unwelcome shadow of the new extension to the M11. There is little outside space. The predominant racial group at the school is Asian, and the predominant religion is Muslim. Domestic duties and pressures mean that many pupils are unable to stay for activities which take place at the end of the school day. There are, quite naturally, also some fears for their safety when travelling home after school, especially during the winter months, as some of the local landscape is less than friendly. There is therefore a wide-ranging programme, involving many staff and pupils, which takes place during the lunch-hour. Among the activities on offer are a steel band, a pen-friends club, a paired reading club, girls football (coaching by Leyton Orient FC), and a car mechanics club. The headteacher comments that 'the activities provided broaden the horizons of many pupils who would not otherwise have the opportunities to participate in certain activities, such as visits to the theatre, visits beyond the immediate locality and interaction with other local groups.' To this extension of learning opportunity should certainly be added the increase in the girls' self-confidence in a sometimes hostile environment outside the school gates, though their training on the very significant assertiveness and self defence training programme. Education Extra made a contribution to the funding of this through an Award in 1993. The successful operation of this project has understandably been featured in the national press.

The importance of a knowledge of first aid is recognised in all schools. King's Somborne School (Hampshire), a small (117 pupils) rural primary school, has a rich and very varied after-school programme, including textiles, cycle training and Morris Dancing. In addition, there is a weekly first aid group which even meets during the holidays in one of the teacher's houses. One of the school's ambitions, for this very popular scheme, was to buy their own 'Resusci-Ann' (the Resuscitation Dummy for First Aid practice) and, through their Education Extra Award in 1994, they were able to do so.

Finally, at the very sharpest end of the personal and life-skills programme after school there is the whole issue of drugs education and the prevention of abuse. There are many and various strategies for drugs education in place already in schools but one of the most innovative involves an after-school project – the 'Cascade' Initiative in Solihull.

CASCADE: A PEER EDUCATION PROJECT ON DRUG ABUSE

The Solihull Peer Education Substance Misuse Project – CASCADE – was started in 1992. It is managed by the Solihull Crime Reduction Programme, a branch of Crime Concern Trust, and was designed to deliver education about substance misuse to school children, using other young people to deliver the message. A secondary school in the north of the borough and a youth club in the south were selected for the pilot, and volunteers were recruited from both places. The objectives were to provide young people with information on risks, to gauge the level of knowledge, to recruit other young people as peer educators and run projects in the school or youth club, and to develop materials for future use.

Two years on, the project is judged to be a major success in the way it has been able to attract and retain volunteers and the support it has received from young people and the schools.

As part of the project, one group of volunteers, aged between twelve and fifteen, were invited to participate in an after-school photographic project which would develop materials in support of the main project. This part of the project ran between January and May 1995 and involved fifteen young people overall. They learned to use cameras, to create studio conditions for photographs, to develop and print, and to make the link between photographic images and literary images. The key images were used in leaflets and information postcards and have been turned into an exhibition which includes the development stage of the project. Six of the young people became further involved with Cascade.[4]

Adding up the added value: recording achievements

In order to put a clear and visible value on after-school achievements it is essential that schools should find as many ways as possible to recognise them publicly. This, in itself, will not only assist in broadening the definition of achievement. It will also help schools to evaluate how after-school activities in themselves can promote higher expectations, self-esteem and skills. There is already a pattern of certification emerging in some school-based schemes. The Duke of Edinburgh's Award Scheme, the Bristol Youth Award Scheme, and the various forms of certification attached to science and engineering education (e.g. CREST) make the point through successful take-up. Some specific schemes give their own recognition or certification (e.g. the after-school club based in Crewe and Alsager Education Department); other schools have their own youth awards or local youth awards to which activities can be attached and recorded. The majority of schools record participation after school within the student's Record of Achievement as a matter of course.

As the headteacher of Matthew Humberstone School in Humberside explains, 'As Records of Achievement become increasingly significant within the school, both teachers and students seek the means of providing evidence of achievement.' Students at Matthew Humberstone refer to extra-curricular activities in their Personal Statements and collect evidence for their Record of Achievement Portfolios. At Patcham High School in East Sussex, every student who attends or supports any club or activity receives a merit which is recorded in their school journal. Students who accumulate fifty merits are given 'a Head's diploma'. If they accumulate two such diplomas they are given a book token.

A record of the extra-curricular achievements of every child is kept at Bulmershe School in Woodley, Berkshire . The school has always had a good tradition of after-school activities and 'in 1992 we decided to extend the range of activities available and encourage all pupils to become involved'. The activities now include literature, gardening, stage lighting, octopush and percussion among others, and parents have got involved in running them alongside teachers. Important features of the new promotion of after-school were to 'establish a house system and a procedure for recording extra-curricular achievement'.

The Dukeries in Newark, Nottinghamshire has been a community college since 1982. With two pits recently closed nearby the college seeks to be a focus for the local people. Adults are admitted into classes and 'it is a place for the family – 365 days a year'. There is a college farm, where many local voluntary workers are involved, and a youth centre on site. (More details about the Dukeries are given in Chapter 8, p. 212.) Roy Sowden, the College's Head, stresses:

> All our activities support the Dukeries Record of Achievement and the Duke of Edinburgh's Award . . . The Record of Achievement should include at 16+ a work based experience, a foreign experience, a residential element and an outdoor pursuit or community service.

At Benfield School, an inner city comprehensive in Newcastle, pupils' participation in out-of-school activities is given a place in their Records of Achievement. The school also holds a special 'Achievements Week' at the end of the summer term. Angley School in Kent is another secondary school where out-of-school activities have now been integrated into the Records of Achievement.

> We believe that pupils need to be provided with opportunities to succeed both within and outside the mainstream curriculum. With the integration of Records of Achievement we

make use of this excellent mechanism for recording participation and celebrating and recognising achievement.

The school kindly made available to Education Extra this example of how a pupil presented her extra-curricular activities in her personal record:

In my third year I gave up my lunchtime to help in the school's library and joined Young Farmers. I also joined a history club which took place on Wednesday lunchtimes [and] the drama club . . . As I was a young farmer I had the chance to look after a calf and go to the Kent Show with the school. I also helped at two boot fairs on the Young Farmers stall. I had the task of making the cakes . . . My last year at Angley I joined Young Enterprise, Mudbank, and became a careers adviser . . . I also stay after school on a Friday to do trampolining.

Conclusion

The schools cited in this chapter have demonstrated with particular clarity how after-school study support can improve children's ability to learn. They can also promote the confidence to take on the formal school curriculum and succeed. Learning support programmes can make all the difference to success in academic work and confidence in the classroom. Programmes of ESOL, Literacy and Numeracy enable students to gain the essential foothold into the curriculum. Supported study, 'clinics' in curriculum subjects, and a calm, quiet and supportive place for homework are a simple and direct means of giving students better chances of success. Special interest groups, which involve learning in indirect and subtle ways, open up whole new areas of interest as well as skill to them. And activities which develop life-skills give young people the personal skills they need to deal with other people and manage their own lives – in and beyond school – effectively.

The flexibility of after-school programmes within the general rubric of 'study support' means they can be adapted to the needs of particular schools and children: pupils struggling at school because English is not their first language, exceptionally able pupils in a disadvantaged area, pupils with special needs who lack opportunities for a social life, and many more, as this chapter has shown. Because the majority of parents see the importance of homework, they are enthusiastic about learning and life-skills programmes. Moreover, the very diversity possible in after-school schemes can make them a great provider of equalising opportunities. Schools, which see in close-up the very different, particular needs of their students, have used time after school to create diverse and innovative programmes to counter disadvantage and to meet those needs.

NOTES

1 OFSTED (1995). *Homework in primary and secondary schools*, p. 2.

2 ALBSU/Gallup survey (1995, January). *Older and younger: The basic skills of different age groups*.

3 MacBeath, J. (1993). *A place for success*. Prince's Trust.

4 Information kindly provided by Helen Thomson, Development Worker with the Cascade Peer Education Project.

5

Learning and the world around us: After-school science and technology

> [One of the] strongest messages . . . concerns the importance of extra-curricular activities
> in science as an encouraging factor for career decision . . . especially for future engineers for
> whom science clubs and competitions . . . were especially influential. It must be hoped that
> the current pressures on science teachers in England to deliver and assess the National
> Curriculum do not mitigate against such activities.
>
> Brian Woolnough (1994), Factors affecting students' choice of science and
> engineering, *International Journal of Science Education*.

In this chapter, in the context of what can be done after school, we are
concerned with three of the central and related elements of cultural and
economic life:

(a) science and technology

(b) their impact on the jobs and lifestyles of the future, and

(c) the emergence of environmental issues and interests as a key theme in the
     lives and preoccupations of children.

Science, technology and the world of work

One of the perceived failures and most common complaints about British
education has been the cultural chasm between arts and science subjects
which has forced specialisation at fourteen. This failure, together with the
emphasis on the virtues of an academic as opposed to a technical or 'practical'
education, has been routinely judged to illustrate the anti-industrial ethic
within education, and, to explain at least in part, the competitive failure of the

British economy.[1] The most recent comparison is with the emphasis on science and education as an element of the success we can now see in the cheap and ruthlessly efficient economies of the Pacific basin.

The criticisms levelled at the traditional education system are, first, that by dividing the arts from the sciences so categorically it has cut down the potential numbers of scientists, engineers and technologists. When it is clear that the jobs of the future will come from the combination of information and technology, the need for scientific and technical literacy becomes more urgent. Second, the present system stands accused of excluding millions of citizens from an understanding of science and technology and its economic and social impact. Above all, it has driven a wedge between two branches of learning which are both essential for a strong economy and a lively culture.

The problems created by this enforced break between the arts and sciences at fourteen – or even earlier is reflected in the unpopularity of science A levels. Only 5 per cent of all seventeen year-olds are taking physics and chemistry at A level; 5.6 per cent take biology; and 7.6 per cent maths. The numbers of young people taking physics has dropped from 33 000 in 1979 to 27 000 in 1993.[2] Two-thirds of those studying science A levels are doing so in combination with non-science subjects, and it is estimated, by the Joint Mathematical Council, that the proportion of the age group qualified to study a science subject at university has fallen by 40 per cent over the decade.[3] This failure has been compounded, historically, by a gender gap which has inhibited many girls from taking up careers in science and technology and which persists most strongly after GCSE.[4] At the same time structural change in advanced economies, and the employment effects of computer and telecommunications technology, have created the prospect of a world where mass employment among young unskilled people may become a permanent and ruinous feature of a world divided into information haves and have-nots.

Modern economies will depend therefore on people who are scientifically literate, technically competent and who have the right range of flexible skills which will passport them through a rapidly changing work environment. That means, in part, an education service which can produce an adequate number of scientists and technologists and which places a far higher premium on the public understanding of science and technology.

In recent years different educational strategies have been introduced to widen interest and competence in science and to strengthen the relationship between the school curriculum and working life. The teaching of primary science is an area of particular concern. The employment of advisory teachers in primary science, prior to the introduction of primary science into the core of the National Curriculum and new television programmes to support primary science funded through the DTI are two such responses. Within the secondary sector, the key change has been the introduction of balanced science rather than two or three separate sciences, the introduction of TVEI to prepare pupils aged fourteen–sixteen to prepare them for the demands of working life, and the Technology Initiative. A total of £135m has been spent on this latter initiative since 1988, distributed through GEST funding. OFSTED report that, along with TVEI, it has provided a resources base which allowed schools to develop IT and to address the requirements of the National Curriculum'.[5]

At the same time, the scientific community itself, represented by the BAAS, the Royal Society and other professional institutions of science and engineering, and the leading science museums, has taken a more aggressive role in promoting the public understanding of science. The Committee for the Public Understanding of Science (COPUS) is evangelical in its concern to involve more young people and adults in the pleasure of science. Science Week, 1995, produced a wealth of imagination and interest. This needs to be sustained, however, by new avenues to lead and keep young people active in science. Indeed, there is a national consensus that specialised A levels must be replaced with a broader qualification at 18, focused on a common curriculum, and a modular structure which will encourage and enable students to make wider choices of skills and careers.

There is a fertile context for the changes that are needed. In 1994, an ESRC report on the teaching of science, criticised the continuing failure of the science curriculum to sustain the curiosity of children in secondary school. Dr Richard Gott, suggested that this 'nosedive in achievement' might be 'the result of an inadequate science curriculum which focused children's attention on the ritual of conducting experiments rather than discovering and understanding the scientific methods behind them.' This was one reason, he felt, for the lack of enthusiasm for science at A level.[6] The National Science Curriculum has been slimmed down twice since its introduction. It is significant, therefore, that in the most recent rewrite of the National Curriculum for Science Sir Ron Dearing has responded, as he put it, to the 'passionate desire to bring back wiring up things, flashing lights and ringing bells – so we have dismissed the Earth and beyond to Outer Space'. At least as far as five to seven-year-olds are concerned, therefore, the science curriculum reflects their boundless curiosity and insistence on making things happen and not merely writing about them.

In fact, it is well observed that children today have far more opportunity for interaction with science and technology in different forms, and are far more likely to be familiar and confident with new technology. Museums are beginning to anticipate and meet this thirst for discovery. Children are avid explorers – evident in the success of 'Hands on' Science and Technology at the Exploratorium at Bristol, the Museum of Science and Industry in Manchester, the Science Museum in London and smaller, lively innovations such as Curiosity in Oxford. At the same time, parents have watched with admiration and amazement as their children revel in computer games which they themselves cannot begin to tackle. As Professor Chris Freeman puts it:

> *Not only do many children concentrate for hours on end on games such as 'Mario is Missing' or 'Sonic the Hedgehog' but they will go on day after day even though the obsolescence rate in these games is high and fashion plays a big part. Yet the same children will often say, 'School is Boring' or 'Homework is Boring' or 'Maths is Boring' or 'Geography is Boring'. Here, surely, is a tremendous challenge for the entire education profession all over the world. Learning should be exciting and interesting, not boring, and often, it should be fun.*[7]

The British Association plays the key role in promoting enthusiasm and interest among young people. It has developed a range of 'informal learning opportunities to foster the interest of young people in science and technology'. The British Association Youth Section (BAYS) offers support and advice for schools, with most of the membership made up of school-based clubs run after school or at lunchtime. There is a wealth of opportunity for age-related participation – exemplified by the CREST Awards, Science Challenge, Young Engineers, or Young Investigators.[8] From the evident enthusiasm there is clearly an appetite for more – particularly for the schemes pioneered in primary schools which encourage maximum participation and involvement and include parents and other adults.

All this evidence reinforces the importance of after-school and out of school opportunities for participation and discovery in science and technology which is evident in the Education Extra Network. Moreover, there is solid academic proof to back it up.

Brian Woolnough, of the Education Department, University of Oxford, has studied the factors which influence the making of scientists and engineers. Drawing on the work of Pell (1985), who demonstrated the strong link between enjoyment and learning, and that of Champagne and Klopfer on the learning benefits of experimentation (1984),[9] he has drawn attention to the vital importance of extra-curricular activities in maintaining interest and enthusiasm for science.

His work demonstrates that, although home background and inspirational teachers were important 'an additional factor came through as being of vital importance to many students, and that was their involvement in extra-curricular activities'. In his in-depth research into science and technology teaching in twelve schools, he found, for example, criticisms of the impersonal, irrelevant and dull teaching of science, 'demonstrating little relationship to the concerns of the student's own world and allowing little opportunity for student self-expression. Creativity and humanity were not associated with the physical sciences or engineering.'[10] Some of the excitement which was missing from the school day curriculum could be offered in the more flexible and free atmosphere after school.

On extra-curricular activities he observed that:

> There was consistent evidence, from the teachers' own experience, from correlations with schools' success, and from the students' own reports, that it was often the 'little bit extra' to the normal science teaching, the extra-curricular activities in science and technology that were all-important factors. These came in different forms; national or local 'great egg' races-type competitions; science clubs, visits, speakers, links with local engineers, national initiatives by professional institutions, BAYS, Crest Awards, and school project or technology weeks. For many students these were significant factors both in influencing their choice of subject, leading towards science and engineering careers and, equally important, motivating and confirming them to continue with such courses into a scientific or technological career.

> [Although] some of the activities, such as science clubs and technological competitions for sixth formers, tended to involve only those who had already made a decision towards the sciences, they were still important in that they reinforced the students' original choices by personalising and making excitingly real the work being covered in an inevitably more prosaic class. The importance of these extra-curricular activities was particularly significant for those going on to engineering at higher education.[11]

Depressingly, however, there was also evidence even in the good schools that the pressure of work imposed on science departments recently (through assessment schemes, administration and curriculum change initially through the GCSE and increasingly through the National Curriculum) was preventing science staff from continuing with such vitally influential extra-curricular activities.

Given the explicit benefits of all forms of clubs, he recommended that science teachers should be encouraged and supported in developing extra-curricular activities. 'Because of the importance of extra-curricular activities,' he suggested that teachers involved in developing them 'should be given an appropriate time allocation in recompense.'[12] He also urged the scientific and engineering institutions to continue to develop their work in building up professional links with schools, linking local enthusiasts and practitioners to schools and promoting a better understanding of the role of the technologist and engineer within society. Alongside this strategy exemplified in practice in some schools already, there is a very positive opportunity, through the relatively mysterious world of science and technology, to attract into schools alongside pupils their parents and even grandparents in an attempt to boost scientific literacy overall.

Environmental issues

For many pupils the link with the world of science comes most easily by way of the issues associated with conservation and the environment, which rouse great passions among young people, both at a local and a global level.

Environmental projects, which range from gardening to ecology, offer vast opportunities for schools to link up with the community, with parental and adult concerns. But within the broad term environment there are, of course, several layers of significance.

There are the initial and basic steps to be taken, to encourage pupils to be concerned about the appearance of the school itself, and to develop a conscientious approach to maintaining a tidy and therefore healthier immediate environment. Even a project as modest as clearing litter can involve enormous out-of-lesson commitment. It is increasingly common practice to find groups of pupils charged with responsibility for keeping areas of the school free from litter and waste; to find a school club or group which takes on responsibility for looking after the school's plants and gardens – or at least plays a part in that process.

And it is a simple logical step for a more sophisticated arrangement to emerge from this, involving parents, pupils, staff, governors and other community members in making efforts to improve the visual and environmental wellbeing of the school – by the judicious placement of greenery, the painting of murals, the provision of quiet areas or retreats, the provision of colourful and attractive resources for games/play (e.g. where groups of parents paint or mark out the tarmac with coloured snakes or numbered squares, which children can enjoy making up games to fit).

Then there are the projects and activities which make whole-school development plans in relation to the environment of the school. This goes a step further, in that it means a positive, proactive approach, rather than simply a damage-limitation exercise (viz. cleaning-up or tidying away). Just a little imagination can transform even the grey and confined playgrounds of Victorian board schools, or the bleak expanses of school playing fields with no trees, which are still much in evidence, by the provision of benches or other points of focus; or by planning the use of space in a systematic way which is related to the needs of the clientele. There are, moreover, in the environmental field, a number of agencies which have tapped into this altruism but which have also brought immediate benefits to the school itself. The work of the organisation 'Learning through Landscapes' has been concerned in part with humanising and improving the actual landscape of the school environment. Their 'Urban Challenge' scheme, launched in October 1992, is precisely targeted on this issue. As LTL's Director, Bill Lucas says: 'We are aware that inner-city schools, and particularly those with tarmac sites, present special challenges . . . we are highlighting innovative solutions to problems encountered in city school grounds.' Even those schools not receiving Awards from the scheme are still eligible to receive help and guidance from LTL in implementing their plans.

It seems sometimes as if the school curriculum leaps from a micro concern with plant life to a macro concern with the rain forests, hardly pausing to consider the importance of growing and caring for plants or for the activity of gardening – one of the most popular of all national pastimes. But there are signs that there is (if the pun may be pardoned!) a growing interest in schools in complementing a positive attitude towards the environment with a positive attitude towards the nurturing of plant and vegetable life. Gardening clubs (to continue with the appropriate metaphors) are springing up everywhere!

From there it is a comparatively small step to the environment of the community itself. Through the learning which goes on within these clubs, etc., there may be some very active encouragement of concerns for world-wide issues relating to conservation and the environmental implications of actions taken. Some of the organisations which support environmental education in schools (such as WWF UK [World Wide Fund for Nature] The National Trust and The Council for Environmental Education) endeavour to assist in the taking of this step.

The examples and case studies in this chapter show how schools are responding to the challenge of involving pupils in after-school science, maths, technology and environmental studies in all their diversity. They range from the simply structured science club, open to all, to the more targeted activities which draw in the high-flyer; from the technology club aimed at lifting the confidence of girls to the gardening project which gives urban children a chance to create a garden for themselves. In each and every way the pupils involved are learning about the natural world.

Science and technology after school

Science clubs

Schools offer science clubs as enrichment and entertainment after school. Indeed, science and technology are relatively unusual in that the scientific and professional institutions have, for some years, promoted different forms of scientific activity after school. In some cases the science club is geared to a particular age group or interest group, and is clearly aimed at the well-motivated pupil. In others it caters for all ages and abilities. Some science clubs stand alone, but in other schools, they take their place alongside a raft of specialised clubs for technology, environment and computing – and encourage personal hobbies such as radio and rocket technology.

Some of the most interesting innovations in science after school are to be found in primary schools where there is a particular delight in discovery.

CLYRO PRIMARY SCHOOL, CLYRO, POWYS:
YOUNG SCIENTISTS IN ACTION

The science club at Clyro Church in Wales School met with an overwhelmingly positive response from pupils when it started in January 1994. Already, two-thirds of all pupils of eligible age choose to take part in it.

Clyro School is a very small rural village school with just sixty-five pupils on roll – one infant and two junior classes. Many of the pupils live out in the country, too far away to walk to and from school, but this does not prevent them turning up enthusiastically to after-school activities. The headteacher admits that 'in truth, although there are Cubs and Brownies in a neighbouring village, there is little else for the children to do out of school.'

The school 'wished to develop National Curriculum science within school hours, but were scarcely prepared for the overwhelming response to the founding of a science club whose main tenet is that Science is Fun.'

The programme of after-school activities has built up gradually out of pupils' requests and the special interests and expertise of staff members and other adults. The school is now in use every night of the week, with a sports club (run by a parent), a gym club where children work towards BAGA awards, a music club with guitar lessons given by two parents, the choir run by the clerk to the school governors (a retired music teacher) and now the science club.

The science club provides a chance for members to enjoy and learn about science outside the rigours of National Curriculum requirements. The children engage in pond-dipping, gardening and other activities, and can work towards the B.A. Young Investigators Award. The club is run jointly by one of the school's three teachers, the school caretaker, parents and high school pupils.

Following the immediate rush of interest in the science club, the teacher who runs it commented in early 1994, 'It is important now to keep up the momentum. We have been lucky in obtaining free "guest speakers" so far, and have used our ingenuity to devise "Water Rocket", "Bubbles" and "Light Entertainment" sessions. As a favour, Techniquest in Cardiff have also lent us equipment (which we were able to share with other primary schools in the cluster group) . . . we now need to stock up on resources and to engage exciting "visiting experts" who can be billed large enough to attract both pupils and their parents, and possibly also a wider audience in the community.'

In 1994 the School won an Education Extra Award for the science club. Part of it was used to buy Newton meters, so a special day was arranged when 'Isaac Newton' (a local science lecturer in full Newtonian regalia!) visited the club to give a talk. Other visitors have included staff from the nearby high school, coming in to give displays and talks about electronics and other special topics. This contact with the high school has an extra advantage for pupils at Clyro – when they themselves go on to high school they will already be familiar with some of the staff, as well as having an insight into some of the subjects to be taught.

Science club is strengthening contacts between the school and pupils' families. One parent helps regularly at the club and a number of others visit frequently. A couple of parents have begun to bring pupils' little brothers and sisters along too. Older brothers and sisters and an auntie (now a university student) have also attended. As Pamela Banks, the teacher in charge of science club, points out: 'Bringing in people from home emphasises that science is all to do with real life. What we do here is try to make it real "kitchen-sink" stuff – we make science fun and accessible.'

Secondary schools have the scope for specialisation – and many take advantage of it

Earlsheaton High School in Dewsbury has a very broad Enrichment Programme for pupils after school which includes information technology, environmental education and an amateur radio club along with a range of other subjects from maths to modern languages. The school has a well-organised 'School Plus' programme, which started in 1993, when staff were given the option of putting directed time into an after-school activity. (More details of this arrangement are given in Chapter 6, p. 159). The school now has 'the most extensive programme of after-school activities in the area'. The school won an Education Extra Award in 1994 for the excellent way it organised activities.

Science is one area where schools can draw on a wealth of support – either from the professional institutions, by involving local enthusiasts (engineers, astronomers, environmental scientists) or by accessing the resources of further and higher education. Some schools have made a feature of exploiting the full resources of further and higher education near the school.

Newlands School in Maidenhead, Berks is a girls' comprehensive with a real commitment to science and technology within and beyond the curriculum. Staff from Thames Valley University come in to the school to run Electronics Workshops for Year 10 pupils after school. Year 9 pupils are also taken to Mathematics Masterclasses at Reading University on Saturday mornings. Older pupils make full use of the Sixth Form computer area to which they have access before school in the mornings. They can also take part in a range of activities to enhance learning, including mathematics master classes and Saturday morning electronics workshops which take place at Reading University. Sixth formers can also make use of a computer area which is open in the mornings before school.

Many schools are already involved after school in the range of certificated activities which encourage young people to work independently or collectively to apply knowledge in practice. Young investigators, young engineers and young scientists clubs all offer after-school links to the curriculum.

CREST AWARDS AND YOUNG SCIENTISTS CLUBS

The BAYS CREST Award (Creativity in Science and Technology) is a popular choice for heads of science departments wishing to involve motivated pupils in particular. They can offer accreditation for a wide range of projects undertaken by students on an individual basis or as members of teams. It is a flexible scheme, which can be adapted to all levels of ability, and which therefore enables pupils between the ages of eleven and nineteen+ to start at any Award level (of which there are three: Bronze, Silver and Gold). This is an established national Award Scheme, which enables teachers to deliver programmes of study appropriate to the curriculum needs of their students.

The scheme provides a structured link to the world of industry, business and the community; it provides a developing sense of achievement and therefore strong motivation to students; and above all provides an enjoyable opportunity for personal achievement. It is not a competition.

Because of its flexibility, CREST is an ideal means of providing some credit for work done outside school hours in the fields of science, technology, engineering and the environment.

As the Director, Alan West, argues, 'A CREST Award is a qualification in enthusiasm.'

There are at present about 2700 schools participating in the CREST scheme. Since their inception, there has been a total of some 70 000 students involved; for last year the figure was 16 500.

One of the most exciting innovations after school has come with the involvement of parents and other adults.

Parents as well as teachers are involved in providing the BAYS science at Shenfield High School in Brentwood, Essex. After-school activities are viewed as 'nothing out of the ordinary – an integral part of the education process'. Teachers welcome them as an opportunity 'to do more with the pupils'. The school also encourages professional men and women to come in and get involved in the activities, whether 'to judge, share, talk, display or lead' them.

Equal opportunities for parents and pupils

One of the most exciting innovations in the field of science and technology after school is the scope it offers for involving families and adults – including local voluntary associations such as the Women's Institutes. Innovations are coming thick and fast in this field as schools, museums and local and national organisations seek ways of breaking down the mystifications of science and technology.

DALE PRIMARY SCHOOL, DERBYSHIRE: FAMILY LEARNING AND SCIENCE

Dale Primary School, in Derby, has been pioneering a Family Learning Project after school over the past two years which has focused on science and technology. 80 per cent of the school's pupils come from Asian families and the intention has been to maximise the benefits of the family unit as a base for learning, and to encourage a practical working partnership between parents and teachers. Over two years about thirty family evenings have been organised, featuring activity-based projects on topics such as flight, nutrition and optics, based in or involving local firms such as Rolls Royce, MacDonalds and Boots the Opticians. The project runs initial and follow-up workshops for parents, teachers and pupils, 'guiding them through innovative activities using very simple, accessible equipment' and relating scientific concepts to everyday life. Breaking down gender barriers is an important objective. Basic learning kits are sometimes provided for follow-up work at home. About one-third of all parents (and grandparents, older siblings and other

127

relations) have taken part in the family evenings which have expanded into other fields, including
literacy.

The project has won a high degree of support, and active, enthusiastic partners, including City Challenge, the Committee for Public Understanding of Science (COPUS) – which have helped fund basic costs, such as supply cover for teachers preparing activities, transport and resources – and The Post Office, which funded the Evaluation. The evaluation exercise conducted with parents in 1994 demonstrated a very high degree of enjoyment – particularly in relation to working together on hands-on activities. When parents were asked what topics they would like covered in the future, there was a very positive response to environmental issues and natural history and consistent interest in the provision of more activities involving computers, science, transport, maths and health and safety. Reasons for participation varied, but above all, the message back to the school was that it provided an incentive for families to do things together and to support the school. Parents said, for example: 'It was just really good fun . . . things that make learning fun', 'I was surprised by how much I learned from other parents' and 'The children were quite keen to come and we like to show an interest in our children's work and what they do at school.'[13]

Another recent innovation, which is taking place after school but away from school, involves not only parents but teachers in training. In this case the club aims to extend the experience of both children and the students involved.

MANCHESTER METROPOLITAN UNIVERSITY SCHOOL OF EDUCATION: PARENTS AND CHILDREN TOGETHER

The opening of a Primary Centre in the Department of Education at the Manchester Metropolitan University, Crewe and Alsager School of Education, provided the ideal base for a new venture aimed at broadening children's understanding of and involvement in science and technology.

Brenda Keogh, Senior Lecturer at the University, was convinced about the positive effect on children's attitudes to science which could be achieved through running science clubs in schools. Research evidence seemed to support this view. She believed that there was the potential within the University for providing children from local schools with relevant extra-curricular experiences which would have an impact on their views of science.

She realised that the heavy demands placed on teachers and, in many cases, their lack of experience in running science activities out of school hours, meant that many schools were unable to offer this kind of experience. The potential numbers involved meant that it was not possible for the University to provide support for individual clubs in local schools. However, one possible solution seemed to be to hold a weekly science club at the University. Even though there was no tradition of educating children on a regular basis on the University site, a University-based science club seemed a promising prospect.

Schools and parents reacted very positively when the idea was discussed with them. They were willing to carry out any necessary administration and to ferry the children to and from the campus. Schools could benefit from regular access to University-based expertise and the strengthening of relationships between teachers and University staff would be an important aspect of the regular contact.

From the University's point of view there was also much to be gained. At the simplest it would provide an opportunity to raise awareness of the University amongst members of the local community. It would enhance the University's partnerships with schools by extending the opportunities for students to work closely with children, teachers and parents. Most importantly, there would be the possibility of giving student teachers an increased understanding of the role of such extra-curricular activities and the confidence and knowledge to start clubs of their own in the future.

The first group of thirty-six children from nine separate schools was welcomed in the University's Science Club in 1994. It is believed that this is the first such club to be organised by a Higher Education Institution.

Students on the Primary B.Ed./B.A.(Hons) course at Crewe and Alsager took responsibility, on a rota basis, for planning and organising the weekly club. Senior managers within the University gave their support and commitment and made it possible to have the science club recognised as a valid part of the students' course. Engaging children in thinking and working scientifically is viewed as an important part of the students' professional work in science. What this means in practice is that some timetabled time is always run at the end of the teaching day in time which the students make voluntarily available.

The students have involved the children in a range of activities. If the students successfully complete the activities then they can gain an award from the British Association for the Advancement of Science. The students claim that they gain considerable pleasure from their involvement and are proud to be associated with the club. Being a science club co-ordinator is beginning to gain status within the School of Education.

The success of this venture was obvious from the start. It has been impossible to meet the demand from schools to let children attend the club and this has meant a limit of four children per school. Children who are unable to attend send in letters of apology to ensure that their places are reserved for them. The level of involvement is high throughout the hourly sessions, with children, and sometimes parents, often reluctant to leave.

Additional benefits have already emerged as a result of the club. For example, the children from one school set up their own science club for younger children; children have continued investigating at home, bringing their ideas with them to following sessions; parents have become involved through trying to solve problems with their children; and teachers are looking for ways of extending the club to other children.[14]

One of the key issues in science education is the need to overcome some of the difficulties which have traditionally inhibited girls from pursuing an academic interest in science and technology. After-school activities can offer girls another positive opportunity to show what they can do, particularly in areas such as mechanics as the following examples prove.

At East Leeds High School, girls as well as boys are involved in go-karting – which involves building and maintaining as well as racing go-karts.

At first we were a little apprehensive and took some stick from the sexist boys in the team who couldn't believe we were good enough. But now we are in the middle of building our own Go-Kart – a Y250 . . . We have marshalled a race at Wigan and had our first race at Chasewater, and still have to race another two times to gain our licences.

Shareen and Joanne, East Leeds pupils.

Many schools have car or bike maintenance clubs, but Connaught High School for Girls, in London Borough of Waltham Forest (see Chapter 4, pp. 111–12), is unusual for a girls' school in having a thriving car maintenance club. Kirkhallam Community School, Derbyshire, has an after-school science and technology club especially for girls.

Some schools have combined maths and technology clubs to fit theory and practice even more closely together. At Marlborough Road Infants School in Salford, for example, where 70 per cent of the pupils claim free school meals and 30 per cent have special educational needs, the technology and maths clubs provide extra learning opportunities for young children from severely economically deprived backgrounds. The after-school activities at Heathcote School, in Stevenage, Hertfordshire, which were commended at the last school inspection, include a club for maths and technology. As well as enhancing work done in curriculum time, the school's headteacher places 'enormous importance' on extra-curricular work for 'its value in developing social skills, levels of active participation, leadership . . . it extends the learning chances of the individual, giving each pupil a sense of pride and self-worth . . . it is these activities, when lessons are a dim memory, which will remind them of the value of education.'

Specialist schools and specialist clubs

Specialist schools or schools with particular provision for technology can open up those resources for the community in a particularly effective way.

DANETRE SCHOOL, DAVENTRY, NORTHANTS: EXPLOITING THE TECHNOLOGY

Danetre is a large comprehensive school (1000 pupils) in the heart of a housing estate in the expanding town of Daventry. The school has superb facilities and equipment thanks to major capital expenditure on it, and seeks to use these as fully as possible after school as well as during the school day. Extra-curricular sports range from basketball and athletics to weight training. Other activities include music, drama and dance, photography, gardening, chess, school magazine and year book clubs. There is also a wide-ranging rural crafts programme (mentioned in Chapter 2 on p. 47).

The technology provision is particularly good at Danetre. The school is fortunate in having excellent technology facilities – now housed in a completely remodelled technology block. Pupils can learn skills like computer aided design both in school and out of school time and in the lunch break. Three members of staff regularly stay on voluntarily after school to supervise the use of computers. 'Lower school pupils tend to use the computers in different ways after school than during class time. Older pupils often take the opportunity to do extra work on curriculum-related projects after school: for instance, Year 11 pupils will use the time and the facilities to "mop up" their GCSE work.'

Links have been forged between the school and the Volvo Company. Volvo has provided funds for publications and has become closely involved with the design and technology department at Danetre. Volvo staff, for instance, have volunteered to come into school to share the benefit of their experience with pupils on a work experience day. Trevor Hopkins, head of Upper School, describes their involvement as 'invaluable help in kind'.

Environmental science-related activities also draw in high numbers of pupils after school. There is a bird club and an environment club. They have been involved in creating and maintaining a nature area, including a pond and bird boxes; more recently they obtained financial support from the local council and some local Trusts which enabled them to clear an area of the school grounds and plant it to create a copse. The environment club has also organised a special environment day for the lower school pupils to show them how a natural disaster could affect the environment.

The Technology Initiative has also opened up new possibilities for schools. In 1993, for example, Kingsway School in Stockport was awarded a TSI grant of

£300 000 to build a new technology centre, and intends to make use of it for twilight courses for members of the community and small businesses as well as school students.

The Middleton Technology School, in Rochdale, caters for a catchment area which is described as 'largely socially and culturally deprived and the housing estates are under provided with leisure facilities'. The school was very successful in 1992 in winning a TSI bid, and was awarded £250 000 for high-tech provision but 'there is much to do in raising aspirations and attainment and in providing cultural and leisure opportunities'. The school runs an extended day for over 400 students between 8.30 and 5.30 p.m in most GCSE subjects.

Being IT rich means students arrive early, and work at lunchtimes and after school in order to gain access to computers in most curriculum areas. The school staff work to make the best use possible of their excellent science and technology equipment and try to provide the students, many of whom come from socially and culturally deprived backgrounds, 'an atmosphere where they can grow'. Among the specialist science activities on offer are technology, maths, electronics and meteorology.

Significantly, given this emphasis on science and technology throughout all aspects of the curriculum the school was aware of the need in 1993, to 'be able to offer more social, leisure and cultural activities at reduced or no cost [which] would encourage students and parents to view the school as somewhere they could attend before and after normal school hours'.

In addition to the general range of science and technology clubs, there are specialised clubs which cater for a wide range of tastes and interests. Radio clubs are very popular, as are rocket clubs, and clubs which provide opportunities for young people to build and maintain machines. Preston School in Yeovil, Somerset, for example, has a radio club as part of an enormous range of after-school activities aided by extensive links which have been built up with local businesses. These include a Prefect Training scheme run in conjunction with Tescos. The headteacher says

As a Community School, Preston is committed to Education as a lifelong activity . . . it has long been our policy to offer a wide range of extra-curricular activity to pupils away from normal timetable.

Marple Hall School in Stockport in 1993, included a rocket club, aeromodelling and a maths and science challenge during an activities week in 1993; Stanchester Community School in Somerset gives budding mechanics the opportunity to work on motor cycles or build a car.

Some schools have particular strengths which have enabled them to develop unique clubs after school.

A school farm, managed and funded by the school, is part of the science department at Angley School in Cranborne, Kent. In 1993, after-school activities included a young farmers' club and a young engineers' club. These were just part of a whole handbook-full of activities provided through the week and on Saturday mornings.

The 1993 OFSTED inspection report commented specifically on the range of after-school activities at South Dartmoor Community College in Devon (*see also* Chapter 4, p. 103), saying that nearly every child was involved in at least one activity. The college's young engineers club is supported by neighbourhood engineers, and has national recognition. After-school extension lessons include electronics and computer programming.

Wodensborough High School, Wednesbury, in Sandwell, is an eleven to sixteen school which looks forward to steady growth from 730 in 1993/4 to 1000 pupils by 1997. The school has an excellent track record in providing after-school activities, including a technology club with sixty members. The school is now developing a young entrepreneurs' club which grew out of two cross-curricular enterprise events for Year 9 in 1993. The two courses brought together Aspects of Enterprise and Designing in Technology.

Two days off timetable saw the launch of various enterprises – culminating in the external judges deciding on the winners. Interest then triggered the establishment of the Young Entrepreneurs' Club. Three teams entered the Sandwell Enterprise Competition and one actually came second, succeeding in selling a custom-made T-Shirt to the Mayor. The most recent success case came in the local area board trade fayre when a team of Year 10 pupils won first prize for the best and most original product and . . . for the most imaginative stall. Working with a mentor from local industry Sweet Xpressions produced children's colouring books and puzzles for sale on their market stall in West Bromwich. . . . This success has been achieved with limited funding. Indeed, the groups have self-funded their projects by issuing shares in their 'Company'.

Education Extra was able to provide some support for the young entrepreneurs' club, in the 1994 Awards, through which the pupil members are now extending their IT and marketing expertise.

Computer clubs

Pressure on resources is particularly acute in IT studies. Sharing computers at school, whether for programming, DTP, accessing information, or games-playing can be particularly frustrating. IT is being used in many different ways after school.

First, schools are providing open access to computers wherever possible. In many schools it is axiomatic that the computer suite will be available for individual use before and after school and during the lunchtime, and sometimes at the weekends if students want to finish project work or homework. Second, there are more specialist computer clubs which focus on designing or playing games, programming, designing newspapers and journals. Third, there is the use of IT as an aid to literacy and basic learning after school; and, finally, there are schools which are using IT facilities as the key source for enhancing learning across the curriculum after school.

In many cases, access to computing facilities is seen as part of the regular commitment to opening up facilities for study support and homework.

Pupils at Mark Hall Comprehensive School in Harlow, Essex, have open access to the computers both at lunchtimes and after school. Organised activities after school include technology, science, maths and homework along with sports, drama and outdoor pursuits. At Walker School in Newcastle, a keyboarding club for Year 11 starts at 8.00 a.m. in the morning; computer facilities are open at lunchtime and after school; and staff are anxious to extend their IT facilities, particularly for pupils with special needs.

The computer activities at Ingram High School for Boys in the London Borough of Croydon are part of a programme (which also includes sports, chess, music and working on allotments) aimed at providing something worthwhile for boys who otherwise 'spend most of their time wandering the streets and getting into trouble because there is little to occupy their time locally . . . and what there is costs a fortune'. In 1993 the headteacher was hoping to expand the range of provision until there is a choice of activities every evening. Many schools are using desk-topping facilities as the key to producing school newspapers and journals. At John O'Gaunt Community School in Hungerford, Berkshire, the computer club is helping publicise itself and the school's whole programme of after-school provision by compiling an After-School Newsletter as part of its activities.

The possibility for bringing parents in to extend their own computer competence is obvious. Literacy schemes based on IT are, for example, being used at Goetre Primary School in Merthyr, Mid-Glamorgan, as a way of promoting family literacy as a whole after school. Pens Meadow Special School in Stourbridge, Dudley, have organised computer workshops for *parents* in the evenings. The acting head explains:

This is an all-age special school with pupils travelling from all areas of Stourbridge, Dudley and Halesowen. Parental involvement is high; parents regularly come into school for their own support group coffee morning, to talk with the staff team, work with their own or other youngsters, or help in fund-raising.

The school took the step of creating a term of weekly computer classes run by a member of staff and a parent because they wanted to offer the parents, who were giving so much, something they would benefit from and enjoy. The experiment was a success, but highlighted the need to look also at the parents' childcare arrangements.

Arranging for babysitters can be difficult for most parents; for our parents it can be even harder. Feedback from parents' computer workshops indicated that more parents would have liked to come, or both parents in some cases, but they were restricted by child care arrangements. A priority now is to run parents workshops where their Pens Meadow youngster, or other siblings, could be left with on site staff who were trained to cater for their needs.

She concludes: 'Offering parents workshops has been an important feature of enhancing our "Parents as Partners" policy.'

Information technology is also being used with particular effect to facilitate all forms of learning after school.

CHAPELTOWN AND HAREHILLS ASSISTED LEARNING COMPUTER SCHOOL

Chapeltown, in Leeds, is one of the most deprived inner city areas in the country with above average rates of unemployment, drugs and crime. 60 per cent of the local population come from the ethnic minorities, mainly Afro-Caribbean. Since 1987, Chapeltown has been the site of one of the most innovative and successful after-school projects in the country: the Chapeltown and Harehills Assisted Learning Computer School (CHALCS).

For two hours every evening and at weekends, under the direction of Brainard Bramah, MBE, 350 young people (50 per cent girls, 50 per cent boys) have come to CHALCS for extra computer-based lessons in maths, English, science and geography. The age range is wide – between seven and nineteen. Science laboratories are also available for practical learning alongside theoretical work, supported by staff from the University of Leeds and qualified tutors. In January 1995 there was a waiting list of 200.

CHALCS works. Pupils attending CHALCS do not truant. They do not have police records, and their work in school improves. They have the academic results to show it. The project can demonstrate that 77 per cent of its 'graduates' had improved in basic academic skills; 82 per cent had become more confident. In 1994, thirty-two CHALCS students achieved more than four GCSEs each. Sixteen are now going on to A level and nine students to college. Since 1992–3 the only four local Black youngsters at university and the only Black sixth former from the area have all been CHALCS students and four more will be going on to university this year. Seven CHALCS students attend a small maths master class run by the University of Leeds.

Another aspect of its work is to provide daytime educational support to children who have been excluded and who are truanting from school for a variety of reasons. CHALCS supports them at a time when they might become attracted to petty crime. It wants to expand its multi-media computer systems to turn these youngsters back on to learning. Brainad Bramah says:

> We want our pupils to develop and acquire skills and qualifications to enable them to compete successfully for employment in the field of new technology and science-based sectors of the economy. We strive to encourage parents to get more closely involved . . . and to help raise expectations and hopes for a better future.

Staff now want to increase the numbers of students to 700–800 to match local demand, and to develop the Microcomputer Science Laboratory to provide more support for science learning. With more pupils going on to A level they want to provide support for their studies too. CHALCS has been supported by funds from central and local government and from Leeds TEC. More funding is now being sought to extend the scheme.[15]

Some schools have taken a successful technology club as the logical basis for expansion into the world of business and industry.

After school and the environment

For children living in inner cities after-school activities which involve growing and gardening projects and wild life gardens in the urban environment are particularly welcome. Some London schools are making strenuous efforts to open up the school environment itself.

Waste ground attached to Christchurch CE Primary School in London Borough of Lambeth is being developed into an area for environmental study. A pond has been dug and plants are being encouraged in a swamp area. Paths are being laid, dividing the area into plots of different character for the pupils to investigate.

At St Alfege with St Peters School in London Borough of Greenwich, a wildlife site is being reclaimed by teachers and pupils as a small oasis in a restricted urban setting. Many of the pupils live in the high rise flats surrounding the school, which is housed in a Victorian building plus extensions and portakabins, on a restricted site, next to a busy main road. Most of the children have nowhere to play out of doors, and no experience outside school of growing plants or contact with animals. The school is now planning to develop the wildlife site to include a bee garden. With their award from Education Extra the school planned to buy tools for the garden, pond nets, magnifiers, trays and containers as well as identification books for the children to note garden development through the seasons.

George Orwell School in the London Borough of Islington is a multi-ethnic inner city school where a third of pupils have refugee status and many others live in temporary accommodation. Like many schools in cities, it has no sports field or even an outdoor dry play area; however the school is giving pupils the opportunity to work on a garden through a wild garden project in partnership with a local nursery school. Science activities after school also take pupils out to different environments; weekend trips include beachcombing and birdwatching.

In other schools the striking feature is the extent to which environmental studies can extend throughout different activities.

Environmental education takes several forms, for example, in the extra activities for pupils at Park High School in Colne, Lancashire. Each year 160 students go on a week-long residential course studying wildlife. In 1993 and 1994 the Year 7 students have had a special Environment Day doing environmental projects. In 1994 a special project was undertaken by the whole school – helping to clean up the local British Waterways reservoir. And the school's fell walking club takes students out into the Yorkshire Dales and other countryside areas at weekends each month. The keenest members can take part in a ten-day hike (such as the 200-mile coast-to-coast walk) which is an annual event during the holidays. (Other features of the comprehensive after-school programme at Park High are given in Chapter 1, pp. 44; 47) Other schools have turned environmental issues into a whole school project.

HARRY CHESHIRE HIGH SCHOOL, KIDDERMINSTER, HEREFORD AND WORCS:
THE GREEN TEAM AND A BROADER VISION

Students and staff of Harry Cheshire High School decided in November 1991 to enter the Wyre Forest 'Cleanest School' competition. A small group of Year 9 students started to meet each Friday after school, cleaning the school site of litter. The group gradually grew to over forty regular member and became the 'Green Team'. Thanks to their efforts, and their influence on the whole school ethos, the school won the high school section of the cleanest school competition in both 1992 and 1993. In 1992 the school also won an environmental award from the Tidy Britain group. The awards carried cash prizes (£300 in total) which enabled the Green Team to expand their work. More importantly they boosted the profile of the school's environmental work and helped to raise interest among the rest of the pupils and their families.

The Green Team has continued its essential work of combating litter problems, but its vision and work have expanded. Students meet several lunchtimes a week as well as on Friday evenings, planning new initiatives and putting them into action. Planting areas are gradually being identified and developed all around the school grounds. Pupils have made bird boxes and set them up in a wooded area to encourage nesting birds. Wild flowers have been planted and long grass areas are being developed to encourage insects and butterflies. In addition, over 6000 bulbs have been planted around the school site by students and parents.

In July 1992 the school held an Environmental Week for all Year 9 pupils. In this large cross-curricular project, a pond was created, a wood on site was cleared of creeping sycamores, a hollow area which had been misused for years for tipping rubbish was cleared and filled in, derelict flower beds were weeded and planted, and new wild flower beds were planted.

The Green Team has also encouraged recycling. Year 9 pupils collect waste paper from around the school for recycling and pupils also bring newspapers etc. from home to be taken to the local recycling skip. Can banks have been set up in four areas of the school and all students are encouraged to bring in steel and aluminium cans for recycling. The aluminium cans can be sold for recycling, and this generates cash which the Green Team uses to buy plants, bulbs, bushes and trees.

The environmental work has brought about closer relationships between outside groups and the school. Parents get involved with bulb planting and other large projects. The local garden centre has been generous in donating bulbs, and its staff have offered expert advice. The Green Team is in regular contact with the British Trust for Conservation Volunteers. Trust members helped with a major project of building steps down a bank between school fields to stop damage to the rest of the bank. The local Leisure Ranger services have also got involved with the school's environmental work.

Concern for the environment has now become part of the whole school ethos. Talks in assemblies raise awareness, everyone is encouraged to get involved with the recycling work and a school environmental policy has been developed and added to the prospectus. Students have even got involved in a 'fertiliser trial' on behalf of BBC Radio 5 and Gardener's World *magazine. Using the new school greenhouse students grew tomato plants using six different mixes of fertiliser, to see which would produce the largest and most flavoursome crop under identical conditions.*

The head of Year 9 told us in 1993, 'Environmentally the school is really flourishing. The Green Team work very hard in "out of school" hours and create some beautiful areas for the benefit of us all.'

Gardening clubs

Gardening clubs occupy a special place in the history of after-school activities. As mentioned earlier in this chapter, many urban schools are now seeking to develop gardens to compensate as far as possible for the fact that the majority of their pupils will come from flats and estates where there are few gardens and very little experience among parents as much as children of gardening as a hobby or supplement to the family diet.

Children at Oakfield Primary School in Cardiff, South Glamorgan, can attend a gardening and environment club every Tuesday. The science co-ordinator told Education Extra, 'We have planted trees and maintain a wood and rock pile for minibeast studies . . . the pond has a variety of inhabitants, both plants and animals. It is used frequently for pond studies in science.' Besides the conservation area and pond the club has been involved in creating three new gardens. Instruction about environmental issues and concerns occurs naturally in the course of the work. The environmental group at Moorfields School in the London Borough of Islington works on the school's gardens and helps maintain the appearance of the grounds. The group is otherwise known as the 'Litter Squad' – the forty-five pupils work at lunchtimes under the direction of the school's premises manager.

Gardening also has a unique capacity to bring parents and grandparents into school – and provides excellent opportunities for partnership throughout the local community. Cavendish School in Eastbourne, East Sussex, for example, offers after-school activities ranging from music to science (including a young engineers group). An after-school project involved the creation of a pond as an environmental project and this has been sponsored by Southern Water. Fulham Primary School, London Borough of Hammersmith and Fulham, is an inner city school newly created by the amalgamation of two schools. This has naturally meant a lot of building work and disruption, but also an opportunity the school seized when the LEA funded the basic costs of creating a new garden. The LEA funding only covered a fence, topsoil and digging a pond – the school and community have done the rest. Deputy head Lorraine Manford told us 'The garden project is extremely important for our children as the majority do not have gardens and have no access to actually looking after or planting a garden. They live in high rise flats, flats in houses and bed and breakfast accommodation.'

The project has proved as important for the parents involved in it as the children. One said, 'I haven't done this since I was a child. I'd forgotten how exciting it is to actually touch soil and plant things'. Ms Manford comments, 'I want our children to have that experience of growing and the long term commitment to looking after something.'

Nettlestone County Primary School, Isle of Wight, has generally poor facilities but can offer pupils the chance to work in and enjoy a garden and nature trail, thanks to a joint effort by the school, the surrounding community and the local gardening society. Local people have donated garden plants, the garden society has helped with expert advice and the project has fostered a very good relationship between the school and local people. Future plans include developing the nature trail and providing a braille guide to it.

The headteacher says, 'We believe in giving our children as broad as possible a range of activities for their enjoyment and development. We consider that by inspiring children in their early years they gain future interests and hobbies. We are being increasing supported by the local community, and mutual respect is blossoming.'

BLACKBURN PRIMARY SCHOOL, ROTHERHAM: AN ENVIRONMENTAL TRANSFORMATION

An outstanding result of Blackburn Primary School's commitment to after-school activities has been the transformation of an ugly area of wasteland and car parking into a large, well-established Nature Reserve. This has been effected in co-operation with the local Boys' Club, whose site adjoins the school, and with the enthusiastic help of parents. Pupils, parents and other community members have worked together, often giving time at weekends, to clean up a stream, clear its banks of rubbish, build bridges and nurture plant life. With several ponds, the site now supports a great of of animal as well as plant life. The school makes the most of the site for environmental studies – the school greenhouse allows for additional gardening activities. Pupils have won prizes at the annual show of the local Garden Society of which the school is a member.

Significantly, these activities are perfectly compatible with the commitment to after-

school activities which is reflected in the way many staff give their time freely at the weekends, after school and at lunchtimes. (Some children are brought to school by coach, so to avoid children being excluded from the extra activities there is a long lunch break (1½ hours) when many activities can take place.) The school's rambling club goes off into the Peak District at weekends. There are weekend chess jamborees, football matches and dance demonstrations. Scottish dancing has become so popular that three separate groups are run. The Scottish dance teams accompany the Sheffield Pipe Band to many events, and travel as far afield as Darlington and Birmingham to take part in competitions. The Maypole dancing group is hoping to take part in an exchange visit with folk dancers from a Swedish primary school.

Staff are thoroughly convinced of the benefits of the after-school activities. Pat Taylor, the school's deputy head, told us:

> We believe that our comprehensive provision of extra-curricular activities benefits our pupils and the local community, as well as improving our own school ethos. We have been able to maintain a stable and well established staff so that many of the activities are a long-standing and well-respected tradition and an unwavering part of our image. Pupils and ex-pupils value the school and its premises because it provides something extra. The opportunities for children to mix with other groups of children and with adults give them increasing confidence. We know that the benefits last long after the children leave school. We also know that whilst the children are in school, we are able to establish greatly enriched relationships with them through our 'extra' efforts. The National Curriculum is by no means 'the Whole Curriculum'.

On the other side of the country, Stocksfield Avenue Primary School has shown great imagination in developing a theme-based garden project.

STOCKSFIELD AVENUE PRIMARY, NEWCASTLE-UPON-TYNE: A DRAGON IN THE GARDEN!

Stocksfield Avenue School serves a wide area in the west of the city of Newcastle, including some designated social priority areas. The school occupies a large, if windswept, site, including two separate buildings and extensive, mainly sloping grounds. There are 460 pupils on roll, including fifty nursery children. 10 per cent of the children speak English as their second language and some speak very little English when they start school.

After-school activities are a regular part of school life. Sports – from football to tennis – are supported by both parents and staff. Pupils in the school's four chess leagues are given tuition by members of the Northumbria Chess Association, with extra coaching on some Saturdays by the National Chess Association.

A particular strength of the after-school programme is the school's environment and science activities. In 1993 Stocksfield Avenue School won an Education Extra Award for its 'Dragon's Lair' environmental project; for a new garden in the school grounds, based around a dragon shape, designed by the children themselves. The garden was in its early stages when the Award was made but already a good deal of interest had been generated among pupils, parents, the local community and local employers, and progress has been rapid ever since.

Members of the school's young environmentalists' club have been centrally involved in the scheme from design to planting. When British Coal offered to supply two very large boulders to mark the entrance to the Dragon's Lair pupils were invited to go to the site and choose the right boulders for the job. There have been positive spin offs for the whole school and the entire school grounds from the project. For instance, the young environmentalists have begun a campaign against litter; they designed posters, and regular litter patrols now clear up the school grounds. The City Works Department have supplied some 2000 daffodil bulbs so every child in school could plant some in the grounds and their employees worked alongside the children to plant the bulbs.

The school is pleased to have support in kind from business, arranged with the help of Newcastle Education and Business Partnerships. National Power and Northern Electric not only supplied eighty wooden sleepers to form part of the Dragon's Lair but their employees gave the time to come and move them into position – and do some imaginative chain-saw work to produce dragon's teeth.

Parents have also become closely involved alongside the children. Several working parties of adults and children at weekends have assisted in the project's progress.

There has been excellent co-operation between the young environmentalists and the school's extra-curricular science club over the project. The science club is affiliated to young scientists and children can work towards gold, silver and bronze awards (which are presented to them at a ceremony at Newcastle University). Four children made a compost bin for the Dragon's Lair garden as part of their gold award.

The project is serving many purposes in the life of Stocksfield Avenue School; as well as generating interest and awareness of environmental issues among pupils it is enhancing their scientific and environmental education and giving them the invaluable experience of being involved in a long-term practical project from design through to completion. At the same time links with parents, other volunteers, local business and the community are being created and strengthened through the Dragon's Lair project.

Conclusion

A knowledge of science and technology, and its social functions has never been more important to young people – and their parents and we need, as a country, to explore as many different ways as possible of keeping alive a life-long enthusiasm for scientific knowledge. The science curriculum, particularly since the latest changes recommended by Sir Ron Dearing, will help achieve that. There is abundant evidence that after-school science clubs – in their manifold forms and open to young people of all abilities – are an essential part of the strategy to spark off and keep alive the fun of science for teachers as well as students. They offer a unique and effective way of mixing knowledge and action on an equal basis for all ages.

We have related here just some of the many examples Education Extra has encountered of after-school activities which make science fun, make it accessible, and show children how it relates to the real world and their own lives. The range of partnerships involved in after-school science and technology is wide and very rich, particularly as the scientific community itself takes an increasing interest in ways of making science more relevant – and more appealing – and as Science Museums lead the way in interactive activities and experiments. The prospects for innovation after school are extremely exciting – not least for involving parents and other adults in developing public understanding of science as a whole.

For older school students after-school science can have a crucial part to play in making them aware of career opportunities and higher education possibilities. Above all, we have seen how after school science broadens young people's horizons and breaks down the mystification which school science can so often generate. By introducing new areas of interest from astronomy to ornithology it can give *all* school students, not only the academic 'science specialist', a more satisfying relationship with the sciences, a more responsible attitude to the environment, and a more comprehensive understanding of the world around us.

NOTES

1 *See*, for example, Weiner, M. (1984). *English culture and the decline of the industrial spirit.* Cambridge University Press; *and* Barnet, C. (1987). *The audit of war: The illusion and reality of Britain as a great nation.* Macmillan.

2 House of Commons Debate, 19 December 1994, c. 922W.

3 Quoted in *The Financial Times*, 17 August 1994.

4 *See*, for example, Harding, J. (1994, February). *Half our future, or the means to survival? Female participation in science and technology.* Paper presented at the Conference on Blackman, S., & Brown, A. (1993, November). *Evaluation of young engineers, Chapter 5: Gender relations and technology*, pp 43–51. Department of Educational Studies, University of Surrey. We are grateful to Dr Harding for her help.

5 OFSTED (1994). *Information technology in schools: The impact of the Information Technology in Schools initiative, 1993–1994.*

6 ESC (1994). *Evidence – a black hole in the teaching of science.* Quoted in *The Times*, 5 September 1994.

7 Freeman, C., & Soete, L. (1994). *Work for all or mass unemployment?*, p. 156. Pinter.

8 I am grateful for information provided by Jackie Zammit and Dawn Mountfield (BAYS Officers), British Association Youth Section, 23 Savile Row, London W1X 1AB.

9 Quoted in Woolnough, B. (1991). *The making of engineers and scientists.* Department of Educational Studies, Oxford University.

10 Ibid., p. 22.

11 Ibid., p. 24.

12 Ibid., p. 34.

13 Evaluation document kindly provided by Allan Randall, B. Ed., M.A., Headteacher, Dale Primary School, Derby.

14 Information kindly provided by Brenda Keogh, Senior Lecturer in Primary Science Education, Manchester Metropolitan University.

15 *See Extra Time*, Education Extra Newsletter, Issue 3, 1994.

6

More time for learning: Using the after-school hours

The staff have no non-contact time during the day so after-school is the only time available to mark work, plan, prepare and attend staff meetings and courses. [We need] more than 24 hours in the day.

Trafford teachers responding to an Education Extra survey.

Time is the most valuable commodity of any school. Indeed, it has been described as its 'coin of the realm'.[1] In no other area of life does the organisation of time play such an obsessive and critical role. And, few other professions face the pressures on their time, after the formal hours of work (the 1265 hours) are ended, to undertake the additional work which is essential to good management and good relations within schools. The timing of after-school activities – the 'when' of our study – not only focuses, the demands and pressures upon teachers, but is also closely linked with the needs that are met by the activities themselves – the 'why' of our study. Those needs, as set out in Chapter 1, are to do primarily with children, but, increasingly, to do with parents, too, as school time cuts across working and, often, leisure time.

Throughout this book we use the term 'after-school activities' as a blanket term to cover the many different options which are available to schools outside those hours when the formal curriculum is taught. In practice, the majority of after-school activities do take place in the twilight hours immediately following the school day. In the Award process in 1993 and 1994, however, we discovered that, both for educational and social reasons, many schools are making the most of other times of the week and the year. Lunchtime activities have been the traditional choice for specialist clubs and activities for many schools, but we were impressed by the fact that in each year a quarter of the schools which entered the Education Extra Awards schemes were offering before-school provision, and half of the schools were offering holiday schemes.

This chapter focuses on those schools which are not simply open as a matter of course before and after the teaching day for the use of pupils and teachers, but which have made a deliberate effort to reconstruct the school day, or to add to the school week and year in specific ways. In examining the alternatives, it looks at the case which can be made for a particular choice of time and the effect this has on the different types of activities which take place.

Choice and necessity in the timing of after-school activities

Behind the choice of the timing of after-school activities lie complex questions about the nature and structure of the school day and the school year both as it reflects the management of time by the school, and the impact this has on pupils and their parents. In a wider context the management of teaching time, political murmurings about the 'extended' day and the trend towards this in GMS and CTC colleges is likely to put this issue onto the political timetable more firmly in the future.

In fact, although the minimum number of teaching hours is fixed by law, there is considerable flexibility in how schools structure the day. Most schools still follow the pattern fixed for our grandparents, but there is now a wealth of experience among schools both pushed by pressures (e.g. a lunchtime which can degenerate into anarchy and encourage afternoon truancy; or concern about bullying, vandalism and the risk of delinquency in the hours immediately after school) or encouraged positively by the school's decision to rethink and replan the school day as a whole. For our purposes, in this chapter, we are concerned with the specific issue of how the shape of the school day is being used to the best effect to provide extra-curricular but supportive activities after the teaching day.

Comparisons abroad

Throughout Europe there are variations in the age for starting school, the pattern of the school day and the length of the school year which make comparisons difficult. Those variations reflect climate and working patterns, as well as education and culture. There is, however, pressure for changes across Europe and in other parts of the world. In Europe, countries as diverse as Denmark and Spain are looking for ways to promote the better use of school resources and finding a better match between school hours and the working day.

By continental standards, British schools have always started late in the day. In some countries in Europe, teaching is concentrated into an extended morning period (Italy, Austria, Germany, Greece, Denmark, Norway and Sweden) with the remainder providing mornings and afternoons, sometimes divided by a long lunch break. To complicate matters, in Greece, Spain, Italy, Portugal and the former Yugoslavia, buildings are often used for school in two shifts. These cultural patterns do not reflect daylight hours, but they do reflect climate and pressure on resources. With such variation, there is, clearly, no one useful model in the form of *the* 'continental day'.

Outside Europe, the most notorious difference is probably that between the UK and Japan, where the average child has an estimated 1500 lessons a year, compared with 950 in Britain. For many Japanese children the result is an educational treadmill which circulates around school and extra classes after school, followed by homework. In the case of some minority groups in Britain, religious observance is also an obligation after school. In practice in Britain, although the number of teaching hours is fixed by law, there is considerable flexibility in how schools structure the day. The public school day has traditionally been mornings-only, with afternoons devoted to team-sports and fostering the house spirit. But, as Brian Knight[2] observes,

> *The great mass of schools still operate school days which are of the traditional form, different only in detail from those of the early part of this century. However, never has there been so much trial of alternatives as in the last ten years. Some of these have been in response to pressures – some of the compressed day changes, for example. But many reflect a systematic attempt to rethink and replan a school's management of time.*

Those alternatives are still being explored in many schools, hastened, we suspect, not only by Local Management of Schools – which has opened up many areas of school life for discussion - but also by the pressures exerted by the (pre-Dearing) National Curriculum to pack into the school day more curriculum segments to meet the statutory requirements. As the many changes in the evolution of the National Curriculum have shown, once part of the timetable is under review the temptation to look at ways of reorganising other parts of the day can become irresistible.

The Government is showing a keen interest in how schools organise time as a whole in school. A recent OFSTED report (July, 1994) concluded after visiting sixty-four schools that, while there was considerable variation in the length of the 'taught week', *neither inspection evidence nor statistical analysis has revealed a relationship between the length of taught time and pupil's educational achievements which would support an increase in the recommended minima for the length of taught time. Indeed, professional staff were aware that this would bring 'a potential reduction in extra-curricular activities'.*

In fact, there have been some recent experiments with a longer school day linked to a five-term school year. This pattern has been adopted by some City Technology Colleges – a move which has increased the number of working days from 190 to 200. Five eight-week terms allow for a shorter summer break while still allowing for family holidays. While advocates are enthusiastic – claiming that an eight-week term maintains the energy and commitment of children and staff, it is acknowledged that this also imposes a strain on families, who are limited to a four-week holiday period. It is also a strain on teachers. A report commissioned by the City Technology Trust acknowledged that 'the 1265 hours stipulated in the Teachers Pay and Conditions Act has little relevance to CTC teachers who typically work a much longer year'.[3]

In reviewing the management of time, Brian Knight also examines some of the individual initiatives in the early 1980s, to make the school day and the school year more flexible, distinguishing between the 'compressed day' or so-called continental day, where the afternoon is set aside for out-of-school activities, and the flexible day, where some afternoons or regular days are set aside for curriculum-related 'electives'. He also reviews some of the attempts made at LEA level (e.g. in Oxfordshire) to open discussions on a flexible day which, while stirring up considerable controversy led to only one individual change, that in Marlborough School, in Woodstock (Oxon). In other areas, e.g. Dorset, attempts to consider a restructured day against a background of cuts in education also brought parental opposition. In Hampshire, however, there was a more general adoption of a compressed day, starting earlier, reducing the lunch-hour to half an hour and finishing at 3 p.m. In September 1987, twenty-five schools had adopted this pattern and the results were positively viewed by all involved. One of the key practical issues in making this choice is, of course, whether the Dining Hall itself is large enough to accommodate one sitting – or whether there has to be a shift system which inevitably reduces options for lunchtime activities.

Whatever changes are made, the impulse will probably always be a push–pull attempt to counteract disadvantage and provide a new benefit. The arguments for the compressed day are, in principle, the concentration of teaching within a shorter period of time when pupils and teachers are fresh and which creates more time at the end of the day for the multiple demands on teachers' time. A shorter lunchtime can also remove or at least reduce the problems and potential chaos of a scenario which features pupils, freed from the traditional format of school meals, unsupervised and aimlessly roaming the streets eating chips.

Increasingly, schools are negotiating their own day. Many schools in the Education Extra Network finish before 3.30 p.m.; some as early as 2.30 p.m.; others have adopted a variable pattern, with early closing on two or three nights a week. In every case that we know of, these changes are being introduced specifically to enable the school to develop new extra-curricular activities, offering different choices in different ways for different children. Those schools which offer such a day say, for example, that 'out-of-school activities can re-grow in the afternoon, which also provides more daylight activities for them in the winter', and speak glowingly of the improvements in homework standards (more time to do it and less conflict). There is also more time available for staff to fit in their own administrative 'extras' after school.

Although past evidence suggests that in theory they are less favourable to change, in practice, parents seem to approve of the new opportunities the day brings – provided that there is some guarantee of activity or supervision after school. For parents who have to commute to work, or who start work early or work part-time or shifts, an earlier start to the school day can be as much of a boon as can any help at the other end of the working day. In terms of traffic congestion alone, a staggered end to the school day could bring direct environmental as well as social benefits.[4] On these grounds, therefore, while the compressed day is still a minority choice, it is under consideration by a number of schools and local authorities. Even where a school rejects a major reorganisation, it is significant what can be achieved by minor changes in the timetable which can introduce welcome flexibility at either end of the day. In each case, full consultation with all staff involved is a pre-requisite for a successful new structure.

The issue of how to make the best of time is as relevant to the school year as to each day. We also look, in this chapter, therefore, at schools which take a day or a week out of the year as time for special, 'extra', themed activities for festivals, or residential experiences, and at the way some schools are responding to the needs of children and parents at half-term and other holidays, and even at weekends.

In practice, schools seem to employ three criteria when it comes to deciding when to offer after-school activities:

(a) feasibility

(b) needs of children

(c) potential for development.

Feasibility

It is self-evident that activities can be offered only when it is feasible to do so. Some activities can only feasibly be done after school has finished. Anything which takes longer than an hour, which involves using space in different ways (e.g. table-tennis in the hall), which involves going off-site or which involves different age groups or children from more than one school will generally rule out lunchtimes as an option.

On the other hand, there is a definite practical rationale for lunchtime activities – particularly for rural schools serving a very wide catchment area. Nothing extra can be done unless there are some school staff available to put on clubs and activities. The staff, parents or volunteers running the activities may only have certain times available. Those with their own children to pick up in the afternoon may prefer to offer activities at lunchtime or on a Saturday morning. Equally important, whereas an 'extra' can sometimes be fitted in during the day, the sheer pressure of administration and relentless round of 'meetings' often cuts down time and energy for 'extras' after school. As one teacher put it to us:

> Meetings used to be confined to an occasional and acceptable time after school. Now they happen constantly, and make it impossible to do many of the things we would prefer to do – and extra-curricular activities have suffered badly.

Most important, the pupils themselves may find some times impossible. Like adults, they too can have other commitments which must be taken into account. Some have after-school jobs themselves; others are responsible for younger siblings. In some cases there are religious and family duties after school. Muslim communities, for example, are strict about religious observation and protective of their children. This often limits the choice of what girls, in particular, can do after school. The comments of the headteacher of Lockwood School (Kirklees) are a typical statement of the issues faced:

> This is very much a multi-racial community. Seventy per cent of our pupils are of Asian origin and the majority of these are Muslims. Their parents require them to attend the local Mosque after school.

For these reasons, for many children, lunchtimes provide the only alternative to do something extra.

Responding to needs

After-school activities in the widest sense meet a wide range of educational and social needs, including the acute needs of working parents.

Not all parents' needs are the same. Working practices are becoming increasingly flexible – especially for women. Some, who work part-time or do afternoon shift work are in desperate need of a helping hand at the end of the day or on Saturdays; others, with full-time jobs and often inflexible employers, need more help during half-term and holidays; others who travel long distances to work or who work early shifts in the health services, for example, would welcome a 'before school' or even a 'breakfast club'. As Chapter 1 emphasised, the Government's own initiative in this field reflects a new awareness of how important the 'family-friendly' workplace is to the economy as a whole, and the pioneering TEC-led initiative will enable more schools to offer more support before and after school.

In different ways schools are helping to meet this variety of need. Teachers see children coming into the school playground well before the start of school, sometimes clearly in need of breakfast. In response, some schools have begun to offer breakfast clubs. Schools see the needs of children as paramount, and in response often provide something extra which goes far beyond the requirements of care for younger children. At Hebburn Comprehensive School in South Tyneside, for example, the lunchtime club was started with the acute needs of younger pupils very much in mind.

Years 7 and 8 feel isolated in the playground area at lunchtime because the older years monopolise the playing area that exists. There are no areas where they feel safe from the older children and they are often the victims of bullying. The club will not only provide a 'safe haven' but will also assist Year 7 pupils in the transition from primary school to senior school.

Schools are even more aware of the risks to unsupervised children after school. For example, in a school where it is estimated one in four children have no adult at home after school, Hebburn School soon added to its provision with activities for eleven–sixteen year olds in the twilight hours, this time in response to the needs of pupils and the neighbourhood.

After-school periods are a major problem for bullying, truancy, vandalism and malicious damage in and around the School and Community Association. The reason appears to be lack of play facilities and constructive activities for school children at these times. The period between 4.00 and 6.00 p.m. also provides a specific problem in that a number of children have no parent at home during that time, and inevitably wander the streets getting up to mischief.

Potential for development

A third criterion is, quite simply, dictated by the resources that are available. Schools which share resources with community associations, or which are designated Community Schools, are often in use throughout the day, with a shifting population of children, young people and adults. The twilight hours can still be problematic, however; a limbo period when neither the school nor the Community Association takes total responsibility for what is offered.

After-school activities can grow more easily if there are already seeds for development within the school. If an art club is already taking place after school, for instance, this means that arrangements are in place for caretaking, later locking up, cleaning and so on. The principle of using some heating and lighting after school is established. In these circumstances it is a relatively simple matter to open up the drama studio next door or the computer room down the corridor for another after-school activity. In many schools the PE and music staff in particular will have pioneered the way for after-school use with their traditions of school sports and music practice.

In the next part of this chapter we look at three different ways of using time. First, we look at schemes which seek to supplement the school day by adding activities before, during or after school; second, at those which complement the school day or the school year by adding activities at the weekend or over the holiday periods; and, third, at those which enrich the school year by adding special days, weeks or residential periods for special extra activities. It also illustrates how schools have overcome some of the practical problems of fitting the basic requirements – cleaning, for example – around after-school activities.

Supplementing the school day

There are three main ways of supplementing the school day. Schools can open up buildings earlier for activities, for breakfast or simply as a safe haven; they can offer clubs and activities at lunchtime; or they can offer activities between 3.00 or 3.30 and 5–6 p.m. They can of course do all three.

Before school: Breakfast and books

A quarter of all schools participating in the Education Extra Awards in 1993 and 1994 were offering some provision before school in the mornings. It was clear that there were three main reasons for doing this:

(a) to provide children arriving in schools early with a warm and safe environment;

(b) to support families who made an early start to work; and

(c) to put the time to specific use for children.

Many of the schools now hosting Kids' Clubs automatically open early (7.30–8.00 a.m.) in order to help parents who work shifts or who have an early start to their working day. St Chad's Primary CE School, on the outskirts of Oldham explains that the 'before and after' club at St Chad's 'was conceived three years ago to accommodate children who otherwise stood for long hours in a bleak moorland playground'. School is open from 7.30 a.m. for the 'before school' club and children can get refreshments as well as doing activities. The Oldham club is an example of how such a scheme can be particularly helpful to those families where the parents have to travel long distances into work – in this case, into Manchester – and who are consequently faced with the choice of leaving children alone or dropping them off at the school playground very early.

The same problems are faced by parents at the other end of the country – on the Isle of Wight. The breakfast club at Brading CE Primary School has been running since October 1993. It was started in response to the fact that: 'many children arrive at school having had no meal and often very early, to enable working parents to go on to work.'

Significantly, the headteacher points out that 'This problem is found across the socio-economic divide and equally affects poor and better off'. The breakfast club provides care, activities, and, of course, breakfast from 8.00 a.m. onwards.

Schools which provide morning schemes not only tend to give consideration to the children's need for nutrition at this time, but also to what type of activity could be most appropriate. An obvious feature is that before school schemes are often geared to ensuring that children spend time indoors on cold or dark mornings. St Nicolas CE First School in Nuneaton, Warwickshire, opened its morning care scheme in September 1993. Parental demand for the scheme was gauged by questionnaire and a charge of 75p per child is made.

Activities will include table-top games, reading, crayoning, a listening library of taped story – i.e. fairly quiet, calm activities suited to the time of day.

One innovative scheme in East London focused as firmly on the nutritional needs of children as well as the opportunities for a little extra reading. The 'books and breakfast' scheme, pioneered by the Open School, and based in the St. Matthias' Primary School, Bethnal Green, London Borough of Tower

Hamlets, and in two nearby schools. The projects brought in volunteers (including ethnic minority families, literary experts and mentors from local companies) as well as teaching and non-teaching staff. The project aimed to provide hungry children with a breakfast and some books to read, using volunteers to provide a warm, comforting start to the school day and an enjoyable story in a relaxed atmosphere. Groups of children were small and drawn from the seven–nine age group. While the projects were too limited to provide conclusions about the educational value, and continuing funding could not be secured, all involved thought it had been a very successful project which offered the potential of something special, not least the opportunity for 'caring in a very safe setting', increased confidence with language, and a good, calm start to the school day.

The benefits of before-school schemes are obvious to children and parents alike. A comfortable start to the day; a warm welcome into the school premises; extra nutrition for children whose breakfast can be very rushed, inadequate, or, sometimes, non-existent; a quiet start to the serious business of learning , or an extra chance to let off some steam before school starts in earnest. Above all, for parents, if work is scarce, employers unresponsive, and travelling distances a problem for all the family, knowing that the child is safe and has a relatively confident start to the day, is a gift beyond price.

A break for lunch

Traditionally, many schools have concentrated their extra-curricular activities during the lunchtime. One of the obvious benefits inherent in fitting extra activities around the school day is that pupils and staff are already on site. Clubs and activities at lunchtime, in particular, solve some problems which make after-school provision an impossibility. Transport arrangements often inhibit rural schools from developing an after-school scheme. Filling the lunchtime can reduce problems of truancy after school and unsupervised behaviour in or out of school.

Rural schools have a particular problem. As Waldegrave School, Richmond-upon-Thames explained:

> The school draws pupils from a wide geographical area and many have difficult journeys involving buses and trains. For this reason most clubs happen at lunchtime, and enabling parents and girls to come to school after the end of the day is not easy.

Some schools have made a significant virtue out of necessity. One of Education Extra's award-winning schools, Connaught School in the London

Borough of Waltham Forest, shows what can be done in the lunch-hour. Connaught is a girls' secondary school with a very high proportion of Muslim girls. It is situated in an area where many parents are unwilling to allow their daughters to walk home alone, even at normal finishing times, especially in the winter. In response, the school has laid on a wide and imaginative range of activities during a longer lunchtime. They have the opportunity to do drama, join the football team, learn how to repair cars, and, as we showed in Chapter 4, pp. 111–12; 130, develop their assertiveness in special courses funded in part by Education Extra.

One of the other advantages of lunchtime activity is that it can ensure more equality of access. Participation rates can be be very high. Dorothy Barley Junior School, in a working class urban area of London Borough of Barking and Dagenham, offers both after-school and lunchtime activities. The majority of pupils tend to take up both the activities available but, as the headteacher reports,

> In a recent survey we found that total club participation is 377 pupils per week after school. This rises to 623 if you include the One O'Clock Club. Pupils have between fifteen and eighteen activities they can be involved in during the year ... A questionnaire to parents showed 82 per cent feeling that we provided an above-average service in terms of lunch and after school clubs. 55 per cent rated us excellent.

There is, however, an alternative argument against using lunchtime as the prime time for activities. As put by the headteacher of Tideway School, this is the observation that they tend to remove from the playground those pupils who can have a positive effect, leaving the field clear to 'the usual miscreants'. This seems to be another reason why many schools have chosen to concentrate their activities after school.

Time after school

In other chapters we have illustrated some of the reasons why schools undertake to provide after-school activities. The most common form of provision, and the one which creates most opportunities as well as meeting the needs of children and parents is, however, that which bridges the gap between 3.30 and 5.00 or 6.00 p.m. The reason why most schools tend to make this the key time is not only because children and staff are still on site but free from lessons, but that the after-school period can be in every sense a creative time, a time when children and staff are more relaxed, responsive and able to develop different relationships, in a freer and more receptive atmosphere than at any other time during the day. Projects which extend over two or three hours, or a series of weeks or evenings can become absorbing and fulfilling in a way which is usually impossible during the intense thirty-five to forty minute lesson periods.

Some schools have chosen to change the structure of the school day and, thereby, to plan systematically for an extension of after-school activities.

Rural schools often have particular problems developing after-school programmes. A shorter school day can bring positive advantages for the community as a whole. Ventnor Middle School, in the Isle of Wight, have developed a twilight programme and a community-based programme which support each other. The school is essentially seeking to create a rural community school serving a wide variety of children from different social backgrounds. It has a very generous programme of activities after school, including art, drama, dance, music, science and technology, history, chess and gardening. Large numbers attend – particularly for the arts and sports – and it means that the school can be open for the community at other times. The headteacher told Education Extra that he had

> changed the school day in 1986 to 8.30 a.m.–2.30 p.m. The 2.30 p.m. finish enables us to run a wide variety of clubs that usually end around 4.00–4.30 p.m. This leaves the school facilities available for local organisations (after cleaning from 5.30–6.00 p.m.). That involves karate, (with over 100 people attending), St Johns Ambulance, Senior Basketball, and Rugby. The programme has evolved gradually over a number of years in response to (a) pupil/parent suggestion (b) teacher interest/expertise and (c) local organisations asking to use our facilities.

Another school on the Isle of Wight – Chale School – offers twilight and evening provision to partly compensate for the fact that there is no local youth club and very little for young teenagers to do. The school is a very small village primary school serving a rural community on the south coast of the island. Over half the children are eligible for free school meals and there are no recreational facilities in the village. In response, in 1993, the school offered activities ranging from textiles to history, technology, gardening, and ornithology after school. There is, most recently, a newly established games club funded through the Sports Council which runs from 6.00 p.m. to 9.30 p.m. (with the under tens collected by 7.30 p.m.) and which offers badminton, table-tennis, kwik cricket and more.

Urban schools are better placed to make the most of after-school links into the community. Chaucer School, in Sheffield, for example, changed its school day, three years ago and now starts at 8.30 a.m. and finishes at 2.55 p.m. This is not only to facilitate a wide range of after-school activities, including a community education programme which provides for 'thousands of members each year', but also reflects the realities of home life for many children: 'Many children have to look after younger children in the evenings whilst mothers do evening part-time work'.

One of the best-known examples of the compressed day in practice is Tideway School, East Sussex which reorganised its school day in 1981.

TIDEWAY SCHOOL, NEWHAVEN:
AFTER-SCHOOL ACTIVITIES FOLLOWING A COMPRESSED SCHOOL DAY

Tideway is a large secondary school (1350 pupils) sited on the hill overlooking Newhaven Harbour in East Sussex. It draws pupils from Newhaven and the urban conurbation of Peacehaven. The changes to the present school day were introduced fourteen years ago by the current headteacher, Ken Saxby, and it is nationally recognised as a pioneering school.

School starts at 8.15 a.m. there is a forty-minute lunchbreak and the day ends at 2.15 p.m. There are six lessons in the morning and two in the afternoon. Ken Saxby is convinced that pupils work better in the morning and a short lunch hour cuts down problems. As he says:

> After-school activities at Tideway are an integral part of the school's philosophy based upon the shape of the day. Our day is designed to leave pupils time after formal teaching to take part in a range of activities . . . with our early start – 8.15 a.m. – an early finish is possible. Lessons finish at 2.15 p.m. while bus passes are valid for homeward travel until 5 .00 p.m. [This enables] all activities to run throughout the year and finish in daylight.

There is a particularly strong emphasis at this school on music, including a choir, two orchestras, steel pans, blues band and a recorder group. Significantly, a primary music centre is also being developed. Team sports – not just for the high achievers or the most talented – is another area of strength. 'We ensure that extra-curricular sport is available for all by devoting Thursday after school exclusively to inter-house sport for all in a range of games.' The drama and stage clubs take place after school and put on evening productions termly. In a joint initiative with Newhaven Council the school is running an appeal to set up a Performing Arts Centre in the Community, based at the school. Linking up with the community and sharing facilities where possible is part of the school's philosophy.

The school's after-school activities 'Phase 1' run till 4.30 p.m. The school is then able to offer with the community 'Phase II' using the leisure centre, music centre, etc., where the pupils can . . . join activities run jointly by the school and the community.

As well as music and sport the activities shared with the community, and specifically supported by Education Extra, include self-supported study, attended both by school pupils and adults. These are free to school pupils but adults are charged. The tutors for self-supported study are paid – teachers run all the other after-school activities on a voluntary basis. After-school activities also have the strong support of the caretaking team who take nothing for covering this time. Use of school facilities goes on into the evenings when various clubs organise a range of activities and the school sports hall/gymnasium is run as a leisure facility.

'Our philosophy,' says Ken Saxby, ' is based on three principles: diversifying pupil's interests . . . optimising time and facilities . . . sharing with the local community.'

It is not only secondary schools which can reorganise their time to accommodate wide programmes of activities. St Clements School in Salford is a prime example of how a small primary school can, with the flexibility of a shorter day, offer a widely different programme of activities for younger and older pupils alike, combined with a limited holiday programme.

ST CLEMENT'S CE PRIMARY SCHOOL, SALFORD: EDUCATION WITH CARE

St Clements School in Ordsall (Salford) has recently been designated a Community Education School. It offers an outstanding example of leadership and innovation in after-school practice. The school is in an area of great deprivation, surrounded by boarded up streets and tower blocks awaiting demolition. The headteacher, Helen Buchanan, is a firm believer in the entitlement of every child to as rich a schooling experience as possible, and in the need to educate the 'whole child'.

With a view to developing a comprehensive after-school programme for all ages and interests, the school negotiated a shorter school day with the LEA and now finishes at 3.00 p.m. There are structured play clubs for infants under seven twice a week between 3.00 and 3.50 p.m., an activities club for 7–11 (twenty-five regular attenders) and specialist activities for all ages, some of which start at 4.00 p.m., with children returning to school to participate. Those clubs include gymnastics, French, jazz-dance, guitar, computing, recorders, and Jesus and Me. Numbers range from ten to forty for each club. There is, in addition, a 7–11 youth club open to children from other schools in Ordsall. During the holidays the school offers a drama school and a music, dance and drama playscheme during August.

There is no management committee; all activities are offered by headteacher, parents, teachers, coaches and community staff under the direction of the headteacher, who invites all new teaching staff to offer activities. Clubs are free or small charges are made for specific costs – e.g. gymnastics, or snacks for the teatime club. Equal opportunities were well catered for in gender terms; children were aware that girls played football, worked at the IT club, and that boys did jazz dance and wanted to do cooking.

The clubs are immensely popular with children and parents. Children point out that: 'We play loads of games you haven't got to do at home' and 'It's fun when you are finding things out for yourself.'

Significantly, the children themselves knew that while they were not 'working' – (i.e. writing or doing maths came within that definition), they were definitely learning and enjoying it.

Some schools which have not sought the upheaval of a new structure to the day, have opened up other possibilities after school by being creative with 'directed time'. Earlsheaton High School in Kirklees, for example, an eleven to sixteen urban comprehensive school, serves a very mixed catchment including an estate where there are very high levels of material deprivation and where post-school facilities are 'almost non-existent for many of our children'. The school offers a very impressive range of activities, including cooking, IT, a D-I-Y group, word processing, amateur radio, modern language clubs, a Youth Award and Duke of Edinburgh's Award. They explain how they have been able to do this:

As in many other schools the number and range of after-school activities decreased significantly as a result of the teachers' action of the late 1980s. Shortly after this, the introduction of the National Curriculum inevitably increased the number of after-school meetings that most teachers were involved in. As a result, after-school activities never had an opportunity in most schools to re-establish themselves.

This was the situation at Earlsheaton High. In order to guarantee attendance at meetings (curriculum, finance, assessment, etc.) we used eighteen hours of directed time for each member of staff. This eighteen hours covered nine meetings per year of two working groups. We were able to release PE/sports staff from this schedule to ensure the maintenance of some after-school sports provision.

Despite the benefits of the meetings cycle for internal staff development and effective planning the negative effect was the lack of available time to spend with children after school. Many of our children – but not all – come from extremely deprived backgrounds where the opportunities for constructive use of leisure time are constrained. Early in 1993 we decided, as a staff, to remedy the situation. We gave all staff the choice of dropping one working group and using the nine hours freed to run or be involved in an after-school activity with the children. Over 90 per cent of staff responded positively – and out of this developed our School Plus programme . . . within a month there were twenty activities running on a weekly basis. Some teachers have kept their involvement to the directed nine hours but many have gone well over.

Another school which has gone further has directly programmed after-school activities into directed time.

JOHN SUMMERS HIGH SCHOOL, CLWYD:
CHOICE AFTER SCHOOL

John Summers High School was the top award winner in Education Extra's 1993 Award Scheme. It is a community comprehensive school with 460 pupils serving an area particularly badly hit by unemployment (the closure of the heavy end of the Shotton steelworks twelve years ago meant the loss of over 10 000 jobs from the area). The school provides a whole array of activities outside the central curriculum, from sports clubs, an after-school club and a youth club, to a residential experience programme and a holiday programme.

The Education Extra Award was made to recognise, in particular, the After-School Enrichment programme which runs twice a week and is attended (voluntarily) by over 80 per cent of the school's pupils.

The scheme is resourced from within the school's main budget.

> We are committed to making the scheme successful and so the staff involvement is within directed time. We encourage ancillary staff to be involved, we pay outside instructors to come in, and we resource the whole scheme generously.

Every Monday and Thursday pupils are offered the option, at the end of the main school day, of either thirty minutes private study or fifty+ minutes of an enrichment activity. Activities include trampolining, rugby, badminton, squash, cross-country, mountain-biking, canoeing, mountain-walking, model-making, silk-painting, gardening, poetry workshop, Welsh, German, music and many others. The activities fall into three main groups: (a) sport, 'the traditional school sports plus a wide range of further activities' put on by hiring the local leisure centre and other local sports facilities; (b) interest activities, 'where members of staff can share their own enthusiasms with pupils', and (c) additional GCSE time. The school offers extra sessions for GCSE maths, drama, art, Welsh and music. The school reports that this resolves many problems but also produces some clashes and that 'we may need to add a third day with a twilight session to accommodate the GCSE dimension'.

Over four-fifths of pupils choose to stay on after hours and demand exceeds the number of places available. Each pupil is guaranteed at least one enrichment activity per week.

Making time for the basics

Using time after school effectively also means solving some of the practical problems: transport, premises costs, caretaking and cleaning are four of the obvious and most intractable problems schools identify.

Overcoming practical problems

Whatever choice a school makes about when it is going to offer activities there is a range of unavoidable practical problems to be solved: primarily transport to and from school, and caretaking and cleaning.

For rural schools wishing to develop after-school activities, transport is a fundamental issue. For schools with a wide catchment area, and for schools with a high proportion of vulnerable pupils, getting home safely, especially in winter evenings, is a prime concern of parents and schools alike. Many schools already make some adjustment to transport arrangements for part of the week to fit in with team sports, or regular activities. Schools which are planning programmes across the week, and offer regular activities, or which are offering play/care facilities for younger children, have negotiated new bus schedules, arranged late buses or additional buses, or, involved parents in a transport rota system. It is not always easy but, as schools such as Tideway prove, it can be done.

The cost and management of premises, caretaking and site management is another area which can be seen as posing insuperable problems. The cost of keeping premises open varies widely, along with the policy of the LEA . Some LEAs simply cover the cost of additional heating, lighting and caretaking. Other schools are able to subsidise twilight activities by renting out premises after six o'clock. In community schools, which are occupied well after six o'clock, twilight activities are often covered automatically.

This question also brings with it the question of charging for the use of premises. As far as activities for the school's own pupils are concerned there is no legal reason why the school's budget should not be used to fund these activities which come under the general heading 'for the purposes of the school'. If the activity involves pupils from other schools there does not seem to be any logical reason why this definition should not also apply in those circumstances. This is essentially left to the judgement of the governors, who can also opt for a definition which includes adult members of the community as well. The problem for schools – and after-school clubs – occurs when they are provided by an independent body using school premises. In this case, after-school lettings which are not for the purpose of the school, e.g for separate play/care, have to bring in sufficient income to cover their costs to the school (*see* Chapter 7 p. 190).

The school caretaker or site manager is often a figure of mythological proportions. He or she rarely turns out to be as uncooperative as the most pessimistic assumptions. In successful schemes maximum consultation and flexibility is the key. Indeed, in many successful schemes, the site manager and other members of the school staff are fully involved, right from the start, and are essential to the success of the scheme. Some schools have made it clear from the start that the caretaker would have a key role. For example, Stoneydown Primary School, in London Borough of Waltham Forest, discussed the school's commitment to after-school provision with the caretaker on interview, and established full personal support for the initiative. In Newfield School, London Borough of Brent, the co-ordinator of the after-school club is the relief site supervisor. In Walker School, Newcastle, the site manager and caretaking staff work a shift system, running from 6.30 a.m. to 10.00 p.m., which facilitates activities after school, every evening and every weekend. The site manager at Walker, Bill Taylor, is clear in his commitment:

> *I'm completely in favour of after-school activities! As site manager it's my task to ensure that the activities take place in a safe and clean environment; this also means ensuring that there are competent people there to supervise the youngsters before they have access to specialist equipment. I'm worried about the danger that school facilities may be becoming too expensive for some voluntary and community groups. It seems to me that the most expensive activity for school premises is keeping them locked up – the more they're used, the cheaper they can be made available. In an ideal world schools might be open seven days a week, twenty-four hours a day!*

There are financial considerations, too. Fitting activities around the school day can minimise the cost and simplify arrangements for caretaking, heating and lighting. For community schools in particular, where community activities start around 6 p.m. heating, lighting and caretaking costs for the twilight hours are already subsidised. Other schools do not enjoy that privilege but, nevertheless, many overcome the practical problems.

At East Leeds High School, one of Education Extra's demonstration project schools, the school site is shared with the East Leeds Community Training Base; consequently, the caretakers are employed and available from 7.30 a.m. until at least 5.00 p.m. Putting on activities for over 300 pupils per week does not involve employing the caretaking staff for extra hours. Fortunately the caretaking team are also very supportive of the school's after-school scheme and do not object to the extra work it creates! The cleaning staff, who begin work immediately after the end of the formal day, are also prepared to be flexible and to 'work around' the many activities happening in school while they are there.

At the same time, the costs of heating and lighting rooms after hours is absorbed in the main school budget as part of the school's commitment to after-school activities. This would be less easy to arrange for the weekends as the heating system for the large site is fairly non-specific and slow-acting. Heating one hall for Saturday morning, for example, would involve having heating on in a quarter of the whole school for eight hours or more.

Adding to the school week and the school year

In 1993 and 1994, the 400 schools which entered for the Education Extra Awards demonstrated how they were making good use of their buildings and facilities outside the school week – particularly during the holidays. The reasons and the benefits for doing so were almost as varied as the activities on offer, e.g. the opportunities to spend more time out of doors during daylight hours; the opportunity for pupils of all ages to spend time on shared activities; the demand for time to revise and prepare for examinations; sports coaching programmes; even the growing seasons of plants, all seem to play their part in determining when schools are accessible outside the formal school week.

King Charles I School in Kidderminster (Hereford and Worcestershire), includes among its activities the restoration and development of a Rose Garden in the grounds which had become badly neglected. Sixth-form students and members of the PTA started up the project together and it has since grown in every way. Strong links have been formed with the local day care centre for disabled people, and raised beds have been installed so that wheelchair users can garden.

The garden is not only a community resource, it is a learning centre too. It is used to enhance life sciences teaching. It includes experimental plots; and a root observation window has been installed in a retaining wall. Pupils work on the garden and on their projects at weekends but involvement does not stop there.

The science teacher told Education Extra that 'Growing seasons and life cycles show scant respect for timetables – such projects involve people at weekends and during short and long holidays as well as before and after school.'

Weekend schemes

It is still relatively rare for schools to provide activities on Saturdays or Sundays, apart from the traditional sports fixtures. There are, however, some local initiatives, building on the example of 'Saturday Supplementary Schools' or evening schemes organised primarily by ethnic minority parents groups, which aim to provide extra learning opportunities for children of all ages. In Birmingham, for example, as the *Sunday Telegraph* reported in December 1994, 400 primary school children received certificates from city education chiefs after completing their first term of Saturday schools. One of the initiators of the Birmingham project – the National Primary Centre – emphasised that the Saturday courses, ranging from maths and English to astronomy and dance, had been heavily subscribed and would be significantly expanded.[5]

There are many outstanding examples of good practice which show what can be done to open up these facilities for youngsters.

At Peers School, Oxfordshire, the 'Saturday Focus' initiative brings in about 100 young people under the age of thirteen who undertake eight programmes such as mountain biking, computers, jujitsu, drama, comic book workshops and the under 7's club. A co-ordinator for Saturday Focus is paid by money raised from charitable funds. The scheme has attracted the support of Children in Need and the Oxford City Council. The deputy head told us that the programme aims 'to provide interesting and challenging experiences which are open to all young people . . . to provide leisure and recreational activities using the school facilities'.

As we have seen in Chapter 4, some schools take children away for whole weekends to enable them to revise or complete project work. Other schools, such as Woodlands School in Basildon, Essex, open the school on Saturday for regular 'extension classes' which support curriculum work. In addition, it regularly runs 'Revision Schools' in the Easter and May holidays to prepare pupils for exams.

For other pupils, Saturday brings an opportunity to pursue a particular interest. In Bridgewater County High School in Warrington, Cheshire, for example, there is a regular Saturday Latin School, supported by the Open School (a charity that aims to increase opportunity and access to education). It provides Latin in an area where no school has it on the timetable, and uses a combination of class teaching and distance learning during the two-year course. It is open to anyone, and caters for a wide range of age and ability. The youngest student is twelve and the oldest is sixty-seven. Motivation varies from those who see it as an aid to their professional careers (e.g. aspiring doctors) to those who simply have a passionate interest in the language and culture.[6]

In Sunderland, Oxclose Community College has taken the Saturday idea overseas. The school has a strong parental involvement and opens seven days a week. Every Saturday, for example, there is a Japanese school.

The only criterion which students and others have to satisfy is that they must be interested in taking part. While excellence is valued, we are much more interested in personal achievement than in comparative achievement. Consequently, a higher number of (a) school pupils and (b) members of the community are involved in clubs.

The high level of activity sustained at Oxclose is assisted by the Community Education Department's involvement (it runs many courses at the school) and the strong Community Association based there.

Opportunities for community involvement, especially in sport, can also be a strong motivating force for weekend and holiday activities. At Kingsway School, a large (1500) comprehensive school in Stockport, staff 'believe our excellent facilities should be used out of school hours to benefit the whole community through a variety of activities'. One of their first ventures was in 1993 to establish a Saturday Club for children in the area from 9.00 a.m. to 12 noon. In 1993 there were about ninety members from the local area coming for dance, trampolining, gymnastics, football coaching and art and design. Members paid £29 a term – but the school was, in addition, subsidising the activities.

Surviving the holidays

In both 1993 and 1994, applications for Education Extra's Awards revealed that over half of all schools which applied were offering holiday schemes of one form or another. Schemes can vary greatly in length and organisation. Some holiday schemes last for days; others for weeks. Some impose considerable charges, others cost very little. Some schemes organise a series of off-site adventures for children, visiting museums, taking them canoeing or orienteering; others use the full school site to offer a range of activities for children from several schools. Most are able to draw in parents or volunteers in support.

Some are organised by teachers with parents in support. Others are run independently by parents, the youth service or volunteers. The Norwich Community Workshop, for example, aims to provide for children in all school holidays with activities ranging from carpentry to ceramics. Some schools offer intensive courses in single sports. Stanley Park High School in Sutton, for example, runs holiday-time 'sports camps'. Other schools have used holiday time to start a holiday arts scheme, linked to community activities as part of the overall programme of community education at the school.

Others open up the school and library to enable pupils to prepare for exams and project work. Easter revision schemes are increasingly common. Tolworth Girls School in Kingston, Surrey, for example, has taken this a bit further by providing an 'open access' policy which means pupils can come into school to word process their work at weekends and in the holidays.

The key factor for many children is that holiday schemes provide something to do – and even, for a minority, the 'holiday' experience they would otherwise not have. Increasing numbers of schools are offering something across the holiday: maybe a week's activities at the end of the holidays prior to the new term, or two weeks of specialist activities in sports or drama. These efforts are greatly welcomed by children and parents alike. The Holiday Workshops based at Abbotsweld Primary School, Harlow, in Essex, were started in response to demand from the community. 'Parents faced with unoccupied children in half-terms and school holidays have asked us repeatedly for activities.' Children pay a minimal amount to participate in the three day workshops where they can do fabric printing, video making, music and so on. Harlow Arts Council has helped in the past to fund the workshops, which cost between £500 and £1000 to put on, depending on the costs of employing experts to run the activities.

Moreover, as the headteacher told Education Extra:

> *Over the past three years the Community Education Team have run a series of projects for young people of Harlow aged between eight and twelve who do not qualify for attention from the youth service. We started junior youth clubs in four neighbourhood community associations, but were constantly being asked for holiday activities. In line with our educational approach we wanted to offer something which would include a learning experience as well as having fun. Little opportunity is open to children of this age to work in the Arts and our projects have included music, fabric and photography. All of these have been a real hands-on experience and our video-making projects have resulted in entries in the Co-op Young People's Film and Video Festival.*

The amount of free time young people have in the holidays can allow for concentrated programmes of activity: academic, sporting, creative and so on. Holiday activities can also provide opportunities to try new activities and learn new skills, or thoroughly to foster the development of particular interests.

Wye Valley School in Buckinghamshire had an excellent spin-off after it offered its facilities to Wycombe Wanderers Football Club. It has now become a centre for holiday football coaching courses run by members of the club. The school has also recently begun to offer multi-activity fun weeks in the holidays. The first, in the spring of 1993, 'was extremely well-attended and successful'. Herne Bay High School, Kent, gets 400 children involved in its 'hugely successful' holiday sport camps. Charges to the children cover the cost of employing expert coaches to run the activities.

Hartcliffe School in Bristol, Avon, first began its holiday scheme in the summer of 1992 – partly in response to the riots which had occurred on the estate the previous summer. Hartcliffe is a vast urban estate on the southern periphery of Bristol with very few facilities for young people and relatively isolated from the rest of the City. After beginning a cricket coaching programme for youngsters (*see* Chapter 3, p. 68), 'It became increasingly clear that large number of youngsters were keen to take part in activities – any activities – as a break from the monotony of "just hanging around".'

The school therefore agreed to try to start a summer school, the costs of which were underwritten in 1992 by the Bristol Initiative (representing sixty local companies). In 1992, the summer school attracted 400 youngsters over a period of three weeks. It has now run for three years, attracts almost 600 youngsters and is supported by a range of business and charitable help – including the Sports Council and the Army. Typical activities, on and off school site, bring in primary and secondary pupils, and have covered all manner of sports (including orienteering and canoeing), arts and crafts (including circus and related skills), and visits to local amenities such as the Exploratorium, zoo, television studios and newspaper offices.

For parents and children who cannot afford holidays summer schemes are an invaluable break. For working parents holidays are often the worst time to make arrangements (child minders and neighbours are on holiday too). A good holiday scheme can be a godsend to a working parent with younger children. They are, however, by common consent, too short, and too few!

GREAT HOLLANDS INFANT SCHOOL:
HOLIDAY PLAYCARE FOR YOUNGER CHILDREN

Many after-school play/clubs extend their cover across the holidays as part of providing an all year round service for parents. One such scheme is the Great Hollands After-School Scheme, started at Great Hollands Infant School in Berkshire. Trisha Bennet, the community development worker based within the social services department, had taken the initiative to explore demand for after-school playcare and identify a local school willing to offer such a scheme. A holiday scheme was seen to be the first priority and after setting up a management committee, training staff and deciding on a charging policy the holiday scheme ran for five weeks in the summer of 1994. Trisha Bennet writes:

> The staff tried hard to provide a variety of activities to meet the needs of all the children attending the scheme. We discussed programmes with them and welcomed any suggestions for activities and games, and included them where possible. The children worked well together during activities and also with tidying up at social times. The age range was four–eleven years which although it gave vast differences in levels of ability, meant that younger children were helped by older children.

One of the key features of this scheme was that each week was focused on a theme. Over five weeks the themes were Circus Week, Our World, Water Week and Fun Week. Activities matched the theme – for example, during Circus week there was mask making, juggling, acrobatics and a circus show; Our World Week involved the children in setting up a tree display, planting cress and recycling machines; Water Week enabled them to make balloon and wool octopuses, create water safety posters and have a water fight; Fun Week offered treasure hunts, junk modelling and face painting. Across the week there were the usual activities and free play.

The Holiday Scheme was judged to be a 'roaring success both with children and parents'. Volunteers gave of their time to provide singing, dancing, parachute games and sports, and, in the words of one school governor, 'Great Hollands is an area that always seems to get a bad press. Now we can show we are doing something positive as a community.'[7]

Special weeks and residential experiences

Many schools make a case for taking time within formal schooling hours on occasion for what might be described as 'extra' or special activities. Schools argue that these activities and experiences are invaluable, even essential to the children's education and development, and meet needs which cannot always be addressed in the regular classroom setting.

In Patcham High School, East Sussex, pupils were offered its first end of term activity week in 1993. It involved taking many young people out of school for a variety of different experiences. Although strictly speaking, 'in-school' rather than after-school, this example offers many ideas which can easily be applied and developed to Activity Weeks offered during the holidays as well. Andrew Money, the teacher-co-ordinator, and Elizabeth Fletcher, the Headteacher, told Education Extra:

In many schools the run down to the end of the academic year is a time when at least some pupils can get out of the classroom for a programme of visits. Those teachers left in the classroom face a losing battle to maintain motivation with decimated classes, warm summer sunshine and the eager anticipation of six weeks' holiday.

In the summer of 1993 the whole school were involved in designing an activity week for all students and staff – an opportunity for everyone to choose their own programme for personal and social education, and an opportunity for developing specific skills. Activities on offer were balanced between on/off site; visits/residential; paid/free. They included camping, cooking, walking, producing newspapers, videos and radio programmes, and a drama workshop, fishing, baby-sitting certificates, riding, writers' workshops, trips to 'Get to Know Sussex' and courses on, for example, 'Positive Images of Women'.

The process of organisation and negotiation lasted throughout the Spring. Seventy per cent of students got their first choice and 96 per cent of students got one of their choices. One hundred per cent of staff responding to the evaluation thought it was 'an excellent way to end the term' and want to participate again. Only 2 per cent of students were disappointed by their choice of activity.

Some of the most memorable school experiences are, however, residential opportunities. While they are usually associated with outdoor activity or specialised course work, the following example shows that they can also work very successfully in respect of study support.

TOM HOOD SCHOOL, LONDON BOROUGH OF WALTHAM FOREST: GETTING AWAY FROM IT ALL

Tom Hood School, an eleven–sixteen school with 730 pupils, in Leytonstone, London Borough of Waltham Forest, has promoted study support with specific strategies designed to focus on revision and examination techniques. 50 per cent of the school's population consists of Afro-Caribbean and Asian pupils; 50 per cent are White. Its catchment area reflects the multiple nature of disadvantage, with local job opportunities clustered in the twilight economy, part-time and precarious. Young people come from families which 'range from the very strict to the laissez faire . . . from parents reluctant to allow their offspring to go on school trips to households in which children are still on the streets in the early hours of the morning. Many of the girls carry a heavy domestic responsibility and are confused by the conflicting role models of their mothers, aspirations of their fathers and expectations of their teachers.' After-school homework clubs do not work because pupils desert the school for 'casual work, domestic duties or other more immediate attractions'.

The alternative, funded through the Prince's Trust Study Support Initiative, has been a series of residential weekends targeted on specific topics (e.g. Shakespeare) or on students preparing for GCSE. Eleven weekends have been run since 1990 at the Isle of Thorns, a residential centre belonging to the University of Sussex and include the opportunity for individual work, and tutorial work with teachers. In addition there were structured sessions at which teachers gave help with approaches to study and study skills – including a mock examination with papers marked and returned in the afternoon, and detailed feedback for students (a 3:1 staff ratio).

Students reported back to the Prince's Trust their appreciation for the additional support. One said: 'I would pay £50 for this. You just can't put a price on it.' And another: 'I never thought I'd do homework until after midnight. It was just the place and the atmosphere. Everyone was working.'

Conclusion

In this chapter we have shown that schools are pioneering new ways of using time for leisure and learning and doing so in ways which are largely unregarded. The good practice we have monitored shows the extent of the innovation at present in our schools in response to widely different needs. The commitment of the staff (and indeed many of the pupils) involved speaks for itself. The range of 'added value' reflected is remarkable – and the willingness of schools to squeeze every ounce of benefit from the day, the week and the year, equally impressive. While activities and staffing are bound to vary according to the time at which they are offered, the quality of activities in the schools cited in this chapter is exemplary. Each of these schools is making the best use of time available, in the interests of the whole school and the whole community. Colin Power, quoted in Brian Knight's study, puts it well:

> *Education is a process which takes time and which can and does occur at points in time other than those which happen to be convenient to an educational institution and its administrators.*[8]

That extra time spent on the whole range of interests covered by our definition of 'after-school activities' is often not 'convenient' to the traditional school, where life is punctuated into thirty-five-minute segments by the school bell. The fact that so many teachers and others are prepared to make that extra time available to pupils and parents shows a generosity and understanding of the educational process which is in itself an 'added value'. It acts as an exemplar for all those who see learning as a process which overturns chronological time frames and which can be taken up and enjoyed throughout a lifetime.

NOTES

1 Power, C. (1980). *Dr Who and alternative ways of organising time in education.* Australian Council for Administration. Quoted in Knight, B. (1989). *Managing school time*, p. 10. Longman.

2 Knight, B. (1989). *Managing school time*, p. 73. Longman.

3 Hagedorn, J. (1993). *The longer school day and the five-term year in CTCs: Some initial observations.* City Technology Trust.

4 By 1990, it was estimated that 900 million hours were spent each year in accompanying children to school. With the extra congestion caused it is estimated that the cost of seeing children to school and back was 1356 million hours, or, in money terms, over £10 000 million. *See* Policy Studies Institute (1991). *One false move.* Quoted in DEMOS (1995). *The time squeeze*, p. 50.

5 *Sunday Telegraph*, 18 December 1994.

6 *See Times Educational Supplement*, 3 June 1994

7 Information kindly provided by Trisha Bennet, Social Services Department, Bracknell.

8 Knight, op cit., pp. 10–11.

7

Managing the learning opportunities: Reasons to be cheerful

The school has become the centre of the community and is 'alive' from 8.30 a.m. to 10 p.m. each night . . .

> The Community Co-ordinator, Shrubland School, Leamington Spa.

Many of the schools which offer successful and innovative after-school programmes have had to find additional resources and ways around practical problems. Many other schools would do more if they knew that they, too, could solve the same problems. This chapter therefore describes how some schools have overcome some of the obstacles which inhibit the development of after-school activities – and how they are planning to make further progress in the future. It is, therefore, concerned with a wide range of management issues. It deals with:

- *leadership and management of schemes* – who is involved in after-school activities and why;

- *resource and funding issues* – how schools have found additional support;

- *site management issues* – how schools have overcome the problems of cleaning or caretaking;

- *partnership issues* – how schools have found local, regional or national partners to help them extend and enrich what they can do.

Working together to make it happen

For schools to undertake the very hard work involved in setting up an after-school scheme, key staff must be fully committed. We looked, in Chapter 1, at some of the educational and social reasons advanced by schools themselves for wanting to be at the heart of the community in this way. The hundreds of activities described in this study are a testament to the determination and goodwill of teaching staff and others who want to offer pupils something extra, want to extend their educational chances, want to share an enthusiasm or a special skill; people who want their pupils to have creative and constructive occupation and decent social opportunities, who want to add real value to young people's lives.

All the teachers and other leaders who have worked hard to create the special opportunities we describe are giving something extra. Some of them – a minority – are paid in money for what they do. Of these, few are paid what they deserve. All of them, paid and unpaid, are certainly giving extra – in time, enthusiasm, good humour, and determination to make things work. All are contributing over and above any call of duty. In difficult times for schools and teachers, when reasons for getting discouraged seem only to proliferate, Education Extra has found hundreds of reasons to be cheerful, in the enduring and willing efforts of so many teachers, leaders, parents, business people, community volunteers, students, and young people themselves .

In describing who runs and staffs after-school schemes we feel it is vital to recognise and applaud the great voluntary effort which alone ensures that most after-school activities happen at all. This chapter examines the ways some schools have managed to acquire some paid help, or to arrange full or part payment for leaders who started out as volunteers. But only a minority of the schools of which we know manage to set up after-school schemes on a fully paid basis. So we also describe here all sorts of alternative ways schools have found to support schemes and their leaders. The range of such alternatives includes grants for equipment, funds for workshops, occasional payments for visiting specialists, access to training and routes to qualification, the use of school equipment after school or the acquisition by an after-school project of equipment that will also be an asset during the school day. All these forms of support go some way towards recognising the voluntary contribution teachers and other leaders are making; they can be the key to enabling leaders and others to do more or to making it possible to do anything at all. Just as importantly they show those involved that their work is valued, and encourage them to go on making the effort.

However much they benefit from voluntary support, sharing of resources and help in kind, most after-school projects run into a need for money at some point. It may be only a matter of a few pounds – the entrance fees to visit an exhibition or fuel costs for a one-off visit. There may be a small regular cost to cover – clay for the pottery club for instance – or a lump sum might be needed to buy a piece of equipment – a kiln, a computer software package, or camping equipment. We will describe in this chapter some of the ways which schools and clubs have found to meet extra costs. Some undertake very ambitious projects, such as converting an under-used wing of the school for out-of-school and community use; running a summer holiday scheme; employing extra staff full or part time specifically to work on extra-curricular projects; building a sports pavilion; or creating a well-equipped area for homework and individual study.

Growing out of the commitment to sharing resources and also the need for support, there has emerged a rich variety of partnerships. Partnership is taking many different forms. Throughout previous chapters we have seen constant reference to partnerships which support excellent and diverse schemes.

For the school, at local level, it can mean finances which will support staffing after school; supply premises; provide subsidies where there are charges for children; or provide one-off grants for the costs of equipment. Just as importantly, it can also mean human resources. It can mean the support of parents and grandparents. It can mean bringing in mentors from local business or from the rich national network of Women's Institutes. It can mean finding other partners from the Education Service itself – feeder schools, local sixth form colleges, and further and higher education, to support coaching, training, supervision, family literacy, specialist sports, and much more.

At an area level it can mean partnerships between schools in a neighbourhood or links between primary and secondary schools. It can mean bringing in some of the most obvious of local partners in a shared project – for example – links with the Youth Service through a youth work post after school; building up an after-school scheme within the general compass of community education; inviting the police, the probation service or St John's Ambulance, to offer support for specialist activities after school; linking up with the Chamber of Commerce or with local employers to develop skills-based activities or provide professional mentoring; bringing in the expertise and enthusiasm of staff and students (including those training to be teachers) in higher education institutions, or of local bodies such as the Women's Institute.

At a strategic level, there are equally practical partnerships to be built. In terms of after-school play and care, the key partners for schools are the local authorities and the TECs – as partners not simply in providing childcare for working parents, but also in providing a framework within which the school can cast its own achievement strategy, and within which the LEAs and TECs can focus a range of supporting strategies. Other strategic partners include the regional arts and sports bodies, regional health authorities, adult and family literacy agencies, which operate nationally (e.g. The Basic Skills Agency, The National Literacy Trust), crime prevention agencies (e.g. Crime Concern and other agencies involved in the Safer Cities programme) national charities which support young people (e.g. The Prince's Trust, Save the Children, Learning through Landscapes, The Wildlife Trust, or the Duke of Edinburgh's Award). Depending on location, there can be in addition, funding through City Challenge, or Rural Development Councils. As many examples show, these partners can work with schools to develop specific elements of a coherent after-school programme, involving, for example, arts, sports, crime prevention, health and safety, environmental improvement or independent achievement.

Within this general framework there are three forms of partnership which deserve particular attention; the role of parents; the role of local business; and the role of community education.

Parents in partnership

There is one set of partners which, however, deserves particular attention: parents themselves. It is now widely recognised that parental involvement in children's schooling is a key factor in educational success. The Royal Society of Arts project, 'Parents in a Learning Society', is symbolic of the attention now being paid at all levels to how home-school initiatives can be promoted in practical ways both to support children and awaken the parents' own interest in their education and personal development.[1]

For parents, after-school activities can offer a direct and powerful link into learning and the life of the school. Michael Fullan, for example, has identified four different forms of parental involvement:

- Parental involvement at school (e.g. volunteers, assistants)
- Parent involvement in learning activities at home (e.g. assisting children at home)
- Home/community – school relationships (e.g. school reports)
- Governance (e.g. governing bodies).

It is significant, from the perspective of after-school provision, that he observes that 'The first two forms of involvement have a more direct impact on instruction than do the other forms.'[2]

One benefit of after-school provision is that it can make a place for parents alongside their children. While research suggests that the majority of parents seem well satisfied with their local schools, too many parents still find schools hostile or alien places, or associate them with negative memories of their own childhood. Hostility, indifference or mere lack of any contact point between school and parents can only be bad for both children and school. The cosy familiarity of the primary school is replaced by the much more forbidding aspect of secondary schools. As so many of the schools already cited show, after-school activities can build bridges between schools and families by providing unthreatening access points to the school, ensures that parents are valued and making a real contribution to school life. They also allow breakthrough contacts to form naturally between school staff and parents away from the formality of academic and disciplinary issues. St Chad's School in Oldham told us, for example, that 'Parents who would otherwise rarely visit the school now feel a partner in their children's education.'

There is no doubt that parents are keenly interested in what schools provide after school. The Keele survey of parents and their attitudes to secondary schools showed, significantly, that parents did not want more involvement in the running of school. Parents did want more information about schools, but not on the measurement of pupil progress. Rather

> *the biggest demand for more information is on extra-curricular activities. About half of all parents would like to know more about clubs and other out of school opportunities. This may be an indirect plea for more provision of this kind . . . And when they are able to they are keen to help. Over 90 per cent of parents think homework is important.*[3]

Schools which have started after-school programmes have noticed within a relatively short time that parents are attracted to the school; they offer it as a specific reason for their choice of primary school (*see* for instance Eardley Primary School, described in Chapter 1, pp. 28–9).

It is also well worth schools considering what they can offer parents through out-of-school programmes, whether in terms of direct involvement or respite from their responsibilities of care. After-school programmes can and do give direct help to parents who are out of work or attempting to enter a new field; they can give valuable experience and even access to training and qualifications. Designated community schools have the advantage of being able to bring in parents through their community networks. Non-community schools have to make a conscious effort and after-school activities can offer a particular opening. Family Literacy (*cf.* Chapter 4, pp. 93–4) after school is an obvious route for parents who wish to support learning, but they can, equally, be offered opportunities to learn word processing and IT skills, and to participate in a range of science-based, environmental and community projects.

For parents who can take advantage of an after-school play/care scheme to return to work, there is the invaluable reassurance of knowing their children are continuing to learn or able to relax and enjoy themselves in a secure environment while they train for, return to, or continue in work. As a result, relationships with the school are strongly cemented.

Schools themselves have a great deal to gain from a high level of parental involvement. An audit of parents' skills can release a hidden torrent of expertise and goodwill waiting to be tapped. Sports programmes can offer extra sessions or activities when parents can take over some of the groups (this is often a particularly successful way of getting fathers, who might otherwise be hard to reach, involved with school) – new activities can start because a parent is willing to share the skills of garden design, cooking, woodworking, repairing cars or putting together a news sheet. Parents are often found willing to take on administrative roles, too, to help publicise a scheme or make special fundraising efforts. All these factors are invaluable for the success of after-school schemes; and all of them have the added benefit of bringing school and parents together with common aims.

Alongside parents are to be found, very often, a wide range of individual volunteers from the community itself. Grandparents and other relatives are involved in activities which range from gardening to lace-making; the Women's Institute, through its interest, for example, in promoting more understanding of science as well as traditional activities, and its wealth of experience and skills, could have an obvious role in the future as a support for after-school activities; local music, drama and special interest groups can help with musical productions, arts and crafts activities (everything from textiles to clog-dancing) and special interest activities such as camera and film clubs, ornithology, astronomy or paleontology. Finding out about and using the local community can enable schools to draw on a much fuller and more exotic range of options. Moreover, bringing young people into schools after school to act as volunteers, to develop new activities and social and community programmes after school could be an obvious expression of a new Citizen's Service.

Enterprise links and community involvement

Opportunities multiply as enterprise becomes involved. In recent years public and private enterprise in general have been seen as vital partners for schools. At the extreme, e.g. the City Technology Schools, they are judged to be not merely partners but lead funders and advocates. Few firms are so involved. There is much more agreement throughout the business community, represented by the CBI, for example, about the proportion of young people leaving school without useful qualifications or even basic competence and about a general ignorance of 'the world of work'. These fears have been compounded by the knowledge that in other parts of Europe more young people are more likely to stay on in education longer, more likely to obtain training for technical qualifications, and more likely to speak more than one language. These are all key skills for young people competing in the future European labour market.

For the majority of schools, therefore, links into the world of business have enabled more bridges to be built into the working world. These bridges are now supported by pillars of qualification, chiefly National Vocational Qualifications (NVQs) and General National Vocational Qualifications (GNVQs). Overall policy has been to set National Targets for Education and Training as proposed by the CBI in 1989 and accepted by the Government in 1991. They involve Foundation Targets (education and training for young people) and Lifetime Targets (for adults already in the world of work). The Foundation Targets include:

- by 1997, 80 per cent of young people to reach NVQ2 or equivalent

- training or education to NVQ3 (or equivalent) for all young people who can benefit

- by 2000, 50 per cent of all young people to reach NVQ3 or equivalent

- education and training provision to develop self-reliance, flexibility and breadth.

These attempts to widen competency across the curriculum and with a new range of qualifications have brought education and business into many different forms of partnership in recent years, particularly through the Training and Enterprise Councils (TECs) and Education Business Partnerships (EBPs) which were tasked with fostering school–industry programmes, bringing them to the forefront of schooling. School–business links have become a feature of the curriculum of both primary and secondary schools. A survey conducted for the Department of Education in 1991–2 showed that 92 per cent of secondary school and 56 per cent of primary schools had links with business, promoted by central and local government through various initiatives, notably TVEI. The pattern is diverse, sometimes chaotic, and evaluation of effectiveness lags behind the rash of individual schemes.

The rationale for these school-business partnerships has been to improve the transition for young people from school to adult and working life by raising standards in career guidance and education, to inform pupils about the economy and industry and to provide 'A resource, context or environment in order to improve the motivation and attainment of pupils.'[4] After-school time and the freedom it offers to innovate, experiment and explore personal enthusiasms, is ripe for involvement by local and national enterprise, as part of existing programmes or as complementary to them. Some aspects of after-school provision will lend themselves particularly well to support from Education/Business Partnerships or Compact schemes which may flourish more freely in time outside the formal curriculum. Our case study report in this chapter on the 'on track' clubs in South London, and other examples of links between schools and businesses, demonstrate how valuable such initiatives can be in broadening young people's horizons and even keeping them away from the brink of school failure.

Many schools in our network have been supported individually by local or national employers who have supplied help in cash and kind. They have obtained sponsorship for improving school grounds, developing gardens, providing information technology and a great deal more. The Education Extra Award for 1994, for example, was supported by thirty separate businesses who supplied resources such as table-tennis tables, outdoor chess sets, scientific instruments and computers to award-winning schools. There is a growing tendency for firms to see the need for this support in local rather than national terms and as a way of fostering the profile of the firm within the local community. There is clearly a great deal more to be obtained through partnership – and some of the most interesting examples of how this is being done come from the United States.

One recent and very effective development in terms of longer term partnership has been the introduction of mentorship schemes. Again, this is an area where after-school activities can open up opportunities for young people to spend time individually or in small informal groups with adults who have time for them, and who can act as role models or advisors.

The Department of Education in the USA reported in 1989 the widespread adoption of 'Mentoring' schemes and their successes in schools. (At that date the Department knew of no fewer than three million mentors attached to individual school pupils.) Marion White-Hood, administrative assistant at Benjamin Taster Middle School in Bowie, Maryland, has given this vivid account of the effective working of one mentoring scheme which enlisted not only teachers and administrators as mentors, but secretaries and cafeteria workers. These 'care-givers' offered care and support through informal and formal activities with students, met with them before and after school, took them out to lunch, visited their homes, or took them on trips.

> *The results were phenomenal. As the mentor program enlarged, it became evident that the role of the school had changed. No longer was school just a place to go each day. For both mentors and students, school was warm, caring, unpretentious and spirited. Students were no longer 'homeless' but 'school enriched' . . . Student goals improved as mentors encouraged gainful involvement in the educational process. They realised that there were 'real important reasons to get an education'. Helping students with homework, providing them with research assistance and challenging them to care, mentors acknowledged students while showing genuine concern and attention. Mentors became part of the cure, and reason to succeed. In addition, our students received fewer referrals for discipline.*
>
> *. . . Often mentors role-played situations that might lead to students' conflict. Students discussed ways to handle difficult people, negative peer pressure, and challenging situations . . . The average daily attendance increased as students poured into the school each day.*[5]

We do not know of any mentoring schemes in Britain which are so far advanced, but there are many instances of in-school and after-school mentoring in the UK. Education Extra is in contact with, for instance, a Tyneside school which brings in young solicitors and other professionals to act as mentors to pupils, and a Sheffield school where qualified professionals and university students visit to indicate to able pupils the possibility of going on to higher education. Winton Primary School, London Borough of Islington, is supported through Business in the Community and the National Westminster Bank for pupils' reading. Bodies like the Citizenship Foundation promote links with the worlds of business and politics. As a senior teacher from Elizabeth Garrett Anderson School, London Borough of Islington, points out: 'The Citizenship Foundation links us with a solicitors' firm and has allowed us to put students into the Motorola National Parliament Competition, and to hold a moot election in connection with the Hansard Society . . . A year 11 student took part in the "Euro Debate" which the Foundation arranged last year.' At the same time large-scale initiatives across the UK can be seen promoting partnerships between schools and industry and seeking to open pupils' eyes to possibilities in the world of work. Large companies including BP, ICI and Rover have taken a lead in this.

These developments signify that many businesses are now moving away from one-off financial investments into schools towards a link which involves voluntary support for reading schemes, study support or a continuing interest in the specific needs and ambitions of local schools. Schools support this development enthusiastically – not only because mentors can bring in new professional skills and outside connections, but because the adults who become involved offer a successful role model for the pupils themselves. Teachers repeatedly cite the wish to *create* aspirations in able pupils whose horizons have never been broadened beyond their day-to-day environment.

The examples and the case studies which follow illustrate how schools have organised and managed their resources to provide after-school activities, and have found partnership potential within the community.

Leadership and management

The role of the headteacher

As in effective schooling as a whole, the impetus which gets after school activities established very often comes from the headteacher or from a key member of the senior staff – a deputy headteacher, head of special needs or, in Community Schools, the community education teacher. Sometimes, especially in small schools, the headteacher will lead by example, personally running one or more after school clubs, consulting with, and helping other staff to do likewise. More typically, heads take a facilitating or managerial role, removing difficulties and enabling staff or other leaders to run the activities they wish to. The backing or direct participation of the head in after-school activities naturally creates an ethos in the school where voluntary after-school activities have been traditionally valued and conditions in which they can flourish.

Andrew Raven, headteacher of St Thomas' CE Primary School near Groombridge (East Sussex) explains how he set out to promote after-school activities at his small village school.

> *I had to lead many myself, actively enthused, and promoted others. Teachers felt they could give one activity per week as they were feeling the stress of work overload from the national curriculum. As a small school we only have four teachers.*

To extend the range of possibilities he sought help 'from parents, local organisations, and professional coaches'. The response to a 1992 questionnaire to parents about after-school clubs was so positive that the school decided to hire professional coaches for tennis, ballet, gymnastics and cricket. A charge of £1 per session had to be passed on to families for those activities run by professional coaches, but these still proved extremely popular and they continue to run alongside the well-established programme of voluntarily run activities (sports and drama, music and homework clubs) led by the head and teachers. Pupils now regularly take a letter home each term outlining the activity options available. Often a club will run twice a week to enable all who are keen to take part.

Many headteachers are fully and actively involved in running clubs themselves. The headteacher of Moorfields Primary School in the London Borough of Islington runs lunchtime library groups for pupils. Three groups, involving sixty children altogether, attend the school library with her to 'play games, listen to tapes, read and generally relax'. Her motivation is 'to offer the children something to do at lunchtimes, which can be boring and unconstructive periods in a child's school day'.

In many schools we have seen headteachers leading activities, which range from jazz-dance (St Clements School, Salford, described in Chapter 6, pp. 158–9), to the junior reporters club (Eardley Primary School, London Borough of Wandsworth).

With strong leadership, the individual enthusiasms of the individual teacher can flourish. That particular factor, the commitment shown by by one or more teachers, is often the primary reason why a particular after-school activity happens at all. Teachers see a need they can meet, work to win the backing of the school for their venture, and will often add an extra aspect to pupils' experience of school, almost single-handedly.

It is impossible to cite the many hundreds of individual examples which deserve particular credit under this specific heading. The following instance illustrates how an individual teacher has committed her extra time.

Jacqui Ambler teaches in the Autism Unit at Chapel Grange Special School, Bradford. She also has peripatetic responsibilities for pupils with Asperger Syndrome (a form of autism) in mainstream schools in Bradford. She saw that these young people and their families had a whole web of needs:

> the need of young people with autism to experience social events and broaden their range of leisure activities (usually severely limited) and learn social skills . . . the need of families to have space and respite during weekends and holidays to be a family (extremely difficult for the families of young people with severe autism) . . . the need of young people with Asperger Syndrome (usually totally isolated in a mainstream school) to meet other young people with the same condition.

In response she decided to establish the young adventurers' club. It runs minibus trips once every half term, usually to safe 'adventure park' type settings (such as Kinderland in Scarborough). Pupils from Chapel Grange and the mainstream schools belong to the club and can be picked up from home for the trips. As well as the fun of a day out and the chance to be with other young people who have Asperger Syndrome the young adventurer trips are valuable opportunities for the young people to go into new environments, extend their horizons and learn about mixing socially both within and beyond their group.

Providing for and paying for after-school provision

Despite all the pressures on schools, it is particularly impressive that many continue to run their after-school provision entirely on a voluntary basis.

Hampstead School (London Borough of Camden), for example, has a packed schedule of activities on every day of the school week, both at lunchtimes and after school. Students can choose to participate in the choir, wind band or show band, join the young investigators award club or take part in design and technology workshops. Those needing support with their work can go to general curriculum support sessions which are held several times a week, or to special subject sessions in most curriculum subjects. The library is also open for an hour each day after school. Hampstead School has recently formulated a written policy on extra-curricular activities, and is working to publicise the opportunities and make sure all students are aware of what is available. In 1994 it received an Education Extra Award to help with the cost of producing a publicity leaflet about its after-school activities.

When *ad hoc* activities develop into a co-ordinated or fully fledged scheme, with study support through to sports every night of the week, the question of whether payment should be made for some or all staff often does arise in an acute form. This development often raises issues of whether staff should be paid for after-school provision in any form.

In principle, Education Extra believes that a teacher undertaking an extra responsibility/activity which is not part of their contract has every right to payment for those services. If a teacher chooses not to ask for or accept payment, then that is a personal decision. It is essential, however, that each school is free to make their decisions in the light of their own traditions and circumstances. The voluntary ethic must not be exploited and that where schools feel circumstances have changed, or that what is being offered has changed and payment is necessary, those resources should be available, on the basis of equity, to be awarded at the discretion of the school governing body. Ideally, as we argue in the Conclusion to this book, for the sake of fair play and expansion, there should be a local budget into which schools can bid in order to extend what they can do. What is not justified is the unchallenged expectation either that teachers should never be paid for after-school provision, or that payment should become a right for some but not others.

Schools are, individually, arriving at some common principles which offer models of good practice for other schools. This particularly applies to the practice of designating posts with responsibility for after-school activities and paying those who hold posts which carry responsibility for coordination and scheme development. In some schools, where there is a designated community teacher, the responsibility for developing a scheme is placed with them, and is essentially part of their normal work. In other cases, staff who take on additional responsibility receive an additional responsibility payment, or can be 'paid' by time off in lieu.

One school which has identified a particular post as carrying specific responsibilities for after-school provision is Islington Green School in London Borough of Islington. This significant step means that now everyone at Islington Green knows where to turn when they want to make things happen after school. As well as liaising with staff, Dan Dickens, the post-holder, works with the Student Council which generates its own ideas 'for improving the range and quality of after school activities' and encourages its representatives to canvass opinions from students about the activities they want. 'This has led directly to the appointment of two additional youth workers to run a games club and a girls club at lunchtime, both of which have proved extremely popular.'

Some schools have set up management teams within the school to develop after-school provision for pupils and community alike. In 1993, the Thomas Telford School (a City Technology College in Shropshire) offers a multitude of after-school activities including dance, cookery, textiles, modern languages and eight sports – as well as a homework centre which runs from 5.30 to 8.30 p.m. all week. The costs are met from the staffing budget with staff contracted to assist in after-school work or paid with time off in lieu. Family members take part in or assist with activities and the whole programme is co-ordinated by a management team of four staff whose jobs include the development and management of an expanded programme to be opened to outside groups with sports and recreational activities through the week and the year.

Where teachers, youth workers or sessional artists are offering specialist activities beyond the traditional scope of the scheme, sessional payments are made often on youth work rates or adult tutor rates. In some cases schools do what they can to encourage staff, e.g. by offering free lunches, or, in the case of residential study workshops, by offering staff involved expenses paid accommodation.

One very recent development in some secondary schools has been prompted by the Out-of-School Childcare Initiative. The development of new and ambitious after-school clubs in selected secondary schools is being funded by Training and Enterprise Councils in Humberside, Leeds, Tyneside, and Merseyside, principally through the payment of school-based co-ordinators to develop coherent schemes or for specific programmes (e.g. IT or study support). These new schemes, which are designed for some hundreds of younger secondary age children will provide not only supervision (and therefore support working parents) but a new range of stimulating and enjoyable activities. These schemes usually make a small charge to parents. It is anticipated that, as they grow in size, the funds raised from parents and other key supporters will ensure that when TEC funding ceases after the first full year, the schemes will be well established and self-supporting.

Many individual schools have worked out their own solutions. The following examples demonstrate how different schemes have worked out some direct methods of using time and resources very effectively.

EAST LEEDS HIGH SCHOOL:
PARTNERSHIP IN ACTION

At East Leeds High School, when the OASIS (Organising After School In School) Project was set up, in 1993, some staff were already putting in time voluntarily to run after school activities. The school wanted to recognise and support this voluntary contribution, yet at the same time wanted to offer some financial reward and incentive when putting after-school activities onto a larger and more formally organised scale.

A solution was found through full consultation with the staff: everyone running an activity agreed to give the first hour of their time each week voluntarily. They then had the option of claiming payment (at youth worker rates) for the second hour of their time. And so on – the third hour was given free, the fourth was paid.

Some of the teachers accepted the payment – and the scheme made it possible for some outside activity leaders to be brought in under the same arrangement (specialists to teach computing, for instance) without the possibly awkward situation of paid and unpaid workers doing the same job alongside each other. Other teaching staff, who had a strong personal tradition of giving their time after school free, declined the payment – but they were able to use the money instead, if they wished, for equipment and supplies for their activities. In addition, all teachers running activities could apply to use part of the funds OASIS raised for their equipment and other needs.

185

In 1993, at Peers School in Oxfordshire, staff involved in the Education Plus scheme (*see* Chapter 4, pp. 104; 164) run classes each Tuesday and Thursday from 3.00 p.m. to 4.15 p.m. Education Plus now involves some 120 students aged thirteen to sixteen. All the staff and tutors who lead activities are paid £14 per hour (in 1993) to do so. There is no charge to participants and the school works hard to raise funds through business sponsorship and charity support, in addition to some assistance from the local Council, to cover the costs. Staff involved in the Saturday Focus programme (*see* Chapter 6, p. 164) are also paid at a similar rate.

At the Education Extra projects based at Swanlea School and Brampton School in East London (both are described in Chapter 6), the co-ordinators of the schemes receive an additional increment to their salary. These additional costs have been paid from funds raised by Education Extra and obtained, for example, from the London Docklands Development Corporation, the East London TEC, the BSA, and local charitable bodies such as the Aldgate and AllHallows Foundation and the Wakefield Trust.

Many schools which offer after-school provision do find that after-school projects can generate their own extra resources, attract extra funds, and that they may be the recipients of special grants or gifts in kind. The school as a whole benefits, and teachers find their conditions of work and the resources they have to work with enhanced, perhaps in small but often very significant ways. For example, the 1994 Education Extra Award won by Chaucer School in Sheffield was a CD-ROM reader; the Award was made to encourage and recognise the after-school Supported Study programme described in Chapter 4 (pp. 88–91) but will benefit all users of the school library in and out of school time. Staff running the computer club at East Leeds High School clearly benefit from school facilities because they use school computers. But funds raised for after-school activities were used to buy 'mice' and extra software for the computer club, and these can now be used both after school and during the school day, so the formal teaching of computer skills has also been enhanced.

Finding the money

Getting hold of money, even small amounts of it, is often seen as the biggest stumbling block in the way of plans for activity after school, and it usually is. After-school activities have no official status and no allocated budget, unless a school decides to grant these to them. Many costs (e.g. room rental, heating and lighting) can be and are waived by some schools with the support of

LEAs to encourage activities to happen. Letting out the school's facilities after 6.00 p.m. can fund twilight activities between 3.30 and 6.00 p.m. Upgrading sports facilities with the intention of renting them out to local sporting clubs can bring in significant funds. Equipment can be borrowed; resources shared.

There comes a point, however, for most projects when they bump up against a need for hard cash. Sometimes only modest amounts are needed because sharing resources has covered many of the costs, but the balance still has to be found. The school, for instance, may make its minibus available without expecting a contribution to overall running costs; but the club has to find enough money for petrol or diesel. The school might make computers and the computer room available but the computer club might want its own software. Art club can take place in the school's art rooms but the cost of materials has to be covered.

As after-school projects grow they often set their sights on more ambitious development, which require higher levels of funding. Starting to provide a modest level of activity often reveals the extent of enthusiasm for provision and activities outside school time; the demand, once tapped, generates more ideas. A school begins to build links with the community; soon it becomes apparent that a community room, or even a community wing, would be a great asset. A homework club starts off, modestly, in a classroom. Over time it becomes clear that the need for this provision would be better served by access to the library or use of a computer area, both of which will then need to be staffed at new hours. The gym club or dance club starts winning local competitions; now they want to start participating in regional or national events.

How, therefore, have active schools resolved this question of resources?

Many schools do support their after-school activity programme financially to some extent. Often this happens in a piecemeal, almost invisible (but nonetheless important) way, with costs being simply absorbed by the school within its own budget. The school, perhaps, doesn't single out the cost of paper and paint used by the art club, or doesn't insist that the orienteering club subscribes for the minibus fuel used on short journeys. This kind of leeway makes a great deal possible.

Financial commitment to extra-curricular time does sometimes go much further however. At Windsor High School in Dudley, for instance, music is given high priority. Music lessons for 100 pupils are paid for out of the school budget.

Woodlands School in Basildon, Essex, provides over £3000 per year from school funds to support its extra-curricular programme. The school's headteacher feels it is a worthwhile investment.

> *This money is used to book experts and venues as well as support families in financial need. Through our extensive range of activities we have created a very positive and vibrant school. Pupils feel valued, and are very positive about the opportunities offered.*

These opportunities include a writer's circle, homework club, drama, music, science and technology activities, a wide range of sports and regular Saturday morning extension classes in subjects ranging from science to Shakespeare. The head stresses

> *Part of our ethos is that we aim to involve ALL pupils regardless of ability and family background. With this in mind we have committed a substantial amount of money to ensuring that no pupil misses out and that our range of activities caters for a wide variety of interests.*

Some after-school ventures require special fund-raising efforts. Schools may find it easier to raise money for a specific purpose than to generate income for general running costs of activities. Newtown High School in Powys has some LEA funding to help with its extensive programme of activities, but in addition it looks for business sponsorship and undertakes a special fundraising effort each year for one special feature of the programme. It seeks to raise £50 for each of ninety students to take part in their annual sixth form residential conference. The conference is themed around a different 'challenge' each year. Pupils stay at a local stately home and work on problem-solving activities, in groups along with local business people and other adults.

At Shrubland Street Community School resources are carefully husbanded and 'recycled' between the Community Education Fund and the out-of-school activity programme. Shrubland Street is a Community First School 'in the heart of the community' in Leamington Spa, surrounded by a mixture of high-rise flats, terraced houses, council estates and modern private housing. Fifty per cent of the children on roll are from ethnic minority groups. The school's Community co-ordinator, deputy head Mrs Y. Cossedine, told us 'there are many social problems and the children need the security of our community school'.

Mrs Cossedine explained how:

staff, governors, caretaker and parents [have become] committed to our work and strive towards providing the facilities required in this area within our building.

The voluntary commitment of staff, parents and other members of the community is vital to the success of the many clubs, which include P.E. club, art club, Bhangra dancing, basketball, music club, classical dancing and two after-school football clubs. A Saturday morning club offers more activities including Tabla classes, art and sport. The school premises are also home to a toy library, a toddler group, and language classes in Punjabi, Hindi and Gujerati.

There is a joining fee of £5 for the Saturday morning club. The club's main source of funding is the lettings fees covered from the Community Education Fund; income from this is 'ploughed back into the School Community Fund to further our work in this field'.

A traditional source of help with funding, fund-raising by the School PTA or Friends' Association, is still the mainstay of many after-school programmes. Ashcroft High School in Luton, Bedfordshire, has an active Friends' Association which raises money to support after-school activities and will accept bids from after-school clubs needing financial help. In 1994, for instance, they gave the orienteering club £200 and the gardening club £400. In addition, the Friends give between £1000 and £2000 to each year group in the school as they reach Year 10. Pupils are then given a taste of democratic decision-making in their choices of how to use this money. The school's extensive programme of extra-curricular activities, and its policy of encouraging pupils to use the school buildings, library and other facilities outside lesson times, were praised in its recent OFSTED report.

Teachers are well versed in the art of making a little go a long way. The after-school activity club at St Anne's Junior School in Rotherham generates its own funds through a snack bar facility run by and for pupils. The club is regularly attended by around 70 per cent of the school's 170 pupils. Children attending the club can choose different activities, one of which is operating the snack bar and making the food for it. Selling the snacks and drinks generates funds (supplemented by the school budget) for the activity club.

Finding financial help locally

The key partners for schools wishing to develop after-school provision are, of course local education authorities and local authorities as a whole. Although it may seem like a counsel of perfection at a time when LEA budgets are so stretched, key development of after-school activities can look for significant expansion to the support of the LEA itself. LEAs with a specific Community Education Budget can support after-school activities far more effectively than those without. One key area is the cost of keeping premises open after school hours, and providing additional heating and light. Community schools may be able to meet these costs more easily. Their school buildings will normally be used after 6.00 p.m., and the transitional period between the end of school and the beginning of the adult evening use can be automatically covered. In addition, community schools in particular can lease out their buildings for evening use, and use those costs to subsidise twilight activities. Schools without that capacity and without that support inevitably face more difficulties.

Some LEAs (e.g. Salford and Tyneside) are now responding to all the possibilities inherent in after-school activities by making it a key element in local community development and enterprise policy. Others, such as Swansea, are supporting after-school provision in individual schools, through the Community Education budget which is helping to fund the cost of after-school staffing.

It is not only the local education authority which becomes involved. Depending on the nature of the provision there are a range of local authority services already involved in after-school partnerships. Leisure and recreation services can support a wide range of sports developments; Arts development officers can help locate funds for arts programmes; Social services departments can subsidise places in after-school care-based clubs for children who have particular needs, and whose parents cannot afford to pay; Employment services officers can help care-based clubs locate funds for schemes designed primarily to help working parents. Where there are co-ordinated education and social services departments they can spearhead integrated care and education provision for school-age children, and help aspiring providers locate local funds for all forms of after-school provision.

There is also a key role for the Training and Enterprise Councils (TECs), already heavily involved in developing out of school childcare schemes. Many TECs are already working in partnership with local authorities and other agencies to develop after-school childcare as part of a general regeneration strategy and a means of supporting parents into training and work. But equally vital, TECs can also support after-school activities as another means of lifting attainment in the drive to meet the National Targets for Education and Training. After-school activities can have a legitimate place within COMPACT schemes, EBP strategies and individual education and training programmes set by individual TECs or determined in partnership bids, for example, for funds under the Single Regeneration Budget or European Funding.

In practice, at the level of the school, there is an enormous variety of partnerships to choose from.

At Ventnor Middle School on the Isle of Wight, the cost of creating a sports pavilion for school and community use is being met by a combination of grants and local efforts; the Parents' Association has raised money, more has been put in from the school fund, and the Local Council Rural Development Commission has given a grant of £800. The 1994 Easter holiday revision programme for Year 11 students at Elizabeth Garrett Anderson School in London Borough of Islington was funded by a special grant from Islington Education Authority. And Moorfields School, also in Islington, received a one-off gift of £500 from Islington Environment Group to encourage it in the work of its litter squad which helps to maintain and improve the school grounds and gardens.

Schools facing the problems of inner-city deprivation can benefit from becoming part of larger-scale regeneration projects as well as local initiatives. A group of four schools in Dudley – Priory Primary, Castle High, Kate's Hill Primary and Wren's Nest Primary – were helped in setting up after-school, lunchtime and Saturday morning clubs as part of Dudley's 'Raising Standards in Inner City Schools' project. Two years of GEST funding enabled them to increase staffing and give staff members special responsibility for setting up and running the out of school clubs and the able pupils' 'quest group' described in Chapter 4 (p. 91). The GEST funding has recently finished, leaving the individual schools to attempt to absorb the future project costs within their own development plans. The LEA has taken on the Reading Recovery section of the programme, and SRB funding is being allocated to the Quest project and work with ESOL pupils.

To charge or not to charge?

When staffing, premises and equipment costs are involved, the question of charging parents often becomes a related issue. The school is not required to charge for after-school activities which are provided for the school's own pupils and which fall within the purposes of the school. In many instances, where activities also involve other pupils (e.g. from feeder schools) schools do not make charges on the same grounds. Where the school has to pay charges for coaching or specialist teaching after school parents are often asked for contributions towards specific costs. Other fully fledged drop-in or registered 'clubs', with their own identify – e.g. a name or a card, often make small token charges to parents – based on a sessional or weekly basis. Some of the newer schemes which bring in a range of specialist activities from outside the school carry higher charges and require parents to book in and register in advance. It is anticipated in such schemes that the after-school 'business plan' will ensure that within a year or so, once the club is established and core funding is withdrawn, the club will sustain itself through income generated in different ways. In such schemes there is a serious question of equal access and opportunity to which the schools involved are deeply sensitive. Wherever possible we have found schools admitting providing subsidies through school budgets or the income to the general scheme to include as many children as possible.

The decision about charging for after school activities can be a difficult one, and it always has to be made in the light of local circumstances. There are circumstances where schools and teachers feel it would be wrong to charge pupils or families anything at all, and they will go to great lengths to cover costs in other ways so no direct charges have to be made. This may be because they wish to offer free participation on principle, as part of the children's educational opportunities. Or they may be aware that a charge, even a very small one, could keep some children away; charging then becomes an equal opportunities issue – and one felt most keenly by teachers themselves.

Where schools feel that charging is acceptable, a sensitive – and sensible – decision has to be made about how much. Some schools told us that the pupils appeared to value their clubs and activities more when a charge was made – if only at a 'symbolic' level. Several youth and FE teachers we spoke to in Tyneside told us that a charge of 50p per session (of about two hours' activities) was acceptable for their local young people because this was the 'going rate' for attending youth clubs. Two of Education Extra's special project schools, both serving severely disadvantaged areas, charge pupils 20p per afternoon session (and, in practice, leaders tend to turn a blind eye when pupils 'forget' their money). These amounts are fairly nominal contributions which cannot cover the real costs of most activities but can significantly help with 'extras' if accumulated over time.

Where charges are made, cross-subsidies from parents who can afford a little extra on behalf of children from poorer families, can be implicit within the Business Plan. In addition, subsidies from Social Services or from Probation Services for children and young people at risk although not easy to access, can be found; while, for children in play/care or supervision-based schemes funded as part of the Out-of-School Childcare Initiative can be supported through an employers' commitment to working mothers in the workforce.

People power

Partnerships with parents and the community

The benefits for after-school activities of partnerships with parents can range from committed volunteers to assist with or lead activities, to experts who can bring in skills for short-term projects or dedicated fundraisers raising money to help the activities happen. Partnerships should, of course, bring benefits both ways. Many parents get involved for the satisfaction of making things happen for their children and other local children. In addition, after-school involvement can have other positive outcomes for them: the chance to share a leisure interest or particular expertise; the opportunity to gain valuable voluntary work experience that could be a route to paid work; and, for some, the chance to follow routes to qualification and broaden their own educational or work horizons.

At St Sebastian's School, Liverpool, parents were running a holiday scheme for over 100 children in 1993; at Gordano School in Bristol, Avon, parents were running a Saturday sports scheme for 150 children; and at Oakwood High School in Salford, parents were running a Wednesday youth club with sports and arts activities and raising additional funding from industry and charitable sources.

At Sedgemoor Manor Junior School in Bridgewater, Somerset, in addition to a range of after-school clubs run by teachers the school supports and promotes after-school activities organised and run by local parents and students. The activities programme has been running successfully for six years, two evenings per week after school, and in the holidays. It makes use of the school playground, its two halls, the kitchen, and occasionally the sports centre at a nearby secondary school.

This programme meets a need in an area with a high crime level and high unemployment. The school's Community Education Co-ordinator told us 'the age range 5 to 11 years is totally under-resourced. I can see a clear need for this kind of provision, especially in our catchment area'. He acknowledges, however, that it can be difficult to maintain a programme on a purely voluntary level. 'With the pressures on parents to find paid work, the number of people prepared to take on after-school activities is dwindling. It is for this reason that where possible we pay the playwork staff a minimum wage (£3.65 per hour).'

One of the most common ways in which parents have taken the initiative in developing after-school provision is, of course, through playcare designed to support families themselves. Indeed, in these instances, parents are often progressing from partners to qualified providers who will be able, in due course, to pursue a career in playcare or playwork. Parents and school staff work together, for example, for the success of the out-of-school club recently started at Gosford Park Primary School in Coventry (*see also* Chapter 1, pp. 24–5) to provide regular facilities and activities for all children at the school who may need to use them regularly or occasionally. The school caters for many one-parent families and is in an area with high unemployment. Many of the parents whose children use the club are attending courses or working shifts; the club seeks 'to allow them to pursue those opportunities at minimum cost and knowing their children are enjoying themselves!'

One of the school's teachers acts as voluntary co-ordinator for the club; two parents and two school assistants are the club's care workers. Families pay £1 per hour for a child to attend, and the four care workers share the club's takings. Suzanne Brown, the club co-ordinator explains, 'this does not amount to a great deal, but as their other income is limited it is appreciated and well-deserved'.

Parents are also involved in qualifying activities at Hebburn School in South Tyneside, where funding obtained for them by Education Extra from the Laura Ashley Foundation has enabled parents to be trained in sports leadership. At Hartcliffe School in Avon, opportunities are offered for parents or other local adults to train and work towards qualifications in sports leadership. In the last two years five adults have gained the Community Sports Leaders Award through participation in the school scheme and two have obtained first aid qualifications. Two have qualified in table tennis coaching; others have become canoeing leaders and trained in orienteering instruction, circus skills and women's football coaching.

Partners within schools and between schools

One of the keys to success in after-school provision is to engage the loyalty, activity and imagination of the young people themselves. Many of the schools in our Network have shown how much is possible once young people themselves are fully involved in developing and managing a scheme. Some schools invite older pupils to supervise after-school clubs for younger children (see Dashwood Primary School); others use their School Council (e.g. Islington Green), or other representative agencies, to ensure that what the pupils themselves want is reflected as far as possible in what can be offered. One of the key aspects of partnership is, of course, partnership between schools, and, particularly between secondary and primary schools. Many of Education Extra's network members pay tribute to the common sense, dedication and imagination of their colleagues from within their own and other schools.

Another key to success is that schools should, wherever possible, use their after-school provision as a way of providing for the eight–fourteen age group – and building stronger bridges between schools. After-school activities provide an obvious opportunity for secondary schools to introduce primary school children to each other, and the wider world of the 'big school', and to ease that transition for parents and children. Franche First School in Kidderminster, (Hereford and Worcs) brings in primary pupils from fourteen schools for its outstanding '425' after-school care club which has its own accommodation within the school grounds and a host of educationally rich activities. Many secondary schools in our Network make a feature of inviting in feeder schools for specific activities such as music and sport. The Fun French programme run by Heathfield Community School is offered to nine local Primary Schools. (*See* Chapter 4, pp. 107–8).

Other secondary schools go even further.

> *The King Harold Grant Maintained School in Waltham Abbey, Essex, is the only secondary (eleven–sixteen) school in the town. It has established a close relationship with its five feeder schools 'to enable the successful 5–16 progression in education of the children of Waltham Abbey'. It houses a day nursery and playgroup on a site which is also shared with the local sports centre.*
>
> *In 1993 the school had been running for four years a creative arts workshop one afternoon a week in the school offering eleven different activities for 6–13 year-olds – and alongside a full programme of activities for its own pupils (including a science club for Years 7 and 8). The activities were managed by the County's Community Education Service and over 120 children were attending. In 1993, the school was offering clay, dance, drama, cookery, football, tennis, keyboards, tapestry, puppet making, dough craft and French. New programmes are put on every term with a core of activities that are constant. The groups are small (twelve to fifteen in number) and the emphasis is on enjoyment and relaxation.*
>
> *By offering these after-school activities we hope to broaden the young people's knowledge and experience of leisure activities both on a short and long term basis. As the King Harold GMs school is the only secondary school in the town it offers the primary age children the opportunity of getting to know the 'big school' and some of the staff before they transfer at the age of eleven. The creative arts workshops have been successful in attracting the younger age group and hopefully this will have the longer term benefits of the children learning to use their leisure time positively.*

The volunteer army

After-school activities is an area which is ready and willing to bring in voluntary support – and one of the great strengths of Britain is the enormous wealth and diversity of the voluntary sector itself – everything from pigeon-fancying to book-binding. As the schools already cited in this book illustrate in many ways, many schools could not manage without the support of other committed adults and voluntary organisations.

At one level, after-school activities are an area where the other adults involved in the day-to-day life of a school often find opportunities to take on an extra role. School auxiliaries, technicians, librarians, nursery nurses and peripatetic staff – all have special skills to contribute – and often it is the involvement of these key staff rather than teachers themselves which can open up key resources such as libraries and laboratories after school.

Peripatetic music teachers, for instance, are often to be found running the school band or orchestra on a voluntary basis. School nursery staff get involved with the school's older children (whom they often already know from their nursery days) in after-school care schemes. Laboratory and computer technicians find the opportunity for a more interactive role with pupils through after-school clubs. At Godshill County Primary School on the Isle of Wight, the school caretaker runs regular football sessions before school in the mornings. Out-of-school activities can thus bring in the whole school community in a non-hierarchical way.

At Sacred Heart RC Girls' School in Newcastle, older girls have become closely involved in running activities at lunchtimes for the younger children. The result has been a closer bonding across the different age ranges, and a closer school community.

Cambridge Park School in Humberside caters for children with moderate learning difficulties and behaviour-related problems. Many are from socially deprived backgrounds.

> The children have special problems and many of them have not yet learned how to play or how to cope with other people. The school therefore set up a series of lunchtime clubs as a trial in order to begin to each children how to play. The clubs are organised and run by teacher aides with the help of dinner-time supervisors . . . these activities fall within their working hours.

The school now intends to increase its commitment to the lunchtime activities further, by 'changing staffing arrangements and the timetable in order to find more staff for lunchtime activities over a period of two years'.

There are also opportunities to bring voluntary help in from outside the school. The following example shows how a fully fledged voluntary after-school scheme in a 'typical' small, urban primary school can be enhanced by the support of individuals from within the community and shows what can be achieved (and how enrichment can work) in relatively unpromising circumstances.

DASHWOOD COUNTY PRIMARY SCHOOL, OXON: VOLUNTARY SUPPORT IN ACTION

Dashwood County Primary School in the middle of Banbury, Oxfordshire, was built in 1902. It is a small school (120), with five classes, and a tarmac playground. There are no fields or playground, and children come from a social and ethnic mix. In 1993, the headteacher wrote that 'The surrounding town centre streets offer few safe play opportunities – either no or little front gardens leading onto busy streets'.

Nevertheless, the school offered ten after-school activities during the week and a Holiday Club, met from the school funds and from 'teachers'/parents' generosity'. The clubs on offer covered soccer, netball, rounders, athletics, art, computers, English, choir, Asian cookery, reading – and woodcraft folk. The school applied for an Education Extra award to raise morale – 'a feeling of support and recognition which would motivate those of us involved to encourage others and thereby extend our options and open them to more participants'.

Education Extra made a Distinction Award to Dashwood School in 1993 which 'made us feel special'. By January 1994 the school were offering eleven after-school clubs and were involving sixth form students, support staff and parents. A lunchtime recorder group had expanded 'with several children taking the opportunity to start learning . . . and in the summer, aerobics and rounders were added for the older infants.'

We now had eight sixth form students giving up their spare time to help our children. Athletics was run by Mr and Mrs Hall from Banbury Harriers Athletics Club. They were very impressed with the talent of the children and encouraged many younger children to take part. Cookery was run by Ann Gilkes, a learning support assistant; the club was oversubscribed and we had to introduce a rota system . . . Aerobics was introduced by two sixth form pupils. That proved so popular that some children joined in after rounders and magazine club. One of our volunteer parents . . . ran the magazine club for the older children. They produced four editions.

Computer skills took up every room in the school and . . . at the beginning of the year [we] ran a book club for the younger children. A parent . . . took this over . . . Wednesdays was a very sporty day. In the winter Mark Andrews took football practice, in the summer Fred Riches [the headteacher] led a cricket club supported by old pupils who dropped in to play on their way home from school. We were able to offer table-tennis when . . . a PGCE student and two sixth formers . . . volunteered. Another popular addition was the reintroduction of badminton on Thursday, led by three enthusiastic sixth formers. The week finished with drama and country dancing run by Gill Blitz and myself.

During the year we have offered a choice of fourteen different after school clubs run by a total of twenty-five volunteers, involving 147 children. In September we hope to be able to add gardening and art to our ever increasing list of activities provided.

Professional workers from other organisations working in the community often come in to lead a particular activity, working independently or alongside teachers. Outside professionals may come in as a one-off – to teach a session which requires a special qualification, for instance – or may work regularly with a group of school students. In some cases they are the key workers who run an entire after-school scheme.

Youth workers run after school projects in many schools, especially where the school has an integral youth centre or community wing. Close co-operation between the school and the youth service workers can make the youth activities a true extension and addition to the school day, while preserving the important difference between formal schooling and what happens afterwards.

In South Tyneside's Community Schools the relationship between school and 'after-school' is bridged by centrally funded youth and FE tutors, qualified in teaching and youth work, attached to each school full time. The schools each have an active community association attached to them, and share facilities and resources. The headteacher of each school also acts as warden of the community association.

Steve Southern is youth and FE tutor at Hebburn School and the Hebburn Clegwell Community Association. He has the leading role in the school's initiative to develop extra options for pupils both at lunchtimes and after school. His first move was to start up a lunchtime club for younger pupils, some of whom were at risk of suffering from bullying if left to fend for themselves outside during lunch breaks (*see also* Chapter 6, p. 151). The lunchtime club is based in the school's youth wing and has quickly become extremely popular, with as many as 100 pupils choosing to attend. Building on the success of the lunchtime scheme (started in early 1994) within a few months Mr Southern started up an after-school club on similar lines, and this too is very well attended. Both South Tyneside TEC and the local task force are giving financial support to the initiative.

Sports clubs, churches, gardening societies – local industry and small businesses – the Red Cross – universities and colleges: schools have found ways to build partnerships with all these.

At Dyke House School in Cleveland teaching staff run an excellent range of after-school clubs and activities from careers club to science surgery, art to computers. Students can study for GCSEs in maths, music, German or CDT in out of school time. In addition to all that the staff can offer, the school makes use of professionals from other agencies to supplement its programme. An outreach health authority worker spends time with the school's students looking at ways to develop healthier lifestyles. A sports development officer works with the school to exploit its sports facilities to the best advantage and encourage excellence in sports. The school also has an adult education section, with tutors providing a range of evening classes.

Another example of the promotion of sporting opportunities comes from College House Junior School in Nottingham where the parents have built a large sports hut on the school field, to allow the use of school facilities at weekends and during holiday times. And at Ashley Primary School in South Tyneside, retired staff members and their partners have retained a close involvement in school life through the Mayor's Award Scheme; they work alongside current teachers taking pupils away on expedition hikes at weekends.

At Cross Hall High School in Ormskirk, Lancashire, for instance, the management team was concerned that pressures on teachers would lead to the loss of after school opportunities for pupils. But building up strong community partnerships has led the school to significant sporting successes. Mike Brown, deputy head, told us 'The problems caused by an understandably diluted staff-based programme of activities have been compensated for by encouraging groups to use the facilities and then encouraging junior sections wherever possible.' There is a very active community association based on the school site, with about 900 members in twenty-one affiliated groups. 'The notion of partnership is very dear to us. We could not work in the way that we do if we were not supported by a District Council and an FE College who both believe in co-operation and common aims.'

The philosophy of partnership and mutual help has led to obvious opportunities for achievement for pupils. 'The best example of this is the fact that the Lancashire Schools Volleyball Team is almost entirely made up of our school pupils who learn their volleyball here on Thursdays via the community association.'

Apart from the involvement of parents, volunteers from the community can be involved in many other different ways. Retired engineers, scientists, astronomers, ornithologists and many other specialists can offer a specialist club or course; local arts, drama, music, chess, or photography societies are rich in enthusiasts and looking for new, junior members; colleges of further and higher education have students with a whole range of interests and skills – apart from teachers in training looking to extend their contacts and experience in school.

Year 9 pupils at Newlands School in Maidenhead, Berkshire, for instance, has links with both Thames Valley University and Reading University. (Chapter 5, p. 126 gives more details.)

Partners from the business community

Apart from links into the voluntary sector, there are now many opportunities for schools to link up with their local business community. Indeed, after-school time may be particularly well suited for the development of initiatives linking schools to business, because it gives room for innovation and flexibility away from the demands of the formal curriculum, and yet can enhance pupils' experience of school and their performance in lesson time.

Our case study on one education/business partnership scheme – the 'On Track' Clubs – carried out in two London boroughs recently, shows how the creation of after-school clubs was made to benefit a whole range of youngsters who might not otherwise have been successful at school during their following two, 'Compact', years. The clubs were targeted on pupils whose particular needs had been identified by their schools. They also fell within the broad band identified by the EBP's own research of Year 9 pupils needing supplementary attention.

THE 'ON TRACK' CLUBS, LONDON BOROUGHS OF GREENWICH AND LEWISHAM: AN EDUCATION BUSINESS PARTNERSHIP IN ACTION

In 1991 a research project called 'On Track' was undertaken by the EBP serving Greenwich and Lewisham, to try to ascertain why some 56 per cent of Year 10 students within the Compact initiative were failing to achieve certain goals in their final two years of secondary schooling. These goals related to punctuality, attendance, completion of course work, work experience and completion of National Records of Achievement. It was clear from the final report that Compact was actually failing the specific pupils it set out to support. A range of support mechanisms were identified by the students themselves which would help them to improve upon their performance at school and support them in dealing with anything which was preventing them from achieving their potential.

In 1993–4 £20 000 of Business Sector funding was acquired by the EBP to set up 'On Track' Clubs in sixteen schools (all of which opted to become involved) across the two LEAs. Partners included Citibank, British Gas, Education Extra and the CSV Student Tutor Scheme. Each of the schools responded in an individual way to the particular circumstances and needs in their own context, but there were three common strands identified as requiring a response from the clubs to the students' expressed needs:

- *Support to be provided outside lesson-time in an informal setting which would thus be distinct from a normal lesson.*

- *Year 9 students to be targeted, as Year 10 was perceived to be too late to reverse negative trends leading to under-achievement.*

- *Careers Advisers to be employed to undertake hour-long, focused counselling sessions, adhering to a standard format devised by the EBP.*

The EBP also suggested that the following elements might be included within the flexible approach:

- *Action Planning*

- *Study Skills*

- *Self-Support Group.*

All these suggestions derived from the students' own requests during the original research project. The EBP themselves offered a network of support services, including funding for a club co-ordinator, additional funds for careers advisers' interviews, business secondees to provide skills training, Education Extra expertise, and degree students to act as extra tutors. The project leader, Bernadette Katchoff, summarises the lessons learned:

> The Clubs have been very well received in the main by schools and their students. There are many areas which can be improved on and developed and this is the task facing both individual schools, careers services, and the EBP as project managers. We have dipped into the great area of under-achievement, and have emerged with one small measure which improves the lives and prospects of a very small group of students considered to be at greatest risk. Whilst there is no doubt it helps, there can equally be no doubt that it is not enough.

It is anticipated that, even with the reduced funding now available, there will be some continuation of the project, and that this may focus on the under-achievement of above-average pupils, as this is 'an area of concern which is becoming more widely recognised'. As the LEAs are also focusing currently on strategies for raising achievement, one knock-on effect of this project may well be a greater inclination towards co-operation on any future LEA-led initiative.

Conclusion

In these ways, the schools described in this chapter are showing not only how to make the most of their own and the community's resources for the benefit of children after school, but are putting the first building blocks of full community partnership into place.

In our concluding chapter we will look at some ways in which schools in this country and abroad are pioneering models of activity and commitment which are anticipating the development of policy for local after-school provision, and fully fledged partnerships.

NOTES

1 More information about this two-year project can be obtained from Dr. John Bastiani, Project Director, and Lesley James, Education Projects Manager, Royal Society of Arts, 8 John Adam Street, London WC2N 6EZ.

2 Fullan, M. (1991, p. 228) Quoted in Barber, M. (1994). *An interim report of a research project in the Centre for Successful Schools*, Keele University, p. 4.

3 Barber, M. (1994). *Parents and their attitudes to secondary schools, Interim Report*, p. 4.

4 Department for Education (1993). *Effective school-business links: A practical guide to improving quality.*

5 Department of Education – USA (1989). *Mentoring in American schools..*

Conclusion:

Learning lessons after school: Policies for the future

This book has been concerned with good practice in after-school provision as it is being developed by schools, and the actual and potential role of after-school activities in helping pupils and schools to succeed. Our research has shown that many successful schools have developed extensive after-school provision. Drawing, additionally, on the experience of other countries, we make the case, in this final chapter, that there should be greater investment and a clear policy to promote this element of schooling as part of preparing all children, no matter which type of school they attend, to meet the pressures of the next millennium.

Good practice and successful schools

On the basis of the evidence presented by schools, good practice follows when:

- after-school activities are seen as central to the ethos and effectiveness of the school and as a fundamental means of releasing the potential of every child

- pupils of all ages and abilities can find something *extra*, over and above the National Curriculum, to suit their personal needs and interests

- schemes are as inclusive as possible; and no child is excluded on grounds of cost

- schemes have a different character from the school day – even when what is offered is some form of curriculum extension. The difference can be explicitly defined, if necessary, by means of informal clothes, different rules, the company of different children, a named club with a logo or T-shirt, or by using a different part of the school or grounds

203

- pupils and parents as well as staff are involved in deciding what is offered and how it is offered

- teaching and non-teaching staff are fully consulted and involved in designing and implementing the scheme

- the scheme is organised and managed by a designated co-ordinator or teacher and funded as appropriate to provide a reliable programme across the week and the school year

- parents are fully consulted and as fully involved as possible

- headteacher and school staff can draw upon support from the local community (either in the form of finance or support in kind), professional advice and commitment from the wider education service and voluntary support from local clubs, societies and individuals

- the efforts of children after school are valued and recorded in Records of Achievement or in individual schemes of recognition

- every advantage is taken of linking into the curriculum and developing in-school confidence and self-esteem.

Not all of these elements need be in place for a scheme to be successful; there are many successful schools which offer excellent programmes on a less structured basis. There is, however, a greater chance that the full benefits will be realised when most of these elements are in place.

Problems and how to solve them

The schools quoted in this study offer a wealth of good ideas. Their experience has also revealed many of the problems schools face which prevent some from getting to the starting block or over the first hurdle. Among the most common problems which prevent start up or development are:

- lack of funding, where necessary, to pay for extra staffing (e.g. a technician or librarian), for co-ordination of activities, for extra coaching, for bringing in outside experts or youth workers, for the co-ordination of school transport for extra equipment (e.g. floodlighting for sports areas; table-tennis tables, furniture for homework rooms)

- pressure on teachers' time and energy

- lack of appropriate space for separate activities and fears of disruption, vandalism and loss of school resources

- lack of support from staff, from non-teaching staff and parents

- fear of setting up an inadequate or inappropriate structure for the scheme which cannot be sustained

- anticipated problems involved with using premises (e.g. insurance/cleaning) or charging for the use of premises under the LMS regulations (if other pupils are involved)

- difficulties in locating or using volunteer staff

- difficulties in ensuring equal access and opportunities for all children

- fears that providing for younger children will lead to schools being involved not in extra-curricular activities but in childminding.

These are real, practical problems. But, as many schools in this book demonstrate, they can be overcome. It is clear, however, that if schools are to do more, and if the full educational and economic benefits are to be realised, there must be a clearer framework for setting goals and making policy, and more resources for after-school provision as a whole.

Good practice in other countries

Britain has something to learn from other countries facing similar problems with similar resources. The problems highlighted by the need for after-school provision both in terms of care and the potential for educational enrichment, are not unique to Britain. Throughout Europe, there is a growing demand for programmes which can equip *all* young people to find a decent living in a highly competitive labour market, and for support to enable families to lift themselves out of poverty through work. This is leading countries as different from each other as Sweden and Spain to look for new ways of using time and resources after school to meet new educational and social demands. As one UK expert has put it:

> *There is an unsatisfied demand in many member countries for the care of young and older children outside school hours. Educational buildings have the potential to meet this demand, but the extent to which they are made available varies from country to country and within countries . . .*[1]

Information about after-school provision and how this relates to education, schooling and care in other countries is, at present, hard to find, and limited – not least because in many countries this is left to the region, the locality or even the school itself.[2] Information about educational enhancement programmes after school is even more elusive than information about care-based programmes. What information currently exists predictably shows enormous variation in provision and policy. Some countries are making a priority of care. Portugal, for example, doubled its commitment to pre-school childcare between 1985 and 1990. New Zealand has pioneered excellent pre-school and after school childcare provision. Belgium is notable for developing policies focused on care and for funding at regional and national level strategies linked directly to employment.[3] Other countries have a tradition of integrating care and education for children of different ages.

The Scandinavian countries are promoting after-school care and educational enhancement as part of local or national education strategies. Some of the American states are developing specific educational programmes by putting school buildings to greater use. Common to each of the examples which follow, however, is that after-school provision is seen as a legitimate and key area of *educational* policy with an obvious relevance to the national economy, and as such they are supported through legislation and public investment. The experience of other countries offers some useful lessons for the UK as it considers the best ways and means of investment in future education policy.

Denmark and Sweden: Integrated after-school provision

Of all European countries, Sweden and Denmark stand out in particular for using the school system to provide both coherent childcare and educational enrichment based in schools. Both countries also share a later school age statutory date – seven years of age.

Swedish policies which enable women to combine care with a career have long offered a progressive model for Europe. Eighty per cent of Swedish mothers with children under the age of eight are in full time or part-time employment. Flexible working, maternity and paternity leave, combined with excellent childcare, offers parents practical support and a real choice; and is seen, essentially, as a right for all children and all parents. Childcare is carried by national legislation and jointly financed by central and local government and parental contributions. Within that framework, the local authorities, who are responsible for pre-school and childcare provision as well as education. This includes out-of-school or leisure-time centres are provided for children between the ages of six and twelve which are open before and after school and during school holidays. Many of these make use of school accommodation or accommodation in school buildings. Two members of staff, often trained recreational instructors and childcare attendants work with each group of fifteen to twenty children.

Significantly, however, there is also a strong tradition in Denmark of the school as the focus of local cultural, recreational and sporting activities. The school day runs from 8 a.m. to 1 p.m. or 2 p.m. and for 200 days a year. The concept of the school as a local cultural centre has recently received specific encouragement through a four-year national research and development programme which involved nearly forty development projects based in schools. Education is provided by the 272 local authorities who also provide childcare alongside social services, recreational services and education. Costs are covered in part by the local authority and in part by parental contributions. The school principal is responsible for educational and childcare provision in the school both during and outside school hours and she/he also appoints childcare staff who work in partnership with teachers.

One of the outstanding features of Danish provision is the degree of pastoral commitment through integrated care and education. Schools appoint 'leisure time teachers' who have close contacts with class teachers as well as with parents and children. Moreover, over the years, the activities which are offered after school are conscientiously designed to offer a wide range of enrichment as well as socialisation. Activities which stress socialisation and 'being together', are placed alongside those which offer opportunities for collaboration, and for sharing knowledge. Drawing, painting, modelling, singing, outings , art and drama, coexist alongside a great deal of structured topic work and voluntary learning. All ages are catered for.

In Albertslund Kommun, in Denmark, for example, in addition to after-school day care provision specifically provided in separate accommodation within the schools, school space is also used by adults in the afternoons and evenings from 3.00 p.m. until 10.00 p.m., and on Saturdays until 1.00 a.m., for sport and educational activities and community groups. Each of the eight municipal schools has an established daycare centre for sixty–eighty places for children of six–ten years old, and a variety of activities for children aged from six to fourteen. Activities include music, drama, sports and so on. In addition, there are community activities. The whole programme is financed by the town council and the children pay a little to join in.[4]

In Aalborg Kommun, the thirty-seven schools have day-care facilities catering for 6000 children (4000 aged from six to nine and 2000 aged from ten to fourteen) across the day from 6.30 a.m. to 5.00 p.m. After the age of fourteen, young people go to the continuation school (the County College) from 2.30 p.m. to 9.00 p.m.

Within the context and reflecting Education Extra's own concerns, it is significant that in Denmark there is a sense that the needs of the age group ten–fourteen need special attention. The Danish Parliament itself has resolved that:

> *It should be noted . . . that many of the people behind the cultural centres especially were surprised at the very real needs of the 10–14 year-olds, who need a place to go. The researchers note in this connection that 'this need, combined with the fact that young people clearly do not mind meeting at the school in their free time, has meant that many cultural centres have felt themselves almost swamped by this age group. If it is indeed the case that cultural centres have felt themselves "swamped" . . . we have here an indication that this group has, to a certain extent, been "forgotten".'*[5]

France and Spain: Educational enrichment and community resources

In other European countries different cultural expectations as well as climate, offer different opportunities. In France the different pattern to the school week is now being used in some local areas for some educational innovation after school. There is no school at all on Wednesdays. The school day runs from 8.30 a.m. to 6.00 p.m. for many children, which limits extra-curricular, leisure and recreation opportunities. These patterns coexist alongside a traditionally high degree of regulation governing the use of schools and a fierce regard for academic achievement. Recent initiatives have encouraged more out-of-school activities during the summer holidays, through the 'écoles ouverts', particularly in areas of high deprivation, and a search for more longer-term solutions which will enable schools to organise learning functions around a school day which allows for the dip in energy and the longer lunch break which is traditional in French life. There is also a drive to develop more local partnerships and contracts between schools and local institutions and individuals, which will bring into schools more of the richness and diversity of the cities and localities around schools – whether that means a contract with a local museum or a group of local jazz musicians.[6]

One area where these ideas are being put into practice is Lyon where the School Affairs Division has taken new responsibility for developing extra-curricular activities.

The Lyonnaire programme consists of a range of complementary activities, organised at schools under the supervision of specialised staff before and after school and on Wednesdays when young children do not attend classes. In nursery and primary schools, childcare services are offered in the morning for thirty minutes to one hour before school begins; directed study programmes which include one hour of study and fifteen minutes of recreation time are also organised. At this time a teacher supervises work being done and offers various types of help to the children. Many nursery and primary schools offer services which extend the day by seventy-five minutes. In the primary schools, the seventy-five minutes are broken down into one hour for doing homework, and fifteen minutes for play. In the evening and on Wednesdays, sporting and cultural activities are also organised. Workshops of the regional branch of the National Conservatory offer music, singing and dance classes and additional classes such as painting, foreign languages, gymnastics, martial arts are also organised for adolescents and young adults.

The Wednesday Educational Sessions offer over 9000 primary school children sports, cultural activities, technological programmes (involving computers, robotics, modelling) and manual activities such as sewing and woodwork. In Lyon, the use of school buildings has been fostered by allowing associations which organise extra-curricular activities to use the school buildings free, even though this extended use engenders additional costs (heating, lighting, water and caretaker's overtime). Increasingly, local neighbourhood organisations, youth groups and social organisations which have no physical base of their own are looking to use school buildings to allow them to offer leisure activities.

In Spain, too, where most schools are also closed on Wednesdays, and where schools often operate on a shift system, there is another recent initiative to provide for the older child after school by bringing in the resources of the community. In the region of Vigo, the local council and the county-based Institute of Sport have taken the lead in developing complementary activities after school. One intention has been to prove that cultural and sporting activities are not educational extras but central to motivation and pleasure in learning; in short, that 'The process of education does not need to be a boring activity.' Another objective has been to develop programmes which integrate the schools and schoolchildren more closely into the life of the local community, to widen their interest and knowledge of civic life and the local environment, and develop personal skills.

The programme has been an aspiration for some time, but in 1994 it finally came to fruition. Schools are now open after school and on Saturdays, especially for sports and parents and ex-students are playing a key role in helping to provide activities. The local Department of Employment offers activities sucy as drama, photography, education about different races and cultures and information technology and organises trips to concerts and the theatre. Twelve different sports are on offer twice a week – from football to karate, and athletics to skating. The programme costs parents £25 for the year. Health and personal safety are enhanced through after-school courses on health issues including AIDS, alcohol and tobacco. The Vigo experiment is now being watched closely in other areas of Spain.[7]

North America: Community use, enrichment and safer cities.

In North America, over the past decade, 'many individuals and organisations have started efforts to reclaim public school buildings and transform them into neighbourhood centers of opportunity, service, and safety for entire families.'[8]

In the inner cities, in particular, some of these programme are a direct response to acute inner city problems. In the City of New York, the New York Beacon Initiative is a publicly funded programme which develops school-based community centres managed by non-profit community based organisation. The centres offer 'safe havens for children, youth . . . parents and grandparents with a combination of supportive services and opportunities to make contributions to their own development and the revitalisation of their neighbourhoods'. The intention is quite specific: 'Funded through the "Safe Streets, Safe Cities" anti-crime program, by offering positive alternatives to the drug and thug culture that pervades some neighbourhoods, the sports, recreation and support programs that Beacons offer help prevent crime before millions must be spent to punish it.'

By 1993 there were twenty such school-based centres, providing opportunities for community service activities for young people, careers advice, family support services, conflict mediation programmes, health information, learning programmes offering, for example, dance and theatre programmes, sports, homework, parenting skills, Afro-American history, IT, languages, literacy and mathematics.

Some North American states also offer some excellent examples of after-school provision managed within a programme which aims to put school buildings to their greatest possible use. One area where there is extended use of school buildings for community and enrichment activities after school is the state of Maryland. The after-school programme, administered through the School–Community Centers Programme (SCCP) has been fully operational since 1970. Local programmes are implemented through the co-operative leadership of boards of education, parks and recreation departments and focus upon services to youth aged seven to twenty-one. The programmes provide a range of supplementary educational and supervised recreational activities as determined by local needs and interests surveys.

State laws provide that county boards are to encourage the use of public school facilities for community purposes and include specific references to the need for day care and for supporting non-profit organisations. The Advisory Committee for Adult and Community Services attached to the State Department of Education provides funding to local schools to enable them to open school facilities during non-school hours (evenings, weekends and leisure time activities for children, youths and young adults). Activities include enrichment programmes. These can involve assistance with homework, computer assisted instruction, science and mathematics clubs, parenting and parent education, arts and crafts, foreign language instruction, youth leadership training, health, safety and nutrition education, instrumental music, 'latch-key' children training and support, and psychomotor development activities. They also include group activities for families and special activities for the physically and mentally handicapped. Research and Evaluation programmes are an integral and regular part of the commitment made.[9]

Partnership and policy in Britain

From these few, and very diverse examples we can see how other countries and regional governments are responding to the evident needs of children and young people after school and how they are drawing out additional benefits from schools themselves. In each case, local and national partnerships have been formed to bring about greater involvement of schools, parents and pupils after school and some funding has been provided to enable the wider use of school facilities and resources and in some cases a statutory framework to support that commitment, for example.

This country has an equal, if not greater, need to give a boost to learning and to provide hopeful and challenging occupation for young people after school. We, too, need to look at new ways of limiting failure by redefining success and preventing the passage of under-achievement across successive generations.

Identifying Good Practice raises some issues about Good Policy. Key questions include:

- How can after-school provision best be promoted within schools, given the mixed economy of voluntary and paid activities?

- How can links with the curriculum be maintained without schemes becoming simply an extension of school and of interest only to those children who are already motivated?

- How can after-school provision achieve the right balance of education with childcare for children of different ages and provided with regard to equal opportunities?

211

- How can policies which link after-school provision to local strategies for raising achievement, creating employment and reducing poverty be best designed or implemented at a local level?

- How can policies for after-school provision at local level be best framed and supported nationally?

In Britain we already lag behind. We have no national policy – or even the national *framework* for a policy for after-school activities or after-school care, other than the limited objectives of the Out-of-School Childcare Initiative, which is geared to employment needs rather than educational opportunity. Moreover, funds for local education, and for mainstream teaching, are being cut in many areas. Likewise, although there is a fine network of designated community schools within the community education framework, the erosion of local authority provision, particularly in relation to non-statutory areas of education, has weakened the ability of schools to attract the sort of partnerships which might frame future expansion in after-school activities and enable them to open up facilities and offer more.

Given the pressures on school resources, on time, and on funding, the future for after-school activities belongs best, we believe, within a framework of local partnership which will enable schools to exploit to the full all the resources which might be available. The schools cited in this book show in many different ways what can be done with limited resources and in very different circumstances. Other schools have pursued the idea of partnership even more fully.

One of the best known examples of local authority partnership in action is probably the Dukeries Complex in Nottinghamshire. The Dukeries Comprehensive School in Ollerton, Nottingham, was at the heart of a mining community which has now virtually disappeared with the closure of its pits. The project, to develop community facilities around the comprehensive school, was unusual 'in that the project crossed the normal bureaucratic barriers of government, and had a team of architects, educationalists, leisure and social service managers working together'. The Dukeries complex is now a 'federation of separate units – the central one being a comprehensive school, now a successful community college', with a splendid after-school programme which in 1992 was offering, among a huge range, archery, textiles, and wood turning.

A different version of the community model and one which explores the possibilities of 'dual use' to its limits, is Stoneydown Park Primary School, in the London Borough of Waltham Forest and its Users' Association which was set up five years ago by the headteacher to promote the co-ordination of after-school activities and the wide use of school premises. The school is in an inner city area of Waltham Forest, with high levels of unemployment and one-parent families and a mixed catchment area. The partnership is supported through a wide range of independent fundraising initiatives, including the Training and Enterprise funding for 'teatime' provision. The school is open around the clock and takes a very evangelical attitude towards community use, promoting open evenings, community lunches and conferences to encourage the greater use of school premises by the community. It provides facilities for twenty-five different organisations catering for all ages, and over 2000 individuals use the site each week.

The Stoneydown Park Users Association co-ordinates the very extensive community use of the school. The concept of Dual Use means that all the equipment is shared and the Users' Association has been able to raise funds and grants over and above what the school itself might be able to provide. For example, the London Borough of Waltham Forest fund the salary of a co-ordinator and assistance; BT paid for the refurbishment of the school's courtyard. Fords Trust paid £1500 towards a new printing machine. The Women's Unit, Adult Education jointly fund the basic English class. Arts and Leisure Department of the Council and the school run the teatime club and the aerobics class with support from the SPUA.

The activities of the school are almost too numerous to mention. The teatime club, funded by leisure services, meets every weekday from 3.30 until 5.30 p.m. There are Tai Chi Classes; a singing class, aerobics, Eastern social dance club; discoverers bible class; children's drama workshop; family French and an African Caribbean association class, and a playscheme.

These schools offer two examples of extended partnership with the community which involves after-school activities as part of wider programmes.

Education Extra believes that, given a clear lead and a local framework of support, most schools could offer more after-school activities which in time could foster more community-based schooling in practice. Giving a lead does not mean formalising after-school provision within educational policy or imposing an after-school curriculum on schools, but enabling schools to enhance the links between after-school education and achievement. This will come, in part, by fostering better home–school relationships and better in-school relationships. All pupils can benefit, but pupils who are low in self-esteem, who lack family support for learning, who are disruptive or disaffected, or who have special needs and special interests, can all benefit in transparent ways from structured programmes. Other benefits will come from:

- **greater efficiency** as school resources and facilities are better used

- **a stronger economy** as young people develop marketable skills and lifelong interests

- **a more responsible community** as schools and communities work more closely together.

All this is necessary but it is made much more difficult by the reduction in community budgets and deficit budgets in many schools which seriously hamper what can be done and frustrate the potential of what is already being done. There is also a limit to what can be done when schools are forced to compete with and bid against each other for scarce funds, when the support which LEAs can offer is constrained, and when govenors and parents know that the main charge on the school budget must be to maintain what happens within the school day. Despite those difficulties, however, there is a strategy waiting to be implemented, and one which will bring benefits all round.

Giving a lead at national level

The creation of the new Department of Education and Employment offers a new opportunity for developing much of the potential held by after-school activities. As such, we believe that the DEE has the major responsibility for bringing about the necessary change. It could now take a lead:

- by formally recognising that after-school provision can make a major contribution to raising achievement and effective schooling

- by recognising that every school-age child should have an entitlement to a range of experiences above and beyond the National Curriculum

- by promoting community schooling and providing resources on a fair and equal basis between schools

- by enabling all schools to fund the organisation and co-ordination of after-school provision as they see fit

- by promoting and funding research as the basis for future good practice

- by promoting partnerships between schools, the youth services, the voluntary services and employers as the basis for more imaginative provision

- by encouraging the Training and Enterprise Councils to invest in the widest range of afterschool provision as part of the means of meeting the National Targets for Education and Training.

In order to achieve this, after-school activities should be included as an explicit element within the school effectiveness segment of the GEST budget to enable local authorities to initiate training, research and development as the first step towards long term programmes. This would enable the training of:

- school co-ordinators

- after-school auxiliary technicians, librarians, sports leaders, and support staff to run courses

- staff to provide personal skills courses, study skills, arts and sporting excellence programmes.

It would enable schools to:

- provide additional space, resources and technology

- develop linked primary and secondary school programmes geared to the transitional needs of the eight to fourteen age group

- identify and draw in, wherever possible, material and human resources from the whole community.

Turning to the related issue of childcare, we would also urge that the Out of School Childcare Initiative should become a coherent element in a long-term strategy for continuing childcare for pre and primary school children. There is a need for continuity as well as security. Only a guarantee of permanence will encourage the provision of after-school playcare clubs which is needed if parents are to look for, take up and continue in work, with confidence. This support for playcare both within schools and within the community can be supported, most effectively, in partnership between local authorities and TECs. Using school resources more effectively in this respect will not only help to dismantle the artificial barriers which have traditionally separated care from education; it will also provide greater opportunities for stimulation as well as socialisation. As part of this policy we would also want to see new programmes, combining supervision with stimulating activities, available within secondary schools, both for primary aged children at the point of transition, and for the first years of secondary education.

Creating a framework at local level

Whatever lead is given by central Government to initiate new policy, it will be essential for schools to remain free to work out their own solutions in terms of what is provided after school and how, who is involved, and whether and how they are paid. The voluntary ethic is too precious to be diminished. However, if schools are to take up new after-school opportunities, they will benefit from the active support of LEAs who will, in turn, need additional funding earmarked for community education to develop a fair and cost-effective strategy. With modest additional resources these opportunities could mean that LEAs can promote coherent after-school provision within all schools.

Creating a local framework therefore means:

- All LEAs, and not simply a dedicated minority, should have a Community Education budget which will support innovative strategies across the LEA

- All LEAs should be able to provide assistance for schools to fund co-ordinators and delegated staff for after school programmes

- All LEAs should be able to provide assistance for schools to employ educational 'auxiliaries' who can help open up resources not simply for the schools' own children, but to develop them as designated centres, capable of offering something extra for children from elsewhere. Working alongside the GEST training strategy, this local after-school strategy would ensure that an after-school policy would be fully rooted in local partnerships and serve the whole community.

It also means:

- Forming closer partnerships to develop imaginative after-school provision aimed at common objectives (economic regeneration/anti-poverty/anti-crime). Such partnerships, in which the Local Authority and the TEC would be lead agencies, could locate funds through the Single Regeneration Budget, the European Social Fund or other national funds for diverse initiatives which could range from providing local study support centres, family learning programmes, or crime prevention

- Creating a co-ordinated budget within the Local Authority, which would bring together different elements of local partnership across education, leisure and arts and community development. This could mean, for example, the release of additional resources for the subsidy of school premises which would otherwise carry a prohibitive charge, and for the development of specialist facilities and shared resources which can become designated centres of excellence, e.g. for sport.

Making it happen at school level

Most schools are already doing more than can be expected at the moment. Our aim is to release the resources which will enable schools to do what they want to do, but to do it with the support that they need to make a real success of these extra efforts. All the recommendations listed will help do that, but, in addition we would urge schools to make more happen. That means:

- Making the most of what you've got. Audit the needs of children and parents; designate a teacher for after-school activities; invite all older pupils, all school staff, classroom teaching assistants, parents, governors, local business and local voluntary organisations to consider what courses or clubs they might be able to offer; look for ways of developing new activities, e.g. with personal skills, core study skills, individual sports; look for ways of bringing in parents alongside students in appropriate clubs; be confident that after-school activities fall within 'the purposes of the school'; and be positive about sharing premises with the community after hours.

- Celebration and evaluation. Ensure that participation is reflected in Records of Achievement which genuinely reflect pupils' specific individual achievements in after-school time. After-school programmes, newspaper clubs, good news stories bring the benefits to a wider audience. Design a simple scheme of evaluation linked, if possible, to schemes of positive discipline, school certificates of attendance and achievement, local or national awards (e.g. the Duke of Edinburgh's Award or the Youth Award). Older pupils who help supervise younger ones or run clubs can be accredited within NVQs. After-school programmes attract parents and students. Monitor and publicise this.

- Making after school part of in-school. Make your after-school provision a fundamental part of your Development Plan and make sure that commitment is clear in all school documents. Make sure your after-school plans, are submitted, positively, and noted by the OFSTED Inspectorate.

Conclusion

We have put forward an ambitious but realistic programme for action. We are optimistic because it means drawing on resources and goodwill which already exists; because it is timely; because it will be seen to be doing something positive to overcome problems which are frustrating social and educational potential; because schools are ready for it; and because Local Management of Schools means greater autonomy and freedom of movement. It involves planning for the long term with a clear framework for policy, a national strategy clearly articulated to objectives in place of inconsistent, underfunded and sporadic initiatives which have usually served simply to stimulate local good practice for a limited time. It also means providing some modest new funding to meet the additional costs.

This is essential if there is to be a significant improvement in quantity and quality. Schools cannot be expected to continue improvising indefinitely, and poor children in poor areas will continue to lose out unless schools can draw on a budget to improve and enhance what they can do.

With this combination of support in place schools will be free to use their imagination in ways which can truly release the full talent of their pupils and staff. Their central role within the neighbourhood will be realised more fully in practice as schools become the visible heart of the working community.

By investing in what schools can do after school, we can draw out the enormous strengths and talents in our education service and our communities. There is a new educational opportunity. This book has been able to give only a glimpse of that and to suggest how other countries are seeking to solve similar problems. Many more changes are also needed to open up access to the right kind of training and qualifications and to provide the right conditions of work if there is to be greater equality and efficiency in the future. A national programme to put after-school activities within the reach of every child should be central to that strategy. To start with what schools can do both with the resources they have and with the support of the community, will be to build on the firmest foundation. And it is the way to build a more effective education service and an economy which can offer a hopeful future to every young person.

NOTES

1 Hacker, M. (Unpublished, March 1994). *A home from home: The use of educational buildings by young people out of school hours.* Paper for OECD Programme on Educational Building. We are grateful to him and to Richard Yelland, of the OECD Programme, for their permission to use this research.

2 Pat Petrie, of the Thomas Coram Research Unit, is currently completing a study, funded by the European Commission, which will set out some fundamental comparisons and approaches throughout Europe in the field of after-school provision. This study, it is anticipated, will be published later this year.

3 Further information on out-of-school childcare in these countries can be obtained from Kids' Clubs Network.

4 We are grateful to Mr Per Hansen, Building Directorate, Ministry of Education, Denmark, for additional information on Danish policy.

5 Danish Parliamentary Resolution, 26 May 1987, Point 1. Quoted in Jensen et al. (1992). *The Danish Folskole*. Quoted in Hacker, M. op. cit., p. 8.

6 We are indebted to Pat Petrie, of the Thomas Coram Research Unit, for current information regarding France.

7 Actividades extraescolares: la letra con vidversion entra. *Faro de Vigo*, 22 September 1994.

8 *Beacons: school-based community centers. A Safe Streets, Safe City Program*. Interim Report, 21 June 1993. City of New York.

9 We are most grateful for this information provided by Dr Yale Stenzler and Charles A. Talbert, Branch Chief of the Maryland State Department of Education, Adult Education and Literacy Services Branch. Mr Talbert has told Education Extra that other States with similar commitment to after-school educational activities include Michigan, Oregon, Washington DC, Virginia, Pennsylvania, Georgia, Florida, Colorado, Texas, Minnesota and Iowa.

Index

LIVERPOOL
UNIVERSITY
LIBRARY

FIAT LUX